Hate Crimes in Cyberspace

Hate Crimes in
Cyberspace

Danielle Keats Citron

HARVARD UNIVERSITY PRESS
Cambridge, Massachusetts, and London, England
2014

First Printing

Library of Congress Cataloging-in-Publication Data
Citron, Danielle Keats, 1968–
    Hate crimes in cyberspace / Danielle Keats Citron.
        pages cm
    Includes bibliographical references and index.
    ISBN 978-0-674-36829-3 (alk. paper)
    1. Cyberbullying. 2. Cyberstalking. 3. Hate crimes. 4. Computer crimes.
I. Title.
    HV6773.15.C92C57 2014
    364.150285'4678–dc23   2014008325

For my family

Contents

Introduction

During the summer of 2008, "Anna Mayer" was getting ready to begin her first semester in graduate school. In her spare time, she wrote a pseudonymous blog about her weight struggles, body acceptance, and other personal issues. She enjoyed interacting with her readers and commenting on other blogs; it provided a support system and sounding board for her ideas.

Before school began, she searched her name and found posts describing her as a "stupid, ugly fat whore" who "couldn't take a hint from a man." Anonymous posters listed her e-mail address, phone number, and dating site profiles. She received e-mails warning that the authors knew where she lived. Posters "outed" her as the author of her pseudonymous blog, taunting that the "confessions she's made about her pitiful fat fucking self are now blasted across teh [*sic*] Internet."[1]

Over the next year, the attacks grew more gruesome and numerous. Sites appeared with names like "Anna Mayer's Fat Ass Chronicles" and "Anna Mayer Keeps Ho'Ing It Up." Posts warned that "guys who might

be thinking of nailing" her should know about her "untreated herpes."
A post said, "Just be DAMN SURE you put on TWO rubbers before
ass raping Anna Mayer's ST diseased pooper!" Posters claimed that she
had bipolar disorder and a criminal record for exposing herself in public. Racist comments she never made were attributed to her. Posts listed
her professors' e-mail addresses, instructing readers to tell them about
Mayer's "sickening racist rants." Someone set up a Twitter account in
Mayer's name that claimed she fantasized about rape and rough sex.
Hundreds of posts were devoted to attacking her.

Mayer could not even guess the identity of the posters. She wondered if
the abuse was in retaliation for defending a classmate who blogged about
her sexual fantasies. In an anonymous comment, Mayer had showed
support for her classmate. There was nothing wrong or unusual in having
fantasies. Might that have gotten people angry?

Whatever the reason the cyber mob turned on her did not matter to
Mayer; she was terrified. Whoever read the posts might believe that she
wanted to have sex and then confront her offline. Posters devoted considerable energy setting up the attack sites. She was stunned that her
attackers could figure out that she was behind her pseudonymous blog.
Every time she closed her blog and started a new one under a different
pseudonym, posters managed to discover her identity and outed her. She
stopped blogging; it was not worth the inevitable abuse.

After graduation, she secured a one-year fellowship with a nonprofit
organization. Shortly after she began working, posts falsely accused her
of having been fired from jobs due to her "sexual misconduct." The name
of her supervisor appeared next to the suggestion that he needs to be told
that she is a "stupid slut." Mayer talked to her supervisor about the posts,
a painful and embarrassing task. As she later told me, although he was
incredibly supportive, she worried that future employers might not be
as understanding.

In our interview, Mayer expressed concerns about finding permanent employment. Many posts were explicitly designed to make her un-

employable. Under the heading "Anna Mayer, Do Not Hire," a post said that anyone "thinking about hiring Anna Mayer needs to learn a few facts about her first": Mayer "will give your workplace a bad reputation"; Mayer has health problems, violent tendencies, and a "lack of discretion"; and Mayer is "financially irresponsible" and does not pay her rent. The posts reappeared in other blogs in what seemed like an attempt to ensure their prominence in searches of her name. They did: 75 percent of the links appearing on the first page of a search of her name were the attack sites and disparaging posts.[2] Given how unusual her real name is, Mayer ultimately decided to include a disclaimer on her résumé, warning employers about what they would inevitably find if they searched her name online.

Mayer's experience is a classic example of cyber harassment and cyber stalking. Although definitions of these terms vary, cyber harassment is often understood to involve the intentional infliction of substantial emotional distress accomplished by online speech that is persistent enough to amount to a "course of conduct" rather than an isolated incident. Cyber stalking usually has a more narrow meaning: an online "course of conduct" that either causes a person to fear for his or her safety or would cause a reasonable person to fear for his or her safety.[3] I will address the two forms of abuse interchangeably because they are accomplished by similar means and achieve similar ends. I will highlight important differences between them where such differences arise.

Cyber harassment involves threats of violence, privacy invasions, reputation-harming lies, calls for strangers to physically harm victims, and technological attacks. Victims' in-boxes are inundated with threatening e-mails. Their employers receive anonymous e-mails accusing them of misdeeds. Fake online advertisements list victims' contact information and availability for sex. Their nude photos appear on sites devoted to exacting revenge. On message boards and blogs, victims are falsely accused of having sexually transmitted infections, criminal records, and mental illnesses. Their social security numbers and medical conditions are published for all to see. Even if some abuse is taken down from a site, it quickly reappears on others. Victims' sites are forced offline with distributed-denial-of-service attacks.

While some attackers confine abuse to networked technologies, others use all available tools to harass victims, including real-space contact. Offline harassment or stalking often includes abusive phone calls, vandalism, threatening mail, and physical assault.[4] As the executive director of the National Center for Victims of Crime Mary Lou Leary explains, "Stalkers are using very sophisticated technology . . . installing spyware on your computer so they can track all of your interactions on the Internet, your purchases, your e-mails and so forth, and using that against you, forwarding e-mails to people at your job, broadcasting your whereabouts, your purchases, your reading habits and so on, or installing GPS in your car so that you will show up at the grocery store, at your local church, wherever and there is the stalker and you can't imagine how the stalker knew that you were going to be there."[5]

Why affix the *cyber* label to the abuse? Why not simplify matters and just call it harassment or stalking? Perpetrators engage in persistent destructive behavior, whether it occurs online, offline, or both. The *cyber* label adds something important, however. It captures the different ways the Internet exacerbates the injuries suffered.

The Internet extends the life of destructive posts. Harassing letters are eventually thrown away, and memories fade in time. The web, however, can make it impossible to forget about malicious posts. Search engines index content on the web and produce it instantaneously. Indexed posts have no built-in expiration date; neither does the suffering they cause. Search engines produce results with links to destructive posts created years earlier. Strangers can put abusive posts to malicious use five days or five years after they first appear. Now and far into the future, victims' social security numbers may be used to steal their identity and their home address utilized to stalk them in person.

Networked technologies exponentially expand the audience for cyber harassment. Why would perpetrators spend the time and money to send letters by mail when the online audience for a given post is limitless and free? Posts that go viral attract hundreds of thousands of readers.

The Internet's ability to forge connections enables *stalking by proxy*, whereby perpetrators recruit strangers to help them stalk victims, and *group cyber stalking*, whereby more than one person is involved in the online abuse.[6] Online harassment can quickly become a team sport, with posters trying to outdo each other. Posters compete to be the most offensive, the most abusive. An accurate name for such online groups is *cyber mobs*. The term captures both the destructive potential of online groups and the shaming dynamic at the heart of the abuse. As the legal philosopher Martha Nussbaum observed, "Mobs from dominant groups are notorious for shaming relatively powerless groups, in taking delight in the discomfort of the excluded and stigmatized."[7] Cyber mobs gather online to harass individuals in degrading and threatening ways.

The Internet's unique features help us appreciate why cyber stalking can fundamentally disrupt victims' lives. Fear can be profound. Marianna Taschinger, a twenty-two-year-old, said that she did not feel safe leaving her home after someone posted her nude photograph, home address, and Facebook profile on a porn site. "I don't want to go out alone," she explained, "because I don't know what might happen."[8] Another woman moved to an apartment building with a twenty-four-hour security guard after her nude photos and contact information appeared online; she no longer felt safe in her home.[9]

In some cases, online abuse has resulted in just what victims' dread: rape and real-world stalking. In December 2009 an online advertisement on Craigslist featured a woman's picture next to her "interest" in "a real aggressive man with no concern for women." The woman's ex-boyfriend Jebidiah Stipe wrote the post; he had previously impersonated several other women in online advertisements.[10] But this time, more than 160 people had responded to the ad, including Ty McDowell.[11] Stipe sent McDowell text messages with the woman's home address and false claims of her fantasies about "humiliation, physical abuse, and sexual abuse." McDowell attacked the woman as she returned home, forcing his way inside. He shoved her into the house and wrestled her to the floor. At knifepoint, he bound and blindfolded her. Then he raped her and abused her with a knife sharpener. During the attack, he told her, "You want an aggressive man, bitch, I'll show you aggressive."[12] The woman was left bound and gagged on her kitchen floor. When caught by the police, McDowell said that the woman had asked him to rape her. He was responding to her advertisement, he insisted.[13]

In 2012 a similar case unfolded in Maryland when strange men began showing up at a woman's doorstep, claiming they had been e-mailing with her and were there to have sex. Her ex-husband had posted Craigslist ads in her name that expressed a desire for sexual encounters with titles like "Rape Me and My Daughters." Other ads offered to sell the sexual services of her then-twelve- and thirteen-year-old daughters and twelve-year-old son; the children's photos appeared next to the family's home address. The woman's fake profiles appeared on popular social networks like Facebook and pornography aggregators like XTube. More than fifty men came to her home demanding sex. Some tried to break in. The woman moved out of state, pulling her children out of their schools. She found a new job, but it paid less and barely covered her bills. Despite the woman's repeated requests to remove the ads, several remain online. "Many people think you can ignore stuff that's posted online," she said. "Virtual reality [can] [become] reality, and it ruins your life."[14]

Cyber harassment victims may go into hiding to protect themselves from further abuse. A hate group targeted the feminist author Jessica Valenti on the radio and online. She received hundreds of sexually threatening e-mails.[15] Her home address appeared on online forums. Valenti removed as much of her personal information from the web as she could and rerouted her mail to a P.O. box. She now uses a fake name when she travels and no longer keeps a public calendar of her speaking events.[16]

Victims change schools to avoid further abuse. Consider the experience of a heterosexual high school student who pursued a singing and acting career. The student maintained a website under his stage name featuring his photograph, a brief biography, and a "guestbook" for visitors to post comments. Students at his school discovered the site and started posting on his guestbook page. Writing under pseudonyms, they attacked the student in a series of frightening and homophobic posts. "I'm going to kill you, faggot," one wrote. According to his father, the threatening postings terrified his son and his entire family. The student withdrew from school and moved with his family to another town.[17]

The professional costs are steep. Cyber harassment can destroy business relationships.[18] Consider what happened to a well-established dentist working in Manhattan. In 2011 she asked a patient to remove negative online reviews that she believed contained baseless lies. The patient sued her after she charged him a fee for keeping the reviews posted in violation of their confidentiality agreement. Although getting patients to sign confidentiality agreements prohibiting bad reviews runs counter to important free speech values and fair competition concerns, those concerns cannot justify what was done to her. News of the patient's lawsuit sparked a torrent of online abuse at the hands of posters who may have had no connection to the patient. Over three hundred anonymous posts attacked the dentist, falsely claiming that she suffers from AIDS and sleeps with her patients.[19] At home and at the office, she received threatening phone calls. Her perfect five-star ratings on popular review sites plummeted to one star. Defamatory posts appeared at the top of searches of her name. Within six months, she was struggling to keep patients and attract new ones. Her medical malpractice carrier raised her insurance rates to an astronomical level. Finally, she closed her practice in July 2012.[20]

Because searches of victims' names prominently display the online abuse, many lose their jobs.[21] Employers fire targeted individuals because they worry that damaging posts reflect badly on them and could distract their employees from their work. Schools have terminated teachers whose nude pictures appeared online without their permission.[22] A government agency ended a woman's employment after a coworker circulated her nude photograph to colleagues.[23] A bank fired a financial sales consultant after someone impersonated her on a prostitution site, falsely suggesting her interest in having sex for money and listing her work supervisor as the person to contact to arrange sexual encounters.[24]

Cyber harassment victims are at a distinct disadvantage when they look for new jobs. Most employers rely on candidates' online reputation as an employment screen. According to a 2009 Microsoft study, nearly 80 percent of employers consult search engines to collect intelligence on job applicants, and about 70 percent of the time they reject applicants due to their findings. Common reasons for not interviewing and hiring applicants include concerns about their "lifestyle," "inappropriate" online comments, and "unsuitable" photographs, videos, and other information about them.[25] According to the social media firm Reppler, 90 percent of employers conduct online searches for prospective hires.[26]

Job applicants usually do not get a chance to explain destructive posts to employers searching them online. Recruiters do not contact them to see if they actually posted nude photos of themselves or if someone else did. They do not inquire about defamatory falsehoods posted online. Targeted individuals cannot refute claims that they harbor rape fantasies, suffer from sexually transmitted infections, or have a poor job history. The simple but regrettable truth is that after consulting search results, employers take the path of least resistance. They just do not call to schedule interviews or to extend offers.[27]

To avoid further abuse, victims withdraw from online activities, which can be costly. Closing down one's blog can mean a loss of advertising income.[28] In some fields, blogging is key to getting a job. According to Robert Scoble, a technology blogger, people who do not blog are "never going to be included in the [technology] industry."[29] When vic-

Types of Online Reputational Information That Influenced Decisions to Reject a Candidate

	U.S. (%)	U.K. (%)	Germany (%)
Concerns about the candidate's lifestyle	58	45	42
Inappropriate comments and text written by the candidate	56	57	78
Unsuitable photos, videos, and information	55	51	44
Inappropriate comments or text written by friends and relatives	43	35	14
Comments criticizing previous employers, coworkers, or clients	40	40	28
Inappropriate comments or text written by colleagues or work acquaintances	40	37	17
Membership in certain groups and networks	35	33	36
Discovered that information the candidate shared was false	30	36	42
Poor communication skills displayed online	27	41	17
Concern about the candidate's financial background	16	18	11

Data from Cross-Tab, "Online Reputation in a Connected World" (2010), 9. Available at: http://go.microsoft.com/?linkid=9709510.

tims shut down social media platforms like Facebook, LinkedIn, and Twitter, they are saddled with low social media influence scores that can impair their ability to obtain employment.[30] Companies like Klout measure people's online influence by looking at their number of social media followers, updates, likes, retweets, and shares. Some employers that see low social media influence scores refuse to hire those candidates.[31]

Our reliance on networked information to assess job candidates will only increase as algorithmic tools become more sophisticated and less expensive. Today human resources rely on Big Data—the collection and analysis of massive databases of information—to identify job prospects. Analytics firms crunch data to search for and assess talent in particular fields. Remarkable Hire scores a candidate's talents by looking at how others rate his or her online contributions. Talent Bin and Gild create lists of potential hires based on online data. Big-name companies like Facebook, Wal-Mart, and Amazon use these technologies to find and recruit job candidates.[32] Will algorithms identify targeted individuals as top picks for employment if they have withdrawn from online life? Will they discount online abuse so that victims can be evaluated on their merits? One can only guess the answers to these questions, but my bet is that victims will not stack up well next to those who have not suffered online abuse.

Along with these professional problems, cyber harassment victims incur legal fees, child care costs, and moving expenses. The average financial impact of cyber stalking is more than $1,200.[33] According to a recent study, individuals who are stalked online take more self-protective measures, pay higher out-of-pocket costs, and experience greater fear over time than individuals who are stalked offline.[34] A computer science professor claimed that online harassment at the hands of her former student and his highly skilled hacker supporters cost her "thousands of dollars in legal fees, hundreds of hours of lost work time, the dismantling of my chosen career, and made it so I cannot use the degrees I worked so hard to obtain."[35]

Elizabeth Cargill, a psychologist who works with cyber stalking victims, explains that when someone is harassed online, it feels like the perpetrator is everywhere: Facebook, e-mail, message boards, and outside the office.[36] As a result, emotional harm and distress routinely accompany the financial costs. Posttraumatic stress disorder,[37] anorexia nervosa, and depression are common.[38] Cyber harassment victims struggle especially with anxiety, and some suffer panic attacks. Researchers have found that cyber harassment victims' anxiety grows more severe over time.[39]

If victims can afford it, they seek help from psychologists, psychiatrists, and social workers. They have difficulty thinking positive thoughts and doing their work. One law student facing cyber harassment said, "I'm a fairly self-confident person. . . . But for the last two months of school, I was absolutely neurotic, glaring at anyone I didn't know who made eye contact with me, and doing my best to not let myself check that stupid board to see what they were saying."[40] Annmarie Chiarini, an English professor, wrote that after her ex-boyfriend uploaded her nude image and the missive "Hot for Teacher—Come Get It!" on porn sites, she "oscillated between panic and persistent anxiety. I would wake up at 3 am and check my email, my Facebook page, eBay, then Google my name, a ritual I performed three times before I could settle back down."[41]

It's not surprising that young people are more likely to experience severe emotional distress from cyber harassment.[42] A national study of middle and high school students found that 45 percent of lesbian, gay, bisexual, and transgender (LGBT) youth who experienced cyber harassment felt depressed and more than 25 percent wrestled with suicidal thoughts.[43] Seventeen-year-old Rehtaeh Parsons killed herself after she was gang-raped at a party and a photo of the rape was posted online. Fourteen-year-old Jill Naber hanged herself after a photo of her topless went viral.[44] Fourteen-year-old Jamey Rodemeyer committed suicide after being terrorized online for being gay.[45] Fifteen-year-old Amanda Todd took her own life after a stranger convinced her to reveal her breasts on her webcam and created a Facebook page with the picture. Just before killing herself, she posted a video on YouTube explaining her devastation that the photograph is "out there forever" and she can never get it back.[46]

These cases are not unique. During the six years that I have been writing and speaking about cyber harassment with academics and members of the public, many have insisted that too much is being made of what they call unusual cases.[47] However, cyber harassment and cyber stalking incidents are devastating *and* endemic. Thousands upon thousands of similar incidents occur annually in the United States. The 2012 National Cyber Security Alliance–McAfee survey found that 20 percent of adults have been affected by cyber stalking, persistent harassing e-mails, and other unwanted online contact.[48] Each year, 3.4 million adults are victims of stalking, one in four of whom experience cyber stalking.[49] The Bureau of Justice Statistics estimated that in 2006, 850,000 people endured physical stalking with an online component, such as threats over e-mail and text, attack sites devoted to them, or harassment in chat rooms, blogs, and social networks.[50] Over 40 percent of the New York City Police Department's Computer Investigation and Technology Unit's (CITU) closed cases from 1996 to 2000 involved aggravated cyber harassment.[51]

Evidence suggests that harassment via networked technologies is increasing. College students report having faced more sexually harassing speech online than in person.[52] Researchers predict that 30 to 40 percent of Internet users will face some form of cyber harassment in their life. Real-space stalking with no online component is more prevalent than stalking online with or without a physical component, but that may soon change. Cyber stalking victimization strongly correlates with time spent online—especially for young people who are online for hours a day.[53] The National Institute of Justice explains that the "ubiquity of the Internet and the ease with which it allows others unusual access to personal information" make individuals more accessible and vulnerable to online abuse.[54] Harassing people online is far cheaper and less personally risky than confronting them in real space.

Personalized Hate in Cyberspace: Hate 3.0

We have moved from a read only (Web 1.0) Internet to user-generated online environments (Web 2.0). Under way is the web's current stage of development (Web 3.0), which involves tailoring our online experiences to our particular habits and tastes. Now, given the ubiquity of networked devices, those choices will follow us everywhere. Cyber harassment and cyber stalking can be understood as Hate 3.0 because they amount to personalized hate, as damaging as this new stage of the web aims to be productive. Both the identity of the victims and the nature of the attacks attest to the bigotry. Let me explain how.

The Impact on Women

Cyber harassment disproportionately impacts women. The U.S. National Violence Against Women Survey reports that 60 percent of cyber stalking victims are women, and the National Center for Victims of Crimes estimates that the rate is 70 percent.[55] For over a decade, Working to Halt Online Abuse (WHOA) has collected information from cyber harassment victims. Of the 3,393 individuals reporting cyber harassment to WHOA from 2000 to 2011, 72.5 percent were female and 22.5 percent were male (5 percent were unknown).[56]

WHOA's findings align with victimization rates in studies covering offline and online behavior that causes a reasonable person to fear for his

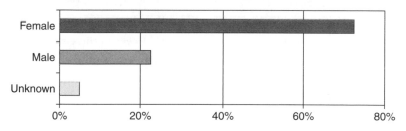

Victims of cyber harassment, 2000–2011. Data from WHOA (haltabuse.org), Comparison Statistics 2000–2011.

or her safety. The most recent Bureau of Justice Statistics report found that 74 percent of individuals who were stalked on- or offline were female, and 26 percent were male.[57]

Law enforcement records support what these organizations were told. From 1996 to 2000, women made up the majority of CITU's aggravated cyber harassment victims: 52 percent were female and 35 percent were male.[58] Academic research also reflects this gender imbalance. The University of Maryland's Electrical Engineering and Computer Department studied online attacks occurring on the chat medium Internet Relay Chat. Researchers found that users with female names received on average one hundred "malicious private messages," which the study defined as "sexually explicit or threatening language," for every four received by male users. User gender had a "significant impact" on the number of malicious private messages sent and "no significant impact" on other kinds of attacks, such as attempts to send files with viruses to users. The attacks studied emanated from human users who selected their targets, not automated scripts programmed to send attacks to everyone on the channel. According to the study, "Male human users specifically targeted female users."[59]

These estimates accord with the experience of women of color. A study conducted in 2009 asked 992 undergraduate students about their experience with cyber harassment. Nonwhite females faced cyber harassment more than any other group, with 53 percent reporting having been harassed online. Next were white females, at 45 percent, and nonwhite males, at 40 percent. The group least likely to have been harassed was white males, at only 31 percent.[60] However, there is no clear proof that race is determinative; for example, the Bureau of Justice Statistics found that 84 percent of cyber harassment victims were white women, and the majority of victims in the CITU cases were white women.

What is beyond dispute is that being a woman raises one's risk of cyber harassment, and for lesbian, transgender, or bisexual women and women of color, the risk may be higher.[61]

By contrast, men are more often attacked for their ideas and actions. John Scalzi, a science fiction author and popular blogger, has found online invective typically situational. When he writes something that annoys people, they tell him so. People do not make a "hobby" out of attacking his appearance and existence as they do female bloggers.[62]

When men face cyber harassment, their experience often resonates with the abuse faced by women. Cyber harassers try to "diminish" male victims' manliness by accusing them of being gay. *Salon's* editor in chief Joan Walsh writes, "When a white male comes in for abuse online, he's disproportionately attacked as gay."[63] Some harassers impersonate men on dating sites and claim an interest in anal rape.[64] Others accuse men of being women and threaten to rape them.[65] They demean their religious affiliations or friends from traditionally subordinated groups.[66] They accuse men of being sex offenders, turning the narrative of abuse upside down.

Consider the experience of the famed novelist and writing teacher James Lasdun, whose former student used the Internet to accuse him of arranging for someone to rape her, of having sex with another student, and of stealing her work. The abuse was riddled with anti-Semitic rants; Lasdun is Jewish. The former student sent the accusations in e-mails to his publisher, literary agency, the school where he taught creative writing, and various magazines, including the *London Review of Books.* She defaced his Wikipedia page and posted Amazon reviews accusing him of plagiarism and sexually inappropriate behavior. Lasdun described the online abuse as threatening "the basic conditions" of his life, jeopardizing his livelihood, and rendering him "unfit for public consumption."[67]

A victim's actual or perceived sexual orientation seems to play a role as well. Research suggests that sexual minorities are more vulnerable than heterosexuals to cyber harassment. According to a study of undergraduate students at the University of New Hampshire by the sociologist Jerry Finn, 33 percent of the students who self-identified as LGBT received "harassing, insulting, and/or threatening" e-mails from strangers, compared to 14 percent of heterosexual students.[68] Similarly, an early study on real-space stalking found gay men at greater risk of being targeted than heterosexual men.

Statistics on young adults follow a similar trend. During the 2010–11 academic year, the American Association of University Women surveyed 1,965 students, ranging in age from twelve to seventeen, about their experience with unwelcome sexual behavior online. Thirty percent of the students surveyed experienced harassment in text messages, on Facebook, or through other social media in the form of sexual comments, rumors about their sexual activity, or claims about their homosexuality. Of those students, 36 percent of girls reported online sexual harassment, compared with 24 percent of boys. Girls and boys were equally likely (12 percent) to be called gay or lesbian in a negative way. Students who experienced online sexual harassment often experienced similar behavior offline.[69]

Hateful Message

The nature of the attacks similarly attests to bigotry's presence. Hate expresses something uniquely damaging. It labels members of a group as inhuman "others" who do not possess equal worth.[70] It says that group members are inferior and damaged.[71] Bigotry conveys the message that group members are objects that can be destroyed because they have no shared humanity to consider.[72]

Cyber harassment exploits these features by exposing victims' sexuality in humiliating ways. Victims are equated with their sexual organs, often described as diseased: "Don't fuck her, she has herpes." They are labeled sexual deviants and their sexually explicit photos exposed.[73] Doctored images depict victims on their knees with penises ejaculating in their face or tied up and raped from behind.[74] Once cyber harassment victims are sexually exposed, posters penetrate them virtually with messages that say "I will fuck your ass to death you filthy fucking whore, your only worth on this planet is as a warm hole to stick my cock in."[75] The feminist legal scholar and philosopher Robin West has observed that threats of sexual violence "literally, albeit not physically, penetrate" women's bodies.[76] Rape threats profoundly impact women: over 86 percent of rape victims are female.[77] Virtual elimination may follow the imagined penetration: "First I'll rape you, then I'll kill you."

The phenomenon of "revenge porn"—the posting of individuals' nude photographs without their consent—illustrates the gendered nature of cyber harassment.[78] Anyone who has ever made a sex tape or permitted someone to take their sexually explicit photo could find their images exposed online. However, most often, revenge porn features women. In a study of 1,606 revenge porn victims, 90 percent were female.[79]

The gender imbalance may be because men are more likely to insist that women share their nude images with them. Countless women have told me that their male ex-lovers pressured them into sharing or permitting them to take their nude photos. Such coercion can be an element of domestic abuse. Gender stereotypes also help explain why revenge porn sites predominantly feature women. Harassers know that women will be seen as sluts whereas men's sexual activity will be taken as a point of pride. Harassers post women's nude images because they know it will make them unemployable, undateable, and at risk for sexual assault.

The "Long Black Veil" of Shame

The critical race scholar Charles Lawrence observed of racist speech that it "evoke[s] in you all of the millions of cultural lessons regarding your inferiority that you have so painstakingly repressed, and imprint[s] upon you a badge of servitude and subservience for all the world to see."[80] Similarly, the demeaning nature of cyber harassment causes some victims to internalize the message that they are damaged and filthy. One woman who faced online abuse noted, "Someone who writes 'You're just a cunt' is not trying to convince me of anything but my own worthlessness."[81] A college student whose nude photographs went viral after her ex-boyfriend posted them online explained that shame about her sexuality wasn't something that came naturally to her, but it is now something she knows "inside and out."[82] James Lasdun said of his experience that it "became an agony" to go into work, as he "felt the literal reality of that elemental attribute of shame, the desire to hide one's face." He felt that he had "re-created" in his "own psyche the America of the Scarlet Letter and the Long Black Veil."[83]

Some victims try to prevent further abuse by disguising their identity. Female bloggers have switched to writing under male names.[84] They have played down stereotypically female attributes to avoid online abuse.[85] According to the sociologists Debra Winter and Chuck Huff, some women believe their only choice is to adopt a "masculine" communication style or forgo posting online altogether in certain online communities.[86] A study of multiplayer online gamers found that 70 percent of females played as male characters to avoid sexual harassment.[87] Revealing their gender risked being constantly propositioned and informed of their incompetence.[88]

This accords with the experience of a young woman who participated in online forums devoted to creationism that allowed participants to send private messages to each other. Having experienced cyber sexual harassment on the forum, she "would try to prevent people from finding out [her] gender, such as by using screen names which sound like male names and trying to write as a male would write." Despite her efforts, forum users discovered her actual gender. They reacted just as she feared. One said, "We do not want you on the forum. Women have no clue about this kind of stuff." She received "dozens of very sexually explicit e-mails and private messages per day." She did the only thing that might allow her to continue on the forum: she changed her identity to another male-sounding name. Eventually, she tired of pretending and stopped participating.[89]

Hiding or playing down one's identity produces feelings of alienation because one must pretend to be something one is not.[90] Performing an unfamiliar identity takes effort.[91] As the student interested in creationism remarked, assuming a male identity was "bothersome." She lost the "pace of any back-and-forth debates" and had to "avoid talking about the same issues in the same ways (otherwise people discover you, find out you are female, and then the cycle repeats)."[92] It is time-consuming to mute female characteristics, such as when refusing to talk about parenting, and to highlight typically male characteristics, such as assertiveness.[93]

Dismissing Victims

Despite the gravity of their predicaments, cyber harassment victims are often told that nothing can or should be done about online abuse. Journalists, bloggers, lay observers, and law enforcement officials urge them to ignore it. Victims are called "whiny baby girl[s]" who are overreacting to "a few text messages."[94] Often victims are blamed for the abuse. They are scolded for sharing their nude images with loved ones or for blogging about controversial topics like sex. They are told that they could have avoided the abuse had they been more careful. A related message sent to victims is that the benefits of online opportunities are available only to those who are willing to face the Internet's risks. They are advised not to expect anything different if they want to make a name for themselves online. The choice is theirs: they can toughen up or go offline.

If victims seek legal help, they are accused of endangering the Internet as a forum of public discourse. The Internet is a free speech zone, a virtual Wild West, that cannot and should not bear the weight of regulation, commenters say.[95] Victims are told not to expect any help: "This is the INTERNET folks. . . . There are no laws here, at least not clearly defined ones."[96]

These views are wrongheaded and counterproductive. Cyber harassment has a devastating and lasting impact on victims. Victims cannot ignore destructive posts because employers, teachers, and friends searching their names will see them now and in the future. Victims could go offline, but it would make their lives worse. Disconnecting from online engagement guarantees the loss of crucial opportunities for professional advancement, political engagement, and self-expression. Victims are not to blame for the abusive behavior of their attackers. Perpetrators are the ones responsible for the threats, privacy invasions, defamation, and technological attacks, not the victims.

The Internet, ever bound up in our lives, is governed by society's rules. Just as television, newspapers, workplaces, and coffee shops can bear the weight of regulation, so too can online spaces and tools. Although the Internet affords new possibilities for interaction, creativity, and productivity, it is not a hermetically sealed space with its own norms. Life online bleeds into life offline and vice versa.

The notion that more aggression should be tolerated in cyberspace than in real space presumes that virtual spaces are cordoned off from physical ones. But when we connect to the Internet, we do not enter a separate space. Networked interactions are embedded in real life.[97] As the cyber law scholar Julie Cohen illuminates in her work, the digital and the physical are enmeshed. We cannot "log out." Harassing posts are situated wherever there are individuals who view them and thus they have a profound influence over victims' lives.[98]

These social attitudes have prevented a robust response to cyber harassment. Most victims do not report cyber harassment to the police because they assume that nothing will be done about it. Sadly, they are right. Law enforcement frequently fails to act on victims' complaints even though criminal law would punish some of the behavior. Some officers do not get enough legal training; because they do not understand the state of the law, they advise victims to buy a gun and to sue their harassers in civil court. Some officers lack technical know-how to track down perpetrators. There is a widespread lack of literacy about matters related to the Internet, a problem to which officers are not immune. Some officers refuse to do anything because, in their view, the abuse is too personal, too messy, and too difficult to address. Victims are told to turn off their computers because "boys will be boys." Experts point out that it is a struggle to get law enforcement to take physical stalking seriously, and this is even more true for cyber stalking.[99]

A Global Problem

The United States is not alone in struggling with cyber harassment. In the United Kingdom, for instance, researchers estimate that approximately 1.9 million individuals a year experience online harassment. During the summer of 2013, high-profile women were subjected to a torrent of online threats.[100] The feminist activist Caroline Criado-Perez received hundreds of graphic rape threats via Twitter after her successful campaign to feature more female images on British banknotes.[101] Members of Parliament and female writers who publicly supported Criado-Perez faced the same, including bomb threats. One tweet featured a picture of a masked man holding a knife with the message, "I'm gonna be the first thing u see when u wake up."[102]

As in the United States, U.K. law enforcement's response is lackluster. Online harassment victims are told that nothing can be done; they are advised to ignore rape and death threats.[103] Online abuse largely goes unreported, or, if reported, is not recorded by the police.[104] Only 11 percent of adults suffering online harassment reported incidents to law enforcement, leaving a considerable majority, nearly 90 percent, unreported. Victims are uncertain as to whether it is a crime or fear the police would not take them seriously.[105] Even when victims come forward, police do not take online harassment seriously because they fail to understand its impact on victims.[106] According to a study conducted by the University of Bedfordshire, over 60 percent of survey participants reported receiving no help from police regarding their cyber harassment complaints.[107] The same story is told elsewhere, from Brazil to India.[108]

Recurring Patterns

We have been here before. Workplace sexual harassment and domestic violence were once viewed as intractable, normal features of everyday life, much as cyber harassment is viewed today. Until the mid- to late 1970s, individuals and institutions trivialized workplace harassment and domestic violence. The reigning idea was that nothing could be done to redress these problems structurally or legally. Wife battering and supervisors' sexual advances were dismissed as "personal matters" and routine "flirting." As a judge explained when dismissing a female employee's sexual harassment complaint, the "attraction of males to females and females to males is a natural sex phenomenon" that "plays at least a subtle part in most personnel decisions."[109] Alternatively, victims were blamed for their suffering because they stayed with abusive bosses and spouses. Sexual harassment and intimate partner violence were ignored because the workplace and home had their own rules and because the law could not accommodate these sorts of highly personal and idiosyncratic situations.

Fighting Back for Civil Rights

In the past forty years, these perceptions have undergone a transformation. The women's movement helped combat widespread, sacrosanct social attitudes that trivialized sexual harassment and domestic violence. Activists educated the public about the harms wrought by both practices. They debunked the myths that protected them from societal scrutiny. They showed the economic, social, and physical harm inflicted by sexual harassment and domestic violence.

Over time, legal and political elites saw these practices as subordination with tangible economic, social, and political costs, and eventually so did the public. Courts and lawmakers brought law to bear against workplace harassment and domestic violence, signaling the wrongfulness of those practices. Many employers, schools, and other important institutions internalized law's lessons. Although change has been slow, society has made steps to combat sexual harassment and domestic violence.

The Civil Rights Movement's New Frontier: Cyberspace

There is much to learn from this history. Social and legal change is a real possibility despite a history of societal dismissal and belittling of gendered harms. As was true for workplace sexual harassment and domestic violence, combating cyber harassment requires persuasion, law, and institutional support. A movement to delegitimize cyber harassment is in its early stages. Advocates are working to educate the public, much as their predecessors did in the 1970s. They hope to raise awareness so that victims are not left to fend for themselves. A number of individuals from a variety of fields have joined the fray to fight back against abusers. While potentially valuable, some self-help efforts have backfired, to the detriment of victims and their supporters.

Victims cannot and should not have to wrestle with cyber harassment on their own. To date, the law has had a modest impact on cyber harassment, in part due to troubling social attitudes. Too few resources have been devoted to training law enforcement about the technical and legal aspects of cyber harassment. That needs to change if we want law enforcement and prosecutors to enforce existing criminal laws against cyber harassers. Civil rights laws are rarely invoked, even though cyber harassment and cyber stalking are fundamentally civil rights violations. Civil rights laws would redress and punish harms that traditional remedies do not: the denial of one's equal right to pursue life's important opportunities due to membership in a historically subordinated group.

That is not to overlook the important role that law has played against cyber harassment. Some perpetrators have been charged with criminal threats, cyber stalking, cyber harassment, and bias intimidation.[110] Some have faced lawsuits for victims' reputational, emotional, and physical suffering. Legal action, however, remains rare.

Law's shortcomings have made combating cyber harassment difficult. Tort remedies for defamation, intentional infliction of emotional distress, and privacy invasions exist only in theory for some victims due to the high cost of litigation and the absence of privacy protections. Traditional criminal law leaves some abuse uncovered, such as stalking and harassment that is not directly communicated to victims and the nonconsensual disclosure of nude images. Another stumbling block for criminal law is that when cyber mobs attack victims, individuals each contribute a little to the attacks. The totality of their actions inflicts devastating harm, but the abuse cannot be pinned on a particular person.

Then too, some civil rights laws are ill suited to address current civil rights problems. Unlike sexual harassment that typically involves employers who are responsible for abuse in the workplace, cyber harassment that deprives women and other minorities of job opportunities occurs in online spaces that are not controlled by employers. Under antidiscrimination law, cyber harassers often cannot be sued for destroying a person's employment chances just because of the victim's gender or sexual orientation. Civil rights laws fail to criminalize online threats made because of someone's gender and sexual orientation, though they cover racially motivated threats.

A Reform Agenda

Legal reforms are essential to make up for law's deficits. We need to enhance criminal, tort, and civil rights laws' ability to deter and punish harassers. State stalking and harassment laws should cover all of the abuse, no matter the mode of surveillance, tracking, terror, and shaming. The nonconsensual disclosure of someone's nude images should be criminalized. Civil rights laws should be amended to cover bias-motivated cyber stalking that interferes with victims' important opportunities.

Other proposals, including those that would permit victims to sue under pseudonyms, aim to provide legal access to victims who might not otherwise seek redress against their harassers. Pseudonymous litigation offers victims the opportunity to pursue their legal rights without further publicizing the abuse connected to their real identity. If we want to encourage victims to bring claims against their harassers, this form of privacy is essential. States have led the way on antistalking and antiharassment efforts; they might be the most effective channels for change.

True legal innovation also means moving beyond a focus on harassers as the sole problem and addressing the responsibilities of a narrow class of online service providers: sites that encourage cyber stalking or nonconsensual pornography and make money from its removal *or* that principally host cyber stalking or nonconsensual pornography. In the Communications Decency Act (CDA), federal lawmakers secured immunity for Internet intermediaries for the postings of others to encourage self-monitoring. Sites make a mockery of that provision by making a business out of online abuse. Campus Gossip guarantees the removal of destructive rumors, but only for VIP members who pay monthly dues. Revenge porn sites offer to remove individuals' nude photographs for a hefty fee. Congress should amend the CDA to exclude these bad actors from its protection.

What about employers? Law can secure procedural safeguards that lessen the chance that employers will hold online abuse against victims. Before employers can use negative search results against employees, they should give victims an opportunity to explain. This approach draws inspiration from rules governing fair credit reporting that permit individuals to challenge false or incomplete information that would otherwise prevent them from obtaining loans or jobs.

Enforcing existing law and adopting these reforms constitute a "cyber civil rights legal agenda." The overall goal of this agenda is to protect the equality of opportunity in the information age. Our civil rights tradition protects individuals' right to pursue life's crucial endeavors free from unjust discrimination.[111] At its core is safeguarding individuals' ability to make a living, to obtain an education, to engage in civic activities, and to express themselves free from discrimination. Cyber harassment deprives victims of these essential activities. The law should ensure the equal opportunity to engage in life's important pursuits.

Free Speech Challenges

Moving that legal agenda from theory to practice will be challenging, given our culture's insistence that the Internet should be a Wild West free speech zone. As the *Guardian*'s Jane Martinson explains, many believe that society ought to tolerate speech online that would not be tolerated offline because the web is viewed as the "new frontier changing the nature of public and personal discourse."[112] This absolutist, almost religious devotion to free speech, however, needs to be viewed in light of the important interests that cyber harassment jeopardizes. Because the Internet serves as people's workspaces, professional networks, résumés, social clubs, and zones of public conversation, it deserves the same protection as offline speech. No more, no less.

Without doubt, the free speech interests at stake are weighty. Free expression is crucial to our ability to govern ourselves, to express our thoughts, and to discover truths. For that reason, government cannot censor ideas because society finds them offensive. Truthful speech must not be banned just because it makes people uncomfortable. Distasteful, offensive, and hateful ideas enjoy constitutional protection so debate on public issues can be "uninhibited, robust, and wide open."[113]

Contrary to the message of cyber speech absolutists, online abuse can be proscribed without jeopardizing our commitment to free expression. Not all speech enjoys constitutional protection. Certain categories of speech can be regulated because they bring about serious harms and make only the slightest contribution to public debate. True threats are not immunized from regulation even though they may be conveyed in words. Defamation can be regulated consistent with our commitment to free speech. Obscenity does not enjoy constitutional protection even though it involves images. Speech integral to crimes is not immune from criminal penalty; the First Amendment does not protect criminal solicitation and extortion. Certain privacy invasions and cruelty amounting to intentional infliction of emotional distress about purely private matters have historically enjoyed less rigorous constitutional protection and can be regulated without trampling on the First Amendment. Civil rights laws comport with the Constitution because they respond to defendants' targeting of victims due to their membership in a protected group and harassment's tangible harm to life's crucial opportunities rather than defendants' bigoted messages.

The law would chill some expression because, after all, cyber harassment is accomplished with words and images. But credible threats, certain defamatory falsehoods, social security numbers, and nude images posted without consent contribute little to discourse essential for citizens to govern themselves and discover truths. Their net effect is the silencing of victims. Victims could blog, post videos, and engage on social networks without fear of destructive cyber harassment. They could raise money using networked tools unencumbered by rape threats, reputation-harming lies, and distributed-denial-of-service attacks. They could take advantage of all of the expressive opportunities available online. Protecting against online harassment would secure the necessary preconditions for victims' free expression.

More broadly, concerns about free speech animate the recommendations at the heart of this book. In Chapter 9 I argue against real-name policies that aim to curb online abuse. Eliminating anonymity is too costly to self-expression and its benefits are illusory. If online platforms require users to use their real names, they run the risk of chilling conversations essential to a democratic citizenry. Without anonymity, people with unpopular views would not express themselves in online spaces. Domestic violence victims, those struggling with their sexual identity, and many others would remain silent to avoid being identified. At the same time, real name policies are not guaranteed to deter bad actors. Determined harassers may be able to figure out a way to disguise their identity. Private platforms should retain online anonymity as the default rule.

The Urgency of Action

Legal solutions need to be implemented sooner rather than later. The longer we wait, the harder it will be to transform conduct, attitudes, and behavior. With the help of law and the voluntary efforts of Internet intermediaries, parents, and teachers, we might someday achieve a free and equal Internet. We need to take action before cyber harassment becomes a normal feature of online interactions. A hostile online environment is neither inevitable nor desirable. We should not squander this chance to combat discriminatory online abuse; it is early enough in our use of networked tools to introduce equality of opportunity as a baseline norm of interaction.

In my work, I have talked to scores of victims. Of those individuals, twenty graciously spent hours talking to me about their experiences. Although many initially sought my help and guidance as a law professor, they ended up providing me with an invaluable education. Their collective experiences inform every aspect of this project. They help us see the need for social and legal change to ensure equality in our digital age.

Part One is devoted to describing cyber harassment and society's tepid response to it. Chapter 1 provides a detailed account of three cyber harassment victims: a software developer who blogged for professional reasons and then faced a vicious cyber mob attack (the tech blogger), a law student with little to do with online life until anonymous message board participants targeted her (the law student), and a PhD student whose nude images appeared on hundreds of porn and revenge porn sites next to her work bio and personal information (the revenge porn victim).

Beginning the book with their stories is deliberate. I want the reader to get to know, through their harrowing experiences, cyber harassment's totalizing and devastating impact—how it trashes victims' professional reputations and careers, discourages on- and offline pursuits, disrupts both crucial and ordinary life choices, and causes physical and emotional harm. As their experiences demonstrate, cyber harassment interferes with victims' ability to take full advantage of the economic, political, and social opportunities of our digital age.

Chapter 2 connects their stories to the social dynamics of networked communications. I explore the reasons why explicit hate is on the rise online even as it has diminished somewhat offline. The Internet is a force multiplier, for bad and for good. Some of the Internet's key features can radicalize human behavior, pushing us to act more destructively than we otherwise would. These features can be the catalyst for cyber mobs that compete with each other in their cruelty, to victims' great expense. The Internet's case of spreading information and the opportunity to manipulate search technology can compound the harm by spreading destructive harassment far and wide.

In Chapter 3 I explore the social attitudes that leave cyber harassment victims invaded, exposed, and unprotected. Whereas most victims hide the abuse because the fewer people who know, the better, the tech blogger, the law student, and the revenge porn victim sought help from the police and talked publicly about their harassment. Overwhelmingly dismissed as overly sensitive "drama queens," all three women were told that online threats were no big deal, that they were making a mountain out of a molehill. Many scoffed at them for going to the police.[114] The tech blogger and the revenge porn victim were blamed for their predicaments. The tech blogger was told that if she wanted to avoid abuse, she should not have exposed her views about software development. The revenge porn victim was admonished for her "poor judgment": sharing her nude photos with an intimate partner was "asking for trouble." All were told that online life is full of crudeness—too bad, so sad, that was the deal.

As these case studies demonstrate and as empirical work affirms, these social attitudes have serious consequences. Victims tend to under-report cyber harassment. Then too, law enforcement underenforces criminal law when victims do come forward. There are some success stories. Victims and advocates have been working hard to educate policymakers, law enforcement, and prosecutors about cyber harassment's harms, and, ultimately, some victims have gotten help. But those victories are the exception, not the rule.

Part Two seeks to chart a way forward by looking back to a momentous victory for women's rights. Chapter 4 takes cues from prior stages of the civil rights movement. Workplace sexual harassment and domestic violence were once viewed, much like cyber harassment is today, as impossible to solve, as something too personal to be amenable to legal recourse. It took decades of hard advocacy and legal work, but now the public accepts workplace sexual harassment and domestic violence as real injuries worthy of legal redress. In the present, as in the past, raising awareness about victims' tangible harms and agitating for legal reform are crucial first steps to achieving equality under digital conditions.

As Chapter 5 explores, persuasion is most effective when paired with law, as it once was for battling workplace sexual harassment and domestic violence. Existing criminal, tort, and civil rights law can tackle some but not all of the abuse. To fill in the gaps in the law, Chapter 6 offers legal reforms aimed at harassers. In Chapter 7 I propose legal solutions aimed at website operators and employers.

Chapter 8 tackles free speech concerns. I contend that we can protect victims from online abuse without threatening our commitment to free speech. The legal solutions proposed in Chapters 5, 6, and 7 do not seek to expand the existing categories of unprotected speech. Instead, they aim to figure out a better way of preventing, deterring, and otherwise regulating unprotected speech or speech entitled to less rigorous protection under First Amendment law.

Chapter 9 tackles the role that Internet intermediaries, parents, and schools can play to change the digital landscape. Silicon Valley exemplifies the private potential for social action. Internet intermediaries, most notably content hosts, often try to influence online discourse. Some are spearheading efforts to prevent and minimize cyber harassment and cyber stalking. Their efforts should be transparent so users can understand what is expected of them. Parents and educators are crucial players in this fight as well. They are often in the best position to teach our youngest online users how to treat other users with respect and to inculcate productive social norms for generations to come.

Part One

Understanding Cyber Harassment

one

Digital Hate

The Tech Blogger

Like many other people, Kathy Sierra started a blog to advance her career. At *Creating Passionate Users,* she wrote about what she knew best: software design. She drew on her experience as a trainer of Java programming skills for Sun Microsystems and as the author of books on software design. With humorous graphs and charts, she argued that the most effective and popular software programs were those that made users feel good about themselves.

From its inception in 2004, the blog was a hit. It attracted vocal commenters, including some who were inspired by her advice and others who found it shallow.[1] Within two years, Technorati, the blog-ranking site, regularly included her blog in its list of the Top 100 most popular blogs. The blog was a boon to her career and visibility in the technical community.

All of that changed in 2007, when she received frightening e-mails and blog comments. In one e-mail, siftee@yahoo.com wrote, "Fuck off

you boring slut . . . i hope someone slits your throat and cums down
your gob." In a comment on her blog, "Rev ED" said he wanted to have
"open season" on her with "flex memory foam allowing you to beat this
bitch with a bat, raise really big welts that go away after an hour, so you
can start again." Someone commenting under the name "Hitler" wrote,
"Better watch your back on the streets whore. . . . Be a pity if you turned
up in the gutter where you belong, with a machete shoved in that self-
righteous little cunt of yours." Others said she deserved to be raped and
strangled.

The abuse extended to the group blogs Mean Kids and Bob's Yer
Uncle, which were spearheaded by Chris Locke. Locke, a technologist and
the coauthor of *The Cluetrain Manifesto*, started Mean Kids to "formalize
(and goof on) the mean kids slur." Frank Paynter, a Mean Kids blogger,
described the site as "purposeful anarchy" for "pointed and insulting satire."[2] Yet as the media blogger Jim Turner noted, the blog devolved into
"'who could be meanest,' 'who could one up the person with their next
post.'"[3] What happened to Sierra next made that quite clear.

A Mean Kids poster uploaded a picture of the tech blogger with a
noose beside her neck to which the commenter "joey" responded, "The
only thing Kathy Sierra has to offer me is that noose in her neck size."
Another doctored photograph of her appeared, this time on Locke's
Bob's Yer Uncle blog. Under the title "I Dream of Kathy Sierra," the
picture depicted her screaming while being suffocated by red-and-black
lingerie.[4]

Sierra was scheduled to deliver a keynote address at a technology
conference days after she received these e-mails and saw the disturbing
comments and posts. She canceled the talk, explaining on her blog, "As
I type this, I am supposed to be in San Diego, delivering a workshop at
the *ETech* conference. But I'm not. I'm at home, with the doors locked,
terrified. I have cancelled all speaking engagements. I am afraid to leave
my yard. I will never feel the same. I will never *be* the same."[5] Sierra was
frightened. She didn't know the identity of the posters and could not

even begin to guess the identities of "Hitler," joey, and siftee.com. She had no idea who posted the doctored photographs.

After she blogged about what was happening to her, the online abuse began again, this time at the hands of a cyber mob whose members may have had nothing to do with the original attack. A self-identified Internet troll called "weev" told the *New York Times* that he posted her social security number and home address all over the web because he didn't like her "touchy reaction" to the harassment. A fabricated narrative about Sierra's career and family life appeared on the web, claiming that she suffered from domestic violence, got plastic surgery to hide her scars, cheated on her former husband with her current spouse, and turned to prostitution to pay her debts.[6] Posters accused her of being an "attention whore" who made up the online abuse.[7]

Some high-profile bloggers and commentators told her she was being a "silly girl" and that this sort of roughhousing was an inevitable and harmless part of online life. She was told to "turn off" her computer if she could not take the "heat in the kitchen." That is precisely what she did. In her final post, she explained, "I do not want to be part of a culture—the Blogosphere—where this is considered acceptable. Where the price for being a blogger is Kevlar-coated skin and daughters who are tough enough to not have their 'widdy biddy sensibilities offended' when they see their own mother Photoshopped into nothing more than an objectified sexual orifice, possibly suffocated as part of some sexual fetish."

The Boulder police advised her to cancel her speaking engagements and sit tight. But their investigation went nowhere because they lacked the technical skills to figure out the posters' identities to institute a criminal case. She did not consider suing her attackers, even if she could figure out who they were. A cyber mob struck back at her just for publicly discussing her experience. She guessed that a lawsuit in her own name would generate more, perhaps worse online abuse.

Many have asked the tech blogger why anonymous posters singled her out. After all, she wrote about technology, a topic that is not especially controversial. On this question she could only guess. Were posters angry about a comment she made a year before in support of a blogger's right to delete uncivil comments? Some have suggested that possibility to her. At the time of her attack, she had no difficult personal dealings that might have led to the abuse. The cyber mob that exposed her personal data and spread lies about her, however, made their goal clear: they wanted to punish her for the "great crime of speaking out." She assured me that she would not make that misstep again.

That was six years ago. To this day, people defend the bloggers who hosted the doctored photographs of Sierra, declaring them the victims of her "imagined" harassment. In 2011 several individuals tried to vandalize her Wikipedia entry with suggestions that she made up the online abuse. The attempted edits described the most recent phase of her life as her "decline." They suggested that her behavior was "erratic" and "incoherent."[8] Wikipedia administrators rejected the edits, but the fact that people were trying to discredit her years after the attack troubled her greatly.

The tech blogger regrets that the harassment was a defining moment in her life. Few parts of her life were untouched by it. She feels less confident of her place in the tech community. She still worries about her family's personal safety. The harassment changed the trajectory of her career, for the worse. Before the attacks, she frequently accepted speaking engagements. Now she rarely does. As she told me, the attacks took away her ability to do what she loves most—teaching and writing about software development—without feeling afraid.[9] She has "stayed mostly offline."[10]

When we spoke in 2012, she had not restarted her blog and doubted she would. On the blog Concurring Opinions, where I am a permanent blogger, she commented on a post discussing her experience: "I do know that 'get over it/grow a thicker skin' (or the more common, 'grow a pair') doesn't work. That is, unless the goal is to get the 'target' to stay offlinc. Unfortunately, that *does* seem to be the goal of those who say, 'can't-take-the-heat-stay-off-the-'net,' and it's working."[11]

The Law Student and the Message Board

At the start of law school, "Nancy Andrews" (whom I will refer to as "the law student") did not engage much online. Although her friends participated in online communities, most of her time was spent studying. But, as she soon discovered, online communities took an interest in her even if she had no interest in them.

AutoAdmit is a discussion board designed to help college and graduate students, but it is also used to harass (mostly female) students. The board attracts a significant amount of traffic, about a million visitors a month. Its operators generate income by hosting advertisements on their site through an arrangement with Google AdSense.

In 2005 the site's users began a contest called "T14talent—The Most Appealing Women @ Top Law Schools." Soon AutoAdmit began hosting discussions about female law students from various schools, including Boston University, Harvard, Northwestern, New York University, Virginia, and Yale. The law student was one of them.

Friends alerted the law student that she had become the topic of conversation at AutoAdmit. She was surprised, having never visited the site. After searching her name, she found several disturbing message threads about her. In a thread entitled "Stupid Bitch to Attend Yale Law," the poster "STANFORDtroll" warned her classmates to "watch out for her."

Pseudonymous commenters responded with sexually explicit threats, such as "I'll force myself on her, most definitely," and "I think I will sodomize her. Repeatedly" (posted under the user name "neoprag"). Under a thread entitled "Which female YLS students would you sodomize," poster ":D" said, "i would like to hate-fuck [law student's name] but since people say she has herpes that might be a bad idea." Poster "Spanky" said, "Clearly she deserves to be raped so that her little fantasy world can be shattered by real life." Posts linked to videos featuring her picture being bloodied and shot.

Posters spread lies about the law student. Poster "STANFORDtroll" stated, falsely, that she got a "159 LSAT score." Readers were urged to "make sure all the Vault 50s know about [her low score] before she gets an offer." The post was referring to Vault's list of top law firms. According to other posters, the law student's low LSAT score proved she got into Yale Law School only because she is a "nigger." Others said she got into Stanford and Yale because she is Muslim. Poster "yalelaw" claimed she bribed her way into Yale, helped by a lesbian affair with the dean of admissions.[12]

The destructive posts gathered steam during the fall of her second year just as she began interviewing for summer associate positions. For law students interested in working at corporate law firms, recruitment season mainly occurs during the fall of their second year. The law student, an editor of the prestigious *Yale Law Journal*, had sixteen initial interviews. She received four callbacks and, in the end, no offers. That worried her. In contrast, her *YLJ* colleagues and fellow editors were struggling with choosing among several job offers.

As a friend suggested to the law student, Google search results of her name could help explain her inability to obtain a summer associate position. During the fall recruitment season, AutoAdmit posts dominated the first page of a search of her name. Perhaps, as the threads suggested, posters contacted their friends at the top law firms to dissuade them from hiring her. She could not know what happened. With the help of her law school mentors, she got a job with a California firm, long after the recruitment season ended.

The harassment interfered with her law school experience. Because several posters suggested they had physical contact with her, she could not dismiss the posts as rants of strangers. Posts provided updates on her whereabouts, the clothing she wore, and her prior jobs. A poster who claimed to be her classmate said she "seemed normal at first but once you get to know her it's clear she is deeply disturbed." At first, she skipped class because she worried that anything she said or did would be posted online. When she resumed attending classes, she avoided speaking. She stopped attending law school events, including those organized by her human rights student group, something that was important to her. She felt self-conscious about people taking pictures of her. She took incompletes in a few courses because she had too many absences. She suffered significant emotional distress and sought out counseling from the student health center. At times, her insomnia was overwhelming, as was her anxiety.

The law student contacted the individuals running AutoAdmit. She asked them to remove the countless threads devoted to her. She e-mailed the site operator and educational director on numerous occasions. The site operators refused to comply with her requests, time and again.

The New Haven Police Department was her next stop. She told the police that she was afraid that someone in her community might be responsible for the threats. But police officers dismissed her concerns. She was told, "Boys will be boys." Officers advised her to work on "cleaning up" her online reputation.

In 2007 the law student and her colleague (who was similarly attacked on the message board) turned to the courts. They sued thirty-nine pseudonymous posters for defamation, privacy invasions, intentional infliction of emotional distress, and copyright violations, among other claims. Mark Lemley, a Stanford Law professor and cyber law expert, and Professor David Rosen at Yale Law School represented them pro bono, which meant they did not have to pay expensive legal fees.

One of plaintiff counsel's first moves was to ask the court to issue a John Doe subpoena to compel AutoAdmit and ISPs to release information that could help identify the posters. The poster who wrote under the pseudonym "AK47" asked the court to deny plaintiffs' request, arguing that compelled disclosure of information about his identity would violate his First Amendment right to speak anonymously. He argued, quite incredibly, that unmasking him could ruin his job prospects. His argument failed.[13] The court recognized that the First Amendment generally protects anonymous speech but that the right is not absolute. Anonymous posters can be unmasked if a plaintiff has solid claims, but they cannot be unmasked if doing so would stifle legitimate criticism. The court ruled that given the strength of the plaintiffs' tort claims, including defamation, "AK47" could be unmasked.

Although the court ordered the unmasking of the pseudonymous posters, most could not be identified. AutoAdmit had stopped logging IP addresses, which made it difficult to trace posters. Some posters had also used anonymizing technologies to disguise their identity. Of the seven individuals who were identified, two voluntarily disclosed their identities: a Yale Law student and a Fordham Law student. Five pseudonymous posters were identified through subpoenas, including a Seton Hall graduate, a University of Iowa graduate, and a University of Texas student. In 2009 a confidential settlement was reached with seven of the thirty-nine posters.[14]

Unfortunately for the law student, the lawsuit produced a wave of retaliatory abuse.[15] Pseudonymous "Patrick Zeke" sent an e-mail to the Yale Law School faculty with the subject heading "Yale Law Faculty concerning pending lawsuit." The author of the e-mail made false and harmful comments about the law student, including that she "is barely capable of reading (159 LSAT)" and "It seems like the risk of contracting herpes from her would convince any rational person to go to a prostitute first." The e-mail also appeared as an AutoAdmit thread.

Posters tried to sabotage the law student's summer job at the California firm. Using an anonymous remailer, someone e-mailed the firm's partners, claiming that the law student was "barely literate" and that she slept with her dean. It urged the firm to tell its clients about her "misdeeds" because they would "not want to be represented by someone who lacks high character." The law student received the e-mail as well. She was mortified and worried it would jeopardize the goodwill she had been building at the firm. Although the firm's partners assured her the e-mail would not impact their assessment of her, it devastated her to know that they were involved at all.

After the summer, the law student took a break from school. She could not bear returning for the fall of her third year; she did not want to have to explain what was going on to her friends and professors. Posters continued to spread lies about her. She returned to school in the spring.

The law student graduated from Yale Law School a full year after her original graduation date. She received a prestigious Luce Fellowship, which meant that she would be working in South Korea starting in the fall. During her interview for the fellowship, she explained what had happened to her and her desire to combat cyber harassment. As she told me, she knew she was taking a gamble telling her interviewer about the lawsuit, assuming that her interviewer did not already know about it. The woman told her that she admired her bravery and her decision not to back down even when the lawsuit seemed to be making matters worse. In the law student's view, it was a lucky break to have someone so understanding making such an important decision about her application.

The law student started a blog to stay in touch with her family during her time in South Korea. She wrote about the interesting food that she ate and cooked while living and traveling abroad. Her blog soon came to the attention of her attackers. On citizen journalism sites, posters claimed that she went to South Korea to dodge a lawsuit when, in fact, she went for the Luce Fellowship. They pointed to her blog as proof that she had failed as a lawyer. She felt she had no choice but to shut down the blog. She did not want to provoke the posters who were bent on damaging her reputation. She stayed offline in the hopes that they would leave her alone.

In 2011 the law student returned to the United States to work in the Honors Program at the Department of Justice (DOJ). The summer before her job started, she taught a course on human rights law at the University of Maryland Francis King Carey School of Law. The law school's website included the law student in its adjunct faculty listing, posting her name and e-mail address. Before the term began, someone using an anonymous remailer wrote to her. The sender claimed to know where she lived and to be watching her. The e-mail warned, "We know all about your lies, you stupid bitch. We are closer than you think."

When she joined DOJ, posters went after her again and focused on her job, reminiscent of what had happened during her summer at the California firm. Posters urged readers to tell DOJ about her "character problems." Under a message thread entitled "DOJ Attorneys beware of lying bitch coworker 'Nancy Andrews,'" a poster accused her of lying "in sworn federal court filings." One poster wrote, "Personally, I don't think it would be unreasonable to contact the Department of Justice, bar associations, and media outlets to find out why someone with a record of dishonesty and abuse of the legal system was hired as a lawyer at a government agency." Another poster listed her DOJ supervisor's e-mail address, and other posts provided her own e-mail address. "Why did these fuckers hire that cunt?? GOOGLE much, you dumbasses??"[16] Individuals tried—and failed—to vandalize a Wikipedia entry mentioning her. They targeted her husband, falsely claiming that he had plagiarized an article he wrote for the *Yale Law Journal.*

As the law student told me, some of the harassment was frightening; some damaged her professional reputation; some was simply bothersome. She worried that the posts could impact her security clearance at DOJ and her character and fitness requirement for the Bar. What weighed her down was the sense that people hated her so much that they were willing to spend time trying to ruin her career and reputation *all these years later.* She had no idea who most of the posters were or how many people were involved. Not knowing made her feel insecure about those around her. She has a hunch that the poster "STANFORDtroll" is a college classmate whose sexual advances she rebuffed, but she cannot be sure because her attorneys could not identify the poster.

The law student now has a job that she loves, and she shared with me her concerns about her reputation and its impact on future opportunities. Because the destructive posts have remained at the top of Google searches of her name, she cannot ignore them. Meeting new people is always nerve-wracking. Do they know about the online abuse? Does she have to explain?

When the law student does alumni interviews for Stanford, interviewees always ask her about AutoAdmit. They've done their research, as anyone would, and they are curious about her experience. For the law student, it seems hard to imagine a time when she will be able to forget about what happened.[17]

The Revenge Porn Victim

In 2008 Holly Jacobs, a graduate student living in Florida, thought she was in love. She and her then-boyfriend used their computers' webcams to video chat and often exchanged photographs. During their two-and-a-half year relationship, some of those communications were sexual. After they broke up, she trusted him to keep them confidential.

In November 2011 an anonymous tipster e-mailed her a link to a website she had never heard of before along with the message, "Someone is trying to make life very difficult for you." When she clicked on the link, she found her nude photographs and a sexually revealing webcam session, which her ex-boyfriend had taped, on a "revenge porn" site. After searching her name, she discovered that her nude photos and a video appeared on hundreds of sites. The posts included her full name, e-mail address, screen shots of her Facebook page, and links to her web bio, which included her work address.

Soon she received countless anonymous e-mails from revenge porn fans. Some were sexual and frightening. The senders claimed that her pictures and videos aroused them and that they could not wait to have sex with her. She kept creating different e-mail addresses, but somehow people figured out how to find her.[18]

On a site devoted to arranging sexual encounters between strangers, a profile appeared in the revenge porn victim's name, listing her e-mail address and alleged interest in sex. Comments on the profile stated that she was out of a job and wanted to have sex for money. A fake Facebook account went up in her name. Her college and high school colleagues received friend requests, which they accepted. When she found out about the profile, she asked Facebook to take it down. Facebook said that it would do so if she provided proof of her identity. But she was afraid to e-mail Facebook a copy of her license. She imagined the havoc that could ensue if her e-mail account was hacked and her license leaked into her harasser's hands. Facebook took down the profile after it learned that the author posted her nude photographs.

Next her education came under attack. The Human Resources Department at her university received an anonymous phone call that accused her of "masturbating for her students and putting it online." Because she taught students as part of her doctoral program, the accusations could interfere with her degree. One of the university's deans asked her if there was any truth to the caller's claims. After she explained the situation, the dean reassured her that everything would be fine.

One night the revenge porn victim received an anonymous e-mail that said her nude photographs would be sent to her boss at her part-time job unless she got in contact with the sender. The e-mail read, "It's 8:15 where you are. You have until 8:37 to reply. Then I start the distribution." After she refused to write back, her colleagues received the photos from an e-mail address that appeared to come from her. Although the firm assured her that no one would pay attention to the e-mails, she could not help but worry about their impact. She received frightening e-mails at work and feared that she would be physically stalked when going home. She bought a stun gun.

The revenge porn victim sought law enforcement's help. She went to two different police stations in Miami and the FBI, only to be turned away by all of them. Local law enforcement told her that they could do nothing. One officer said that the online posts were technically legal because she was older than eighteen. Another explained that because she had sent some of the pictures to her ex-boyfriend, he owned them and could do what he wanted with his "property." Still another officer said his department lacked jurisdiction over the attacks because they occurred on the Internet. State police failed to investigate the abuse even though Florida criminalizes repeated online behavior designed to harass another person that causes that person substantial emotional distress. When she talked to the FBI, agents told her they could not do anything because the online abuse was not related to "national security." Even though federal law bars anonymous electronic harassment, cyber stalking, and extortion, the FBI told her the "dispute" belonged in civil court and urged her to get a lawyer to sue her harassers and to buy a gun for protection.[19]

The revenge porn victim did what she could to protect herself. She spent hours upon hours contacting site operators, informing them that the video and photos needed to be taken down as required by federal copyright law. She owned the copyright to some of the pictures because she was their original creator.[20] Under federal law, copyright holders have exclusive rights to reproduce, distribute, and publicly display their copyrighted work.[21] Online service providers can avoid liability for copyright infringement if they have a reasonable notification system in place for copyright holders to inform them of an apparent infringement and, upon being notified, act expeditiously to remove the infringing material.[22]

Many site operators simply ignored her request. A few sites said that they would be happy to remove the photos for a fee. The rare site took down the videos and images, but as soon as those sites did, more nude photos appeared on other sites. It was a nightmare game of whack-a-mole, which she kept losing. Her efforts to get the photos and web-cam session taken down ultimately failed. To date, they appear on countless revenge porn, regular porn, and torrent sites.

The revenge porn victim's online reputation was totally destroyed. In early 2012 approximately 90 percent of the first ten pages of a Google search of her name featured the nude video and pictures with demeaning captions that cited her name and former workplace. Because she could not imagine that future employers would consider her application if she kept her real name, she legally changed her name from Holli Thometz to the more common name Holly Jacobs. As she explained to me, she did not want to change her name but felt she had no choice because she "wanted a professional future."[23] She did everything she could to keep her new name as private as possible. She even asked a local judge to seal the records documenting her name change. Unfortunately the county posted her request to seal those records online—precisely what she had wanted to avoid.

The revenge porn victim felt terrorized. "I just feel like I'm now a prime target for actual rape," she explained. "I never walk alone at night, and I get chills when I catch someone staring at me. I always wonder to myself, 'Are they staring at me because they recognize me from the Internet?'" She withdrew from online activities. She closed her Facebook page and LinkedIn profile. She covered up the web camera on her computer to ensure that no one could hack into her computer and turn on the camera.

What would happen after she got her doctorate, she worried? Would she have to tell prospective employers about her name change? Should she disclose her cyber stalking struggle in her cover letters since employers might be able to independently discover the ruin of her former identity? Would raising the issue before she even got an interview disqualify her application? As she observed with great sadness, she felt like a criminal who had to give employers a full account of her "record" by explaining the nude pictures and videos appearing online. She told me that she had toyed with the idea of starting a private consulting practice with a friend who agreed to keep her name out of the marketing materials.

By February 2012 she had grown weary of feeling helpless and un-protected. She started a site called End Revenge Porn, an online hub for victims and advocates to discuss revenge porn. Comments on her site were mostly supportive, though some blamed her for her predicament. She was essentially asked, What did you expect would happen when you sent your boyfriend your nude photographs? It's your fault that the photos now appear online, some said. To that response, she explained, "I let my guard down and trusted [my ex-boyfriend] in ways that I would not with others. I shared intimate moments with him because we were in a relationship." She insightfully noted, "We should not blame the victim" and "It's like blaming someone who was raped and saying that they should not have worn a certain outfit." In her view, blaming vic-tims "gives the perpetrator an out," even though it was the perpetrator who intentionally invaded the victim's privacy and sought to shame and embarrass the victim, and worse. This is just "a new version of victim blaming," she said.[24]

Through her work on her site, she has connected with other victims both in the United States and abroad. She started working with a group of activists, including myself, to think about ways to educate the public about revenge porn and other forms of cyber harassment and to press for innovative legal solutions. The group's members have advised state and federal legislators who are interested in criminalizing revenge porn.

While working to put an end to online abuse, she continued to be victimized. In the summer of 2012 she was scheduled to present her thesis at a conference for the American Psychological Association when someone published the date, time, and location of her talk alongside her nude photos. The poster told readers to "check her out and see if she'll have sex with you for money because she's obviously out of a job." After she received anonymous e-mails alluding to the post, she canceled her appearance. She could not risk the possibility that those individuals might confront her in person.

That incident prompted her and her mother to get in touch with U.S. Senator Marco Rubio. The revenge porn victim told the senator's legislative aide about law enforcement's refusal to help her. The senator's office jumped on the issue and sought help from the Florida State Attorney's Office. In March 2013 she got word that a state attorney would take the case. Investigators traced one of the porn posts to her ex's IP address. (That post falsely suggested she was available for sex.) The Hillsborough County prosecutor's office charged him with misdemeanor harassment. Her ex denied that he had released the photos, contending that his computer was hacked.[25] A month later she sued her ex for intentional infliction of emotional distress, defamation, and public disclosure of private fact.

With the backing of the state attorney and the support of private counsel, she felt ready to talk about her experience publicly. In the past, whenever I talked to reporters about online harassment, I suggested that they interview her because I knew she wanted to share her experience but would do so only if reporters agreed to keep her name a secret.[26] Now she wanted to come forward in her own name to reclaim her public voice and reputation. She was tired of hiding and feeling "like a criminal."[27] She hoped that by sharing what she is going through, the sorts of social and legal changes that this book seeks might come to fruition.

What do we know about the harassers? Some research exists on harassers' gender. A recent national survey reported that women were more likely to be stalked off- and online by men (67 percent) than women (24 percent).[28] More than 80 percent of CITU's cyber harassment defendants were male.[29]

Although one might assume that harassers target only people with whom they have a personal connection, WHOA has found that nearly 50 percent of cyber stalking victims who could identify their attackers (about 60 percent of all victims) had no relationship with them.[30] And rather than a single harasser, groups are routinely involved in the abuse. A recent Bureau of Justice Statistics report estimates that a third of stalking incidents involve more than one offender.[31]

Sometimes victims have a strong sense of their attackers' identities and motives. In some cases, victims believe that their ex-lovers have gone after them because they are angry about the dissolution of the relationship. Other victims, like the tech blogger, say that they know nothing about their anonymous attackers. Cyber harassers leave scant clues about their identities. Although the law student suspects a Stanford classmate initiated the message board attack, she has no idea who most of the posters are, some of whom continued to harass her years after the attacks began.

Can we infer anything about cyber harassers? Cyber mobs often harass victims on sites with distinct subcultures, which can tell us something about their members' interests and values. Some victims have been attacked on sites explicitly devoted to hate, such as the neo-Nazi Stormfront.com. The site's culture of bigotry provides an obvious explanation for the abuse.

Sometimes online abuse involves what Professor Brian Leiter has labeled "cyber-cesspools," understood broadly as sites that encourage users to post abusive material about specific individuals usually to make a profit through ad sales.[32] The culture of cyber cesspools is one of shaming and degradation. Campus Gossip calls on users to post gossip, which tends to involve deeply personal, homophobic, misogynistic, and racist attacks on students and professors.[33] TheDirty.com features sexually explicit posts and pictures of individuals, mostly women.[34] There are approximately forty sites that traffic in revenge porn. The site IsAnyBodyDown featured the full names and contact information of more than seven hundred individuals whose nude photographs were posted.[35] The site's operator, Craig Brittan, described the site as profitable entertainment; he earned $3,000 a month from advertising revenue.[36] Texxxan.com published intimate photographs of young women alongside their personal information, without their permission.[37]

Consider the purported goals of one revenge porn operator, Hunter Moore. Of his endeavors, Moore explained that the more embarrassing and destructive the material, the more money he made. When a reporter told him that revenge porn had driven people to commit suicide, Moore said that he did not want anybody to die, but if it happened, he would be grateful for the publicity and advertising revenue it would generate: "Thank you for the money . . . from all of the traffic, Googling, redirects, and press."[38]

Cyber harassers also gather on sites devoted to "trolling"—"pulling pranks targeting people and organizations, desecrating reputations, and revealing humiliating or personal information."[39] To be sure, trolling cultures are multifaceted and complex. Some trolling sites engage in light-hearted pranks; some seek to embarrass people who annoy them; some generate funny Internet memes and videos like LOL cats. These sites are also home to nontrolling activity, including helpful advice to those having emotional troubles. Some encourage trolls to harass each other, not people outside their orbit. Some engage in activities that expose hatred.

Nevertheless, much trolling is devoted to triggering or exacerbating conflict for purposes of amusement.[40] The ethnographer Whitney Phillips explains that when people "*describe* themselves as trolls," they are saying that they revel in the misfortune they cause.[41] The phrase "I did it for the lulz (laugh out loud)" conveys the desire to disrupt another's emotional equilibrium.[42] As an ex-troll explained, "Lulz is watching someone lose their mind at their computer 2,000 miles away while you chat with friends and laugh."[43] Gabriella Coleman, a noted anthropologist, characterizes trolls as seeking to "invalidate the world by gesturing toward the possibility for Internet geeks to destroy it—to pull the carpet from under us—whenever they feel the urge and without warning."[44]

The identities of many trolls would be difficult to discern given their anonymity.[45] Trolls often crowd-source their attacks, which means a bewildering array of trolling cliques with different values may be involved. As Coleman explains, trolling cliques, such as GNAA, Patriotic Niggars, and Bantown, "justify what they do in terms of free speech."[46] Other trolls seek a negative reaction from the media as much as they want to provoke individuals. Some trolls are just in it for the lulz. Because trolls disavow the seriousness of anything, trolling is often described as "schoolyard" performances. Nonetheless, experts surmise that some trolls who attack individuals in vicious ways are "bigots and racists of one stripe or another who are expressing their real opinions."[47]

A well-known trolling stomping ground is 4chan's "random" forum (known as /b/), which attracts over 300,000 posts per day.[48] /b/ is a "nonstop barrage of obscenity, abuse, hostility, and epithets related to race, gender, and sexuality ('fag' being the most common, often prefaced with any trait, e.g., 'oldfag,' 'straightfag')." A common response to someone claiming to be a woman is "tits or GTFO" (meaning "post a topless photo or get the fuck out"). The forum's culture abounds with shock and offense. At every turn, users aim to press the "bounds of propriety."[49]

/b/'s message board trolls attack individuals and groups.[50] Trolls post individuals' phone numbers, addresses, and social security numbers (called "doxing"). They spread lies, expose private information, and inundate individuals with hateful e-mails. They order unpaid pizzas for delivery to their homes and make prank calls.[51] Trolls use technology to shut down sites. Troll attacks and other "Internet drama" often appear on Encyclopedia Dramatica, a wiki devoted to all things lulz, which the Urban Dictionary describes as "the high school cafeteria of the Internet."[52]

For instance, self-professed trolls embedded flashing computer animation in links on an epilepsy support group message board. Users who clicked on the links saw images flashing at high speeds, triggering migraine headaches and seizures in several epilepsy sufferers.[53] In another case, a young Philadelphia boy posted a picture of his penis on the /b/ forum. Trolls set out to identify the teenager and torment him. Once they figured out his identity, the troll Matthew Bean Riskin sent the photo to the young man's principal, claiming to be a concerned parent. Other /b/ participants said they hoped that the boy would be so humiliated that he would commit suicide.[54]

Some trolls behave like virtual vultures, targeting victims after others have done so. As Phillips explains, trolls are attracted to *"exploitable situations."*[55] For trolls who think it is "fun" to go after people whose emotions are likely to be disturbed, cyber harassment victims are perfect targets. We have seen trolls partake in the second (or third) wave of cyber harassment. Recall that the tech blogger initially faced harassment on her blog and group blogs. The self-identified troll "weev" and his cohorts got involved only after she spoke out against her harassers. Trolls documented their abuse on Encyclopedia Dramatica; the tech blogger's entry includes a false narrative about her alongside the doctored photographs first posted on the group blogs.[56]

It is important to differentiate trolls from the contemporary collective Anonymous, whose roots lie in the /b/ forum. In 2008 groups affiliated with Anonymous started to turn away from trolling and toward activist pursuits.[57] As Coleman insightfully explains, groups affiliated with Anonymous have "contributed to an astonishing array of causes, from publicizing rape cases in small-town Ohio and Halifax to aiding in the Arab and African Spring of 2011."[58] Anonymous was responsible for the distributed-denial-of-service attacks to take down the websites of PayPal, Visa, and MasterCard after they ceased processing donations for Wikileaks.[59]

Anonymous activists defy the trolling creed, though their tactics may be troll-like. A group affiliated with Anonymous launched a campaign to destroy Hunter Moore's revenge porn site. Group members posted Moore's personal information online, including his home address and the names of his family members. KY Anonymous, the operative who launched the campaign against Moore, explained, "We won't stand by while someone uses the Internet to victimize and capitalize off the misery of others."[60] KY Anonymous told Gawker's Adrian Chen that he took on Moore because his friend had been posted on Moore's revenge porn site, and it had come close to ruining her life.[61]

To bring this discussion full circle, recall the harassment of the graduate student I described in the introduction. Commenters on her blog targeted her with sexual threats and lies. Posters on cyber cesspools attacked her in demeaning and sexually threatening ways. Unnamed individual(s) created attack sites in her name, which monitored her whereabouts and spread lies about her. Sometime in 2011 an Encyclopedia Dramatica entry entitled "Fatass Denial Bloggers" discussed the woman, repeating the abuse that appeared online. Although she hired a forensic computer expert, she could not determine the identity of the posters on her blog and elsewhere. As for the Encyclopedia Dramatica entries, self-identified trolls surely had something to do with them, though whether they did it for the lulz or other reasons is unknown.

These experiences raise the question, Is there something about the Internet that fuels destructive cyber mobs and individual harassers? Does the Internet bring out the worst in us, and why?

two

How the Internet's Virtues Fuel Its Vices

When Jeff Pearlman, a writer for *Sports Illustrated,* began his career in journalism in the 1990s, readers rarely attacked writers' intelligence or character. Though readers often disagreed with him, they did so in civil terms. Things have radically changed since then. His readers regularly take a nasty tone when commenting on his work online.

Perplexed by the shift, Pearlman reached out to his commenters to figure out what was happening. After some sleuthing, he discovered the telephone number of Andy, who, in a tweet, had called him "a fucking retard." When they talked, Andy was clearly embarrassed. He told Pearlman, "You know what's funny. I enjoy your writing. But I disagreed with you and I got caught up in the moment. When you read something you think is bullshit, you're going to respond passionately. Was I appropriate? No. Am I proud? Not even a little. It's embarrassing: the internet got the best of me." Pearlman tracked down Matt, a college student, who, via Twitter, sent him snarky comments and a link to a "nasty" pornographic site that would make "even the most hardened person vomit." On the phone, Matt was meek and apologetic: "I never meant for it to reach this point."[1]

The Internet's social environment had a lot to do with Matt's and Andy's behavior. Some of the Internet's key features—anonymity, mobilization of groups, and group polarization—make it more likely that people will act destructively. Other features, such as information cascades and Google bombs, enhance the destruction's accessibility, making it more likely to inflict harm. Yet these same features can bring out the best in us. The Internet's anonymity allows people to express themselves more honestly; networked tools enable us to spread knowledge far and wide. These capabilities are the reason why billions of people flock to the web and other networked communications. The Internet fuels our vices and our virtues.

Anonymity: If You Would Not Say It in Person, Why Say It Online?

The message board posters who attacked the law student and her colleague wrote under pseudonyms. "Paulie Walnuts," "Unicimus," "Whamo," ":D," "neoprag," "Yale 2009," "STANFORDtroll," "HitlerHitlerHitler," and "AK47" said disgusting, frightening things that they surely would never have said to the law student's face. A poster whose real identity was uncovered admitted as much to the journalist David Margolick: "I didn't mean to say anything bad. . . . What I said about her was absolutely terrible, and I deserve to have my life ruined. I said something really stupid on the fucking internet, I typed for literally, like, 12 seconds, and it devastated my life."[2]

Anonymity can bring out our worst behavior, just as this poster admitted. It can nudge us to do terrible things. Not surprisingly, most cyber harassment is accomplished under the cloak of anonymity. Why do people behave differently when they feel anonymous? Or, as an anti–cyber bullying advertisement asked, "You wouldn't say it in person. Why say it online?"

Uninhibited

Anonymity frees people to defy social norms. When individuals believe, rightly or wrongly, that their acts won't be attributed to them personally, they become less concerned about social conventions.[3] Research has shown that people tend to ignore social norms when they are hidden in a group or behind a mask.[4] Social psychologists call this condition *deindividuation.*[5] People are more likely to act destructively if they do not perceive the threat of external sanction. Anonymity is often associated with violence, vandalism, and stealing.[6] This is true of adults and children.[7] People are more inclined to act on prejudices when they think they cannot be identified.[8]

A classic study conducted by the social psychologist Phillip Zimbardo involved female college students who believed they were delivering a series of painful electric shocks to two women.[9] Half of the students wore hoods and oversized lab coats, their names replaced by numbers; the other half received nametags that made it easy to identify them. The study found that the anonymous students delivered *twice* as much electric shock to subjects as the non-anonymous students. The anonymous students increased the shock time over the course of the trials and held down their fingers even longer when the subjects twisted and moaned before them. That the students ignored the pain of those affected by their actions showed the dramatic change in their mentality and empathy when they were anonymous.[10]

Is anonymity's influence muted in online interactions where people's identities are known? When individuals join social networks, create video blogs, or send e-mails, they often reveal their names, pictures, and affiliations. But despite the ability to be identified, people often perceive that what they say or do online won't stick to them. This certainly seems counterintuitive. Computer-mediated interaction, however, occurs in a state of *perceived* anonymity. Because people typically cannot see those with whom they are interacting, they experience their activities as though others do not know who they are.[11] They are less self-aware because they think their actions are being submerged in the hundreds of other actions taking place online.[12] This feeling of anonymity influences how people act online.[13]

Out of Sight, out of Mindfulness

Users' physical separation exacerbates the tendency to act on destructive impulses. People are quicker to resort to invective when there are no social cues, such as facial expressions, to remind them to keep their behavior in check.[14] As *Jezebel*'s Anna North explains, she has been called evil, ugly, and sexless online, but she doesn't experience that kind of abuse offline. In her view, people recognize others' humanity when interacting face-to-face but forget when they are separated or, alternatively, hide their rage until consequence-free opportunities arise for them to express it.[15]

We lash out more when the negative consequences of our actions seem remote.[16] The operator of online forums that published nude pictures of young girls and women without their consent explained that his pseudonymous character was merely "playing a game."[17] Electronic Freedom Foundation vice chair John Perry Barlow aptly remarked, "Cyberspace has the potential to make people feel like information artifacts. If you cut data, it doesn't bleed. So you're at liberty to do anything you want to people who are not people but merely images."[18] Telephone interactions also exhibit these tendencies. Call centers are an important case in point. The sociologist Winifred Poster has shown that Indian workers experience an enormous amount of racial abuse by U.S. customers.[19]

A 2003 study explored the connection between anonymity and hate. It focused on a newspaper's online forum designated for readers to share their views after a group of African American, Hispanic, and Caucasian youths murdered a local resident. The newspaper neither moderated the forum nor required posters to register with the site. During a three-day period, hundreds of posters weighed in on the incident. Of the 279 online comments examined, nearly 80 percent were "vitriolic, argumentative, and racist denunciations of the youths, their families, and various socio-political institutions." Forty percent attacked the youths and their families, often with calls for violent retribution.[20] The study attributed the violent expression of racism to users' anonymity, at least in part, because of the posters who expressed prejudice, only 25 percent revealed their e-mail addresses, while 53 percent of all other posters included their contact information.

We can better appreciate anonymity's influence by thinking about what happens when it is lost. When people are reminded of their potential traceability, they tend to retreat from destructive behavior. Holly Bee, a former moderator of a technology news and chat forum called The Register, explained that when online comments got "very ugly," she would try to calm things down by e-mailing posters who provided their e-mail addresses during registration. She would tell them, "Even though you are not writing under your real name, people can hear you." Posters wrote back immediately and were contrite, almost as if they had forgotten who they were. Bee explained, "They would send messages back saying, 'Oh, I'm so sorry,' not even using the excuse of having a bad day or anything like that."[21]

Anonymity's Virtues

Anonymity is not all bad. Quite the opposite: anonymity can be essential for some people to speak the truth about themselves and the world as they see it. There is substantial evidence that people express their views more freely online than offline because they believe they cannot be identified.[22] Freed from concerns about reprisal, people tend to speak more honestly.

Examples abound of the importance of anonymity for commentary on politics, culture, and social matters. Political dissenters document governmental abuse on micro-blogging sites because they can disguise their real names. Teenagers share their concerns about coming out to family and friends on LGBT sites because they are not worried about being identified. Under the cloak of anonymity, new parents are more willing to be honest about the difficulties of raising children without worrying about being labeled a bad parent.[23]

Anonymity's substantial costs must be understood in light of its great benefits. As I explore in Chapters 8 and 9, anonymity's benefits must be carefully balanced along with its costs.

Networked Tools Bringing Us Together: Facilitating Anonymous Cyber Mobs

In 2008 a journalist blogged about the film *The Dark Knight*, criticizing it and the studio's marketing strategy. In short order, her post was read over ten thousand times. More than two hundred commenters attacked the journalist personally: "Get a life you two dollar whore blogger, The Dark Knight doesn't suck, you suck! Don't ever post another blog unless you want to get ganged up"; "If you were my wife, I would beat you up"; "I hope someone shoots then rapes you." The journalist had no idea who the anonymous posters were: "Are they working at the desk next to you? Are they dating your sister, your best friend, your mother, your daughter—you?"[24]

The Internet was key to the formation of the anonymous cyber mob that attacked the journalist. It is easy to bring large groups of people together online. Gone are the physical and time restraints that make it difficult and expensive for people to meet in real space. All that is needed is an Internet connection. Whereas cost and geography once prevented individuals from finding one another and from meeting, search engines make it happen with little effort. Networked technologies remove practical barriers that once protected society from the creation of antisocial groups.

Consider the way the Internet has fueled the rise of online hate groups. In the past fifteen years, we have seen astronomical growth in extremist groups online. In 2000, 1,400 hate and extremist sites appeared online. Today there are over eleven thousand, and their numbers grow every day.[25] It is safe to say that many of these groups would never have formed in real space.

In the present as in the past, anonymity has contributed to the rise of bigoted mobs. People are more inclined to join antisocial groups when they do not have to disclose their identities.[26] The hoods of the Ku Klux Klan were key to the formation of mobs responsible for the death of African Americans. In our time, anonymity has encouraged the formation of destructive cyber mobs like the ones attacking the tech blogger and the law student.

Together for Good

Of course, the Internet does not facilitate just cyber mobs. Online groups come together for prosocial reasons: political campaigns, fundraising efforts, and school projects. They form to counter bigoted messages. The "It Gets Better" online campaign provides support for sexual minority teens bullied because of their actual or perceived sexual orientation. A week after the project was initiated, its website had more than thirty thousand entries, and 650 videos were uploaded to its YouTube channel. Much like our concerns about anonymity, the Internet's ability to mobilize groups can be positive and negative.

Moving to Extremes: Group Polarization in Cyberspace

Recall the young actor whose fan site was overrun with homophobic taunts and graphic threats. A poster (later discovered to be one of the actor's high school classmates) explained that at first, the comments seemed "derogatory, though jesting." Soon, however, the "postings became increasingly bizarre and weird, it became apparent . . . that everyone was competing to see who could be the most outrageous." After someone wrote that the actor deserved to die, the poster added his own message to what he called the "Internet graffiti contest." He acknowledged writing, "I want to rip out your fucking heart and feed it to you. . . . If I ever see you I'm going to pound your head in with an ice pick." He offered this explanation for his words: "I wanted to win the one-upmanship contest that was tacitly taking place between the message posters." As he noted with regret, his "desire for peer approval . . . induce[d] [him] into acting like an idiot."[27]

Group dynamics contributed to the poster's abusive behavior. The legal scholar Cass Sunstein explains that when groups with similar views get together, their members hear "more and louder echoes of their own voices."[28] Learning that others share their worldviews boosts their confidence.[29] People embrace more radical views because they feel more confident and because they want to be liked.[30] They often exaggerate their views to convince others of their credibility, which leads to the sort of competition for persuasiveness that the poster described.[31] This phenomenon is known as group polarization. We have seen that it is easy for like-minded people to find each other online; the feeling of anonymity minimizes perceived differences among online users so they feel part of a group.[32]

Online hate groups have shown this sort of shift to extremes.[33] The work of Magdalena Wojcieszak, a political communications scholar, demonstrates the growing intensity of hate on white supremacist sites. Based on surveys of 114 individuals and posts on neo-Nazi sites during a six-month period, one of her studies found that although extreme people tend to turn to radical groups in the first place, their participation in online hate groups nudges them to greater extremes. Forum discussions were instrumental in changing "fence-sitters" into white nationalists, for instance, "When I first saw this site I figured it was just a bunch of wack-o white supremacists crying 'white power.' . . . But I started reading anyway. . . . I thank the members here for their hard work and dedication in researching the facts they present and for opening my eyes to the real world. I am now a White supremacist and damn proud of it." Even short online exchanges resulted in more radical thinking. The White Power online forum asked participants whether they preferred extermination, segregation, or slavery as punishment for the hated group. Posters who initially opted for segregation changed their vote to extermination after hearing others' replies.[34]

An early case study tracked the rapid escalation of sexual harassment in an online discussion. A male participant, "ViCe," initiated the harassment by telling a male administrator, "Aatank," that he's "got women here u'll fall in love with!" and by providing him with a "babe inventory." Aatank responded by telling female participants, "U can call me studboy. What color are your panties?" ViCe cheered on Aatank, who, in text signaled as "actions," "rushed" up to the women and "yanked" off their "panties." Comments grew increasingly abusive toward female participants as commenters encouraged each other. The study's author analogized the harassment to "gang violence, where two or more individuals together may commit more violent acts than they would have had each been alone."[35]

Cruelty Competitions

Group polarization is evident in the activities of cyber mobs. Cyber mob members engage in an ever-escalating competition to destroy victims. The sheer volume of the abuse ups the ante. The crowd-sourced nature of the destruction disperses feelings of culpability for some individuals, even though the effects are concentrated to the extreme. The tech blogger observed, "Horrific behavior online—fueled heavily by anonymity—is strengthened and repeated because it is reinforced. For way too many years, the most hateful comments were not just tolerated but high-fived (see YouTube, Digg, and the many blog and forum comments). Worse, the online hate comments then escalate in a need to one-up the previous high-fived hateful comments and we went from 'you are a moron' to 'you deserve to be raped and murdered, and here is how it should be done in explicit detail (bonus for Photoshopped example!)' over the course of a decade."[36] The blogger Jim Turner described the attack on the tech blogger this way: "Suddenly the game began to be a 'who could be meanest,' 'who could one up the person with their next post?' Someone then crossed the line."[37]

Hearing supportive voices for the abuse encourages more abusive behavior. A forty-nine-year-old man known as "Violentacrez" created over six hundred online forums exposing sexually revealing pictures of women and girls who never consented to their pictures being displayed. The forums were named "Choke a Bitch," "Rape Bait," and "Jail Bait." In an interview taken after the journalist Adrian Chen revealed the man's actual identity, Violentacrez attributed his behavior to the fact that he was "playing to an audience of college kids." His "biggest thrill" was his audience's support for what he was doing. He was compelled to keep going to please his outsized fan base. He received 800,000 "karma points," which means that 800,000 users positively endorsed his forums.[38]

The actual extent of group polarization online is not known. There are no solid answers to questions about how often it happens and whether some groups depolarize given the diversity of online users. Just by looking at the comments sections of blogs and political news sites, one can conclude, though nonscientifically, that people are often polarized and aggressive to the detriment of others.[39]

Socially Productive Extremes

At the same time, online group discussions can push people in more positive directions if group members embrace norms of respect.[40] In one well-known study, high school students answered surveys about their racial attitudes. Unbeknownst to the students, researchers used the surveys to form different groups of like-minded individuals. After a round of discussion among like-minded participants, the groups who initially leaned toward prejudiced attitudes became even more prejudiced, and the groups of relatively unprejudiced students became even more tolerant.[41] Much like the Internet's other key features, group polarization is neither good nor bad; it can be both.

Spreading the Abuse: The Information Cascade

Aside from radicalizing our behavior, the Internet can magnify victims' injuries by spreading the abuse far and wide. Consider how fast harassing posts spread after 4chan trolls targeted an eleven-year-old girl. Trolls exposed the girl's real name, home address, telephone number, and social media accounts. They claimed that her father beat her and that she had tried to commit suicide. The posts went viral after social bookmarking services and blogs picked them up. Typing the first three letters of the girl's first name into Google produced search prompts featuring her name.[42] Within days, there were thousands of web postings about her.[43]

The young girl was caught up in a dynamic known as an "information cascade." Everyday interactions involve the sharing of information. Because people cannot know everything, they often rely on what others say even if it contradicts their knowledge. At a certain point, it is rational for people to stop paying attention to their own information and to look to what others know. People forward on what others think, even if the information is false, misleading, or incomplete, because they think they have learned something valuable. The cycle repeats itself, spreading information to many others in an information cascade.[44]

Once an information cascade gains momentum, it can be difficult to stop. Social media tools highlight popular information, laying the groundwork for its continued distribution. Consider social network sites like Facebook that recommend stories read by "people like you." After seeing friends' recommendations, users tend to endorse them. It's all too easy to push the "Like" button and increase the visibility of a friend's post. When filtering algorithms preferentially weight our friends' information, as they often do, their recommendations are drawn from relatively homogeneous groups. Social media tools surround us with ideas with which we already agree, which we then spread to others. And on it goes.

Search engines contribute to the escalation of information cascades. Popularity is at the heart of the tools that run most search engines. Search engines index, monitor, and analyze hyperlinks, the pathways between webpages, to ascertain which sites best answer users' queries. Google's PageRank algorithm, for instance, ranks sites with the requisite search terms based upon the number and importance of their inbound links.[45] Roughly speaking, if enough *other* pages link to a website using similar anchor text, it has a greater likelihood of achieving prominence in searches of that text. As websites accumulate more visitors and links, their prominence in search results continues, even if their information is untrustworthy.[46]

Google's feature Autocomplete operates in this fashion. When users input search terms, Google displays related searches based on similar queries of previous users. Google explains the feature this way: "Start to type [new york]—even just [new y]—and you may be able to pick searches for 'New York City,' 'New York Times,' and 'New York University' (to name just a few)." Google's "predicted queries are algorithmically determined based on a number of purely objective factors (including popularity of search terms) without human intervention." In turn, information appears in Autocomplete prompts, which users select and recommend to others.[47] When searching the law student's name, Autocomplete prompts include her name with the words "LSAT" and "AutoAdmit," which lead to the harassing posts on the message board.

Networked technologies are perfect tools to generate information cascades of sexually charged comments, lies, and suggested violence. As a society, we are predisposed to respond to certain stimuli, such as sex, gossip, violence, celebrity, and humor.[48] The Internet amplifies this tendency. This explains the popularity of gossip sites like Campus Gossip, TheDirty.com, TMZ.com, and PerezHilton.com. It's no surprise a Google search of "Jennifer Aniston" produces Autocomplete prompts such as "Jennifer Aniston pregnant" due to false rumors of pregnancies. Because Google knows our interests and produces search results based on them, future search results feature more of the same—more sex, more gossip, and more violence. As in a maze, once you enter a certain pathway online, it can be hard to find your way out.

Cascading Truths

Of course, information cascades do not necessarily propagate destructive harassment. Social media tools can spread truthful information, correcting lies about cyber harassment victims. Truthful posts might gain so much attention that they appear prominently in a search of victims' names. Destructive lies could drop down into the third or fourth page, relative obscurity in the world of search. Social news sites could recommend truthful information to others who do the same. Information cascades can help restore victims' good names, just as they can undermine them.

The headlines are filled with examples of the Internet as a tool for spreading truthful information.[49] Arab Spring protesters spread videos and photographs of police torture, leading to the toppling of tyrants. After the death of a government dissident at the hands of the Egyptian police, an anonymous human rights activist created the Facebook page "We Are All Khaled Said" that posted cell phone photos of the dissident's battered and bloodied face. Within six months, 473,000 users had joined the page, spreading the word about the timing and location of protests. Protestors shared videos and photographs of Egyptian police torture and abuse on Twitpic, Facebook, and YouTube.[50] As a result, thousands upon thousands gathered at protests. The journalist Howard

Rheingold refers to such positive information cascades as "smart mobs." Information cascades can indeed be forces for good or bad.

The Google Bomb: From Information Cascades
to Malicious Manipulation

In 2010 the law student put up a LinkedIn profile, hoping it might replace abusive posts at the top of searches in her name. But once message board posters saw she was trying to create a positive online presence for herself, they countered her efforts. They announced they would not let her "influence google rankings by getting her name out there for things other than this thread." Posters asked message board participants to help them manipulate her search rankings. Their goal was clear: "We're not going to let that bitch have her own blog be the first result from googling her name."

Mission accomplished. To this day, a search of her name produces an Autocomplete prompt with her name and the message board's name. If the prompt is selected, the *first* page includes links to the destructive posts with titles suggesting that she is a liar and a racist. Even if users ignore the Autocomplete prompt, they will see that the fourth entry on the first page of the search results asks if she is a "lying bitch." Other abusive posts appear below that entry, including "DOJ attorneys: Beware of lying bitch coworker."

How did posters do that? Search engines can be gamed to elevate rankings of destructive pages. In a relatively harmless form of manipulation, people engage in search engine optimization, which helps promote the visibility of favored content. A site may repost certain content in popular sites, for instance, to attract more visitors.

A more troubling form of this practice is called a "Google bomb." Google bombs enhance the prominence of favored posts in searches of particular terms, such as a name (like the law student's). Individuals can accomplish this by linking to their favored webpages with anchor text—the relevant name, for instance—in as many other webpages as possible. They deliberately create thousands of phony web links to elevate a particular page to the top of search engine rankings despite the lack of any authentic relevance for its contents.[51] The more sites that link to a page along with anchor text, the more popular that page will seem to search engines. This strategy is particularly effective when links to a page appear in sites deemed important by search engines, such as Wikipedia.

The end result is the public's deception about the genuine relevance of links to search terms. A well-known example of a Google bomb involved efforts in 2006 to ensure that the top result for a search of the term "miserable failure" was the official George W. Bush biography. President Obama inherited the prank when he first took office. In 1999 the search phrase "more evil than Satan himself" returned the Microsoft homepage as the first result.[52] In February 2011 the first entry in a search of "murder" was the Wikipedia entry for abortion.

Unlike the "miserable failure" hoax, most Google bombs are not obvious. They are never "recognized as such because the mechanism that detonates [it] is a common utilitarian device (anchored text link) put to use for good and bad every day, and many times over."[53] Google bombs can be deadly to people's careers precisely because obvious signals of fraud are missing. That was certainly true for the law student attacked on the message board. It's hard to recognize that a Google bomb has distorted searches without clear cues of manipulation.

Turning the Tables: the Counter Google Bomb

Cyber harassment victims could engage in Google bombs to counteract cyber mobs. The feminist blogger Jill Filipovic's supporters did just that after anonymous posters targeted her on the message board Auto-Admit. The blogger tigtog called for "personal-political collective action" to diminish the prominence of harassing threads in searches of her name. Readers were instructed, "Please feel free to copy any or all of what I've written here to your own blog in order to help change the top-ranked search engine results for Jill Filipovic. If you don't have your own blog then please at least link to one of Jill's post[s] listed below at your preferred social networking site and give it the tag 'Filipovic.'" Linking to Filipovic's blog posts, web bios, and writings would raise the search engine rankings of these results over the rankings of harassing posts.

The effort to "correct an injustice" against the feminist writer paid off. The blogger's Google bomb instructions spread like wildfire all over the Internet. By March 2007 the top results for a search of "Jill Filipovic" included her web bios and publications. The destructive threads dropped to the bottom of the first page rather than appearing at the top. As tigtog explained, "Anyone googling [Filipovic's] name should now never be under any misapprehension that the sexist cyber-obsession about her was something she volunteered for or in any way agreed to take part in."[54]

Some Google bombs devolve into an arms race. That was true after a virulently anti-Semitic website, Jew Watch, appeared as the first entry in a Google search of the word "Jew." Jewish activists urged people to link the word to a Wikipedia article so that search engine users would more likely see that article first rather than the Jew Watch site. Neo-Nazi sites launched a counter Google bomb, which put the anti-Semitic site right back near the top, where it remains today.

Explicit hate has found a powerful outlet in the Internet, and understanding the Internet's key features helps us understand why. In a speech at the Web 2.0 Expo in 2009, the social media expert danah boyd offered these insights: "Our bodies are programmed to consume fat and sugars because they're rare in nature. . . . In the same way, we're biologically programmed to be attentive to things that stimulate: content that is gross, violent, or sexual, and gossip, which is humiliating, embarrassing, or offensive. If we're not careful, we're going to develop the psychological equivalent of obesity. We'll find ourselves consuming content that is least beneficial for ourselves and society as a whole."[55] We are already substantially there. The Internet helps fuel the desire for salacious, sexually degrading, and hateful content and spreads it far and wide.

Of course, the Internet's key features could be marshaled to combat this inclination and bring out our best selves. Herein lies the challenge. The Internet's key features have powerful positive and negative potential. Given their benefits, they should not be constrained without serious thought. These features are what make the Internet so important to economic, social, and political activities, even as they can destroy them.

Regulating online interactions embroils us in a difficult balancing act, which I will soon explore. But before we can even engage in that endeavor, we need to consider the social attitudes that prevent us from seeing cyber harassment as a problem deserving intervention. The next chapter explores those social attitudes and their costs.

three

The Problem of Social Attitudes

In November 2011 the British newspapers *New Statesman* and the *Guardian* interviewed female bloggers about their experiences with online abuse.[1] No matter their ideological bent, the women regularly "g[ot] called bitches or sluts or cunts" who deserved to be "urinated on and sexually abused."[2] Anonymous commenters detailed "graphic fantasies of how and where and with what kitchen implements" the bloggers would be raped.[3] According to the *Guardian,* some of the "best known names in journalism hesitate before publishing their opinions," and others have given up writing online because they could not stand the abuse.[4]

The *Telegraph*'s Brendan O'Neill called attempts to combat the personal attacks a "Victorian effort to protect women from coarse language." In his view, "fragile" and "particularly sensitive" female bloggers were threatening free speech because their "delicate sensibilities" had been "riled." O'Neill remarked, "If I had a penny for every time I was crudely insulted on the internet, labeled a prick, a toad, a shit, a moron, a wide-eyed member of a crazy communist cult, I'd be relatively well-off. For better or worse, crudeness is part of the internet experience, and if you don't like it you can always read *The Lady* instead."[5]

O'Neill spoke for many others who dismiss cyber harassment as no big deal. This response stems in part from stereotypes that women tend to overreact to problems. Commenters insist, for instance, that unlike "real rape," words and images on a screen cannot really hurt anyone.[6] The trivialization of cyber harassment is also connected to the tendency to blame victims for their predicaments. Victims are told that they should have seen the abuse coming because they chose to blog or share their nude images with intimates.[7] After all, commenters say, the Internet is the Wild West, like it or lump it. The message is that no intervention is warranted.

In this chapter I explore prevailing social attitudes and take stock of the fallout. Victims often do not report online abuse because they assume that law enforcement will not do anything to stop it. Their intuition is regrettably accurate. Law enforcement agencies often fail to follow up on victims' complaints because they are not trained to see online harassment as a problem and feel uncomfortable getting involved, even when the law suggests that they should.

Trivializing Cyber Harassment: Drama Queens and Frat Boy Rants

The public often accuses victims of exaggerating the problems they face on the Internet. Commenters insist that victims have forgotten the childhood saying "Sticks and stones will break my bones, but words will never hurt me."[8] According to a popular criminal law blogger, concerns about cyber harassment are wildly overblown: "It's all a grand conspiracy to discriminate against women and stop their voices by hurting their feelings, even when their feelings aren't hurt at all. And men are shooting gamma rays at them to cause premature menopause too, right?" In his view, cyber harassment victims are "overreacting" to speech that is not "vagina friendly."[9]

The tech blogger was told the same. In a post entitled "Why the Lack of Concern for Kathy Sierra," a *Huffington Post* blogger wrote, "A lot of people think that the entire brouhaha about the death and rape threats Kathy Sierra received have been vastly overblown."[10] Recall that the abuse included comments like "Fuck off you boring slut . . . i hope someone slits your throat and cums down your gob"; "Better watch your back on the streets whore. . . . Be a pity if you turned up in the gutter where you belong, with a machete shoved in that self-righteous little cunt of yours"; and "The only thing Sierra is good for is her neck size" next to a picture of her head with a noose beside it. Nonetheless, the tech blogger was dismissed as a "hysterical drama queen" who needed to "toughen up."[11] Because the abuse involved hurt feelings, it was not worth anyone's attention or time.

Victims are told not to complain because cyber harassment is "nonthreatening satire."[12] According to online commentary, the tech blogger turned "nasty but ambiguous words and images" into "concrete threats to her well-being."[13] The writer Jay Geiger argued that the tech blogger faced "a bunch of stupid kids saying stupid things" who "will probably cry in front of their mom" when they get caught.[14] Markos Moulitsos, the founder of the liberal blog *Daily Kos*, described the tech blogger's "situation" as a big "so what?" He expressed dismay that she took the threats seriously. He questioned her sanity and her veracity: "Look, if you blog, and blog about controversial shit, you'll get idiotic emails. Most of the time said death threats don't even exist—evidenced by the fact that the crying bloggers and journalists always fail to produce said 'death threats.' But so what? It's not as if those cowards will actually act on their threats."[15] Not that it would warrant abuse, but the tech blogger did not write about anything "controversial" at all; her blog explored software design.

The response to the law student's experience struck a similar chord. David Margolick, a former *New York Times* reporter and a longtime contributor to *Vanity Fair*, told National Public Radio that the posts were "juvenile," "immature," and "obnoxious," "but that's all they are . . . frivolous frat boy rants."[16] Other commenters dismissed the abuse as the "shtick" of digital natives: "The whole auto-admit thing does have a generation gap component to it. Some of the stuff you kids say just doesn't make any sense to me (DHAPMNG and WGWAG for example), but I see that it makes YOU laugh . . . and I realize that it isn't there for me. . . . As I had jokes my parents didn't ever understand, so shall you."[17]

Along these lines, the University of Wisconsin law professor Ann Althouse said that the law student had no cause for complaint: "Too beautiful to appear in public? Too hot to be hired? Come on! What rational employer would deny you a job just because idiots chatted about you online in a way that made it obvious that the only thing you did was look good?"[18] The University of Tennessee law professor Glenn Reynolds remarked that the law student needed thicker skin about the "Internet trash-talk": "Isn't 'the scummiest kind of sexually offensive tripe' exactly what we always used to say people had to put up with in a free country?"[19] Of harassing posts the law student faced, another commenter said, "Rape/violence threats are so common on the internet that it's pretty much impossible to take them as anything other than hyperbole."[20]

Recall the young actor attacked on his fan site with frightening, homophobic comments, including threats to kill him.[21] After the media covered his lawsuit against the posters, a commenter wrote, "If the kid with the 'singing career' can't handle criticism and the occasional over-the-top fan threat, then his singing career is already over." Others said that the case involved simply "harmless teenagers who posted hateful remarks on the Internet."[22]

Another Trivialization Strategy: Blaming Cyber Harassment Victims

Blaming victims is another common response to online abuse.[23] Commenters say that victims have no one to fault but themselves.[24] The tech blogger was told, "If you aren't comfortable with the possibility of this kind of stuff happening, then you should not have a public blog or be using the Internet at all."[25] *Daily Kos*'s founder chastised her for staying online if she could not "handle a little heat in her inbox." The law student was blamed for her predicament because she did not ignore it. The revenge porn victim has gotten countless e-mails telling her that because she chose to share her photos with a trusted intimate, she could not "complain" when her "stupid" decision came back to bite her.

Revenge porn victims have told me that the overwhelming response to their struggles is that they are responsible for their nude photos appearing online. The operator of the revenge porn site Texxxan.com told the press, "When you take a nude photograph of yourself and you send it to this other person, or when you allow someone to take a nude photograph of you, by your very actions you have reduced your expectation of privacy." Ironically the site operator refused to disclose his real name to a *San Francisco Chronicle* reporter because he didn't "need the headaches that publicity brings."[26]

Some journalists have echoed the sentiment. In response to Maryland delegate Jon Cardin's proposed bill to criminalize the nonconsensual publication of sexually explicit photos, the *Baltimore Sun* columnist Susan Reimer urged young people to stop "sharing their naked photos." She acknowledged, "This point of view puts me dangerously close to blaming the victim. . . . But we should be telling our daughters and our young women friends that they cannot count on the police, the courts or the legislature to protect them from the consequences of their own poor judgment."[27]

Many believe that writing about controversial topics is an invitation to abuse. On Sex and the Ivy, Harvard University student Lena Chen blogged about her hookups, alcohol use, and "feeling like a misfit at an elite school where everyone else seemed so much more self-assured." Anonymous commenters attacked her not with substantive criticisms of her opinions but rather with death threats, suggestions of sexualized violence, and racial slurs.[28] On the gossip blog Ivy Gate, someone posted her sexually explicit photos, taken by her ex-boyfriend, without her permission.[29] Her nude photos were reposted all over the Internet.[30] The abuse continued even after she shut down the blog.[31] The woman was accused of provoking the abuse by "making a blog about her personal sex life."[32] She was labeled an "attention whore" who deserved what she got. Commentators said that she leaked her own nude photos to get attention.[33] Others said that she wrote about sex because she wanted posters to make sexual advances.

We have been blaming cyber harassment victims since the earliest days of the Internet. In 1995 a participant in the virtual world LambdaMOO proposed legislation entitled "Hate Crime," which would impose penalties on those who harassed others on the basis of race. The petition's detractors argued that legislation wasn't "important" because those offended could have but declined to hide their race in their self-descriptions. A user named Taffy wrote, "Well, who knows my race until I tell them? If you want to get in somebody's face with your race then perhaps you deserve a bit of flak." Another wrote, "Seems to me, if you include your race in your description you are making yourself the sacrificial lamb."[34] Today's current lackluster law enforcement response owes much to the claim that victims can avoid their problems themselves.[35]

Dismissing Cyber Harassment:
Unique Rules for the Virtual Wild West

Some defend online abuse as a "normal" feature of the Internet. Abusive commentary is "part of the territory—if you want to write a blog like this, you're going to deal with unpalatable people."[36] According to Althouse, the blogosphere is "like the Wild West," where people can "use any technique" to "climb to the top," including "push[ing] women out."[37] The phrase "It's the Internet, innit [Isn't it]" captures the notion that the Internet is exempt from social norms. People allegedly assume the risk of abuse by using networked tools. Simply put, we cannot complain if the roughhousing turns in our direction.

Reactions to the tech blogger followed this thinking. Many people said to her, "'Get a life, this is the Internet.'" A letter to the *Salon* editor entitled "It's the Blogosphere, Stupid" argued that the tech blogger should not have been surprised by the attack given the Internet's norms.[38] She was told to "cowboy up" like everyone else.[39] The writer Rich Kyanka said the same: "Can somebody please explain to me how this is news?" Kyanka summarized what happened in this way: "1. Someone writes a blog. 2. Somebody reads this blog. 3. The person who reads the blog sends the person who writes the blog a message informing them they would be killed. Am I missing something here? Nobody was murdered. No crimes were committed. The same thing that's been happening on the internet for two decades has happened yet again. The faceless masses make baseless asses of themselves."[40] Of the doctored photos that depicted the tech blogger with a noose beside her neck and being suffocated by lingerie, the tech guru and author Chris Locke said, "Evidently, there are some people who don't much like her. The same could be said of myself or indeed of anyone who blogs much. It comes with the territory."[41]

This view is pervasive. According to the *Information Week* journalist Mitch Wagner, "The sort of language used against [tech blogger Kathy]

Sierra is outrageous, unacceptable, and, unfortunately, it's become normal on the Internet. Name-calling is routine, and death threats aren't particularly unusual. It's hard to read any public forum on the Internet without wanting to wash your hands."[42] Until the attacks on the tech blogger, the blogger Laura LeMay thought that "constant harassment was so common and so obvious it wasn't even worth mentioning." It had "gone on for so long and I had gotten so used to it that it hadn't occurred to me that this is anything other than what it means to be female on the Internet." She remarked, "Maybe this isn't normal and maybe it shouldn't be."[43]

The Same Story: Sexual Harassment at Work and Domestic Violence at Home

Not long ago, society viewed workplace sexual harassment as no big deal, just as many view cyber harassment as frat boy nonsense. Until the late 1970s, employers and judges defended male supervisors' "amorous" activity as a normal and healthy development. Sexual harassment was a "game played by male superiors" who "won some" and "lost some."[44] A state unemployment board, for instance, ruled that a woman lacked good cause for quitting her job after her boss demanded that she sleep with him and told male clients that she would have sex for the right price. According to the referee assigned to her case, "Today's modern world requires that females in business and industry have a little tougher attitude towards life in general."[45] In a case involving a male supervisor who repeatedly tried to molest two female employees, the judge ruled that federal law could not interfere "every time any employee made amorous or sexually oriented advances toward one another."[46] According to the judge, "The only sure way an employer could avoid such charges would be to have employees who were asexual."[47] These decisions were not unique.[48]

Society's response to domestic violence was the same. Spousal abuse was viewed as "lovers' quarrel[s]."[49] Judges told complainants, "Let's kiss and make up and get out of my court."[50] Unless abuse involved "permanent injury," husbands and wives were advised to "work things out on their own."[51] Law enforcement's training manuals echoed this sentiment. The police officer's role was to "soothe feelings" and "pacify parties" involved in "family matters."[52] One Michigan judge explained, "Law enforcement agencies say, well, that's just a domestic problem and you should see your lawyers and handle it in civil court. A domestic call is not serious in their view."[53]

A young mother's experience in 1974 demonstrates our indifference to intimate partner violence. For seven years, the woman's husband regularly beat her. One night, when the woman asked her husband what he wanted for dinner, he hit her in the eye, then in the nose and mouth. Badly bleeding, the woman called the police. Officers told the woman that she and her husband should work things out on their own. After they left, her husband beat her and threatened to strangle her if she called the police again. After the woman moved out of the family home, her husband tracked her down and beat her in front of her children. This happened repeatedly. Each time, she called the police, and each time, they refused to arrest her husband. When officers finally arrested the husband after the fifth call, the court dropped the assault charge because the husband promised he would never hit her again.[54]

Just as contemporary commenters regularly tell cyber harassment victims that they brought their predicaments on themselves, society once said the same to sexually harassed employees and battered wives.[55] Female employees were told that they "asked" supervisors to proposition them by dressing provocatively.[56] A broadcasting executive claimed, "You know, some women dress so that people look at their breasts."[57] Courts legitimated this view by permitting employers to defeat sexual harassment claims with proof that female employees invited employers' sexual advances.[58] In a *Redbook* story about congressmen who hired female staffers if they agreed to sleep with them, the reporter Sally Quinn criticized the women for having chosen "to compromise [their] bodies."[59]

Some said that employees could not complain about sexual harassment if they chose to stay at their jobs.[60] By remaining at work, female employees showed that they enjoyed their supervisors' advances.[61] Society minimized the culpability of sexually harassing employers and maximized the responsibility of sexually harassed employees.[62]

Twentieth-century judges and caseworkers similarly treated battered women as the responsible parties rather than their abusers.[63] If only they had cleaned their homes and had dinner ready for their husbands, they would not have been beaten. Battered wives were advised to improve their appearance to prevent their husbands from beating them.[64] Police training guides instructed officers that it would be unreasonable to remove abusive husbands from the home because they were simply responding to their wives' "nagging."[65] Psychiatrists reinforced this view with a medical diagnosis: battered wives allegedly suffered from "feminine masochism" that propelled them to nag their husbands into beating them; they derived pleasure from the abuse, or so doctors explained.[66]

Judges dismissed assault cases if the abused spouses did not leave their batterers.[67] Judge Richard D. Huttner, the administrative judge of New York City Family Court, recalled a colleague's reaction to domestic violence victims: "Why don't they just get up and leave? They have been taking these beatings all these years and now they want me to intercede. All they have to do is get out of the house. What do they want from me?"[68] Judges required battered women to prove that they had done everything to rid themselves of their abusive partners, including divorce, to warrant taking the assault seriously.[69] A woman's decision to remain with her abusive partner was treated as evidence that the abuse never happened or was not serious.[70]

Just as today many claim that the Internet has its own norms, society once contended that special rules governed the workplace because it was a private arena. There, men could engage in sexual harassment; it was a perk of the job. Courts dismissed sexual harassment complaints because employers were expected to deal with them.[71]

Society similarly turned a blind eye to domestic violence on the grounds that the family, not the state, governed the home.[72] Courts treated the home as "uniquely unsuited to regulation by law" because it was separate from civil society.[73] The home had its own "government," designed to suit its "peculiar conditions." Like fights on the playground, where the school is deemed the appropriate disciplinarian, the family was best suited to address violence in the home.[74] Police officers treated wife beating as a "private" matter.[75] A 1970s Detroit police manual instructed, "When a police officer is called to a private home having family difficulties, he should recognize the sanctity of the home" and "create peace without making an arrest."[76] Some officers viewed arrests in wife battering cases as attacks on the family unit.[77] Courts and police argued that arrests would "blow up" marriages.[78]

The Cost of Social Attitudes: The Underenforcement of Criminal Law

In the past, societal attitudes left domestic violence victims and sexually harassed employees without help from law enforcement or the courts. Now, as then, similar views about cyber harassment are costly. Victims fail to report cyber harassment, and even when they do, law enforcement often ignores their complaints.

Cultural views explain why many victims do not report cyber harassment.[79] A 2009 National Crime Victimization survey found that only 40 percent of the estimated two million stalking victims—of which 25 percent experienced cyber stalking—reported incidents to law enforcement, with men and women equally likely to report. Why did the majority of stalking victims fail to contact the police? Thirty-seven percent of survey participants thought the abuse was not important enough to report; 17 percent believed the police would not help them because they would not take it seriously or because they would blame them for the harassment; 13 percent thought the police lacked legal authority or sufficient tools to address the problem. Three percent of those surveyed attributed their failure to report to feeling ashamed.[80] A study of female college students found that more than 83 percent of stalking incidents were not reported to police or campus law enforcement officials. Seventy-two percent of the students explained that they did not know stalking was a crime; 33 percent of the students thought the police would not take it seriously.[81]

As cyber harassment victims suspect, state and local law enforcement have difficulty addressing cyber harassment complaints. At times, officers resist dealing with victims' reports for the same reasons that laypeople refuse to take online harassment seriously. The majority of law enforcement agencies do not investigate cyber stalking complaints because they lack training to understand the seriousness of the attacks, the technologies used to perpetrate them, and the usefulness of existing laws.

Police officers in local and rural communities rarely have any training about the problem of cyber stalking.[82] Parry Aftab, an attorney who runs an online safety and education nonprofit, explains that small-town officers have trouble advising online harassment victims because "they don't know the laws." They "encourage the victims to ignore the abuse, even if it requires intervention, because they're embarrassed to say that they don't know how to handle it."[83] For instance, in Allegheny County, Pennsylvania, only 30 percent of police departments have a staff member capable of investigating cyber stalking cases.[84] When the journalist and *Slate* writer Amanda Hess went to law enforcement after being repeatedly and graphically threatened on Twitter, the officer asked her, "What is Twitter?" The officer told Hess not to bother with using Twitter; that way she could avoid the abuse.[85]

According to Jim Beurmann, president of the Police Foundation, victims often have to educate state and local police about existing stalking and cyber stalking laws. The advice that police give to victims is to stay offline. As Beurmann notes, that is like telling someone not to go outside. "Why should you have to change your life because this jerk's traumatizing you?" he says. "This is one of the areas in which police need the most training."[86]

Federal cyber stalking laws are also woefully underenforced. My review of federal court records reveals only ten cases involving cyber stalking charges from 2010 to 2013.[87] After the FBI pursued a cyber stalking complaint against General David Petraeus's biographer Paula Broadwell (which exposed their affair and led to his resignation as CIA director), a former federal prosecutor told *Wired* magazine, "This is highly irregular. Highly, highly irregular. With a case of e-mail harassment, we'd normally say: we're kind of busy, contact your local police. You know that old cliché 'let's not make a federal case out of it?' Well, in this case, it rings true."[88]

Part of the problem is officers' poor response to stalking generally. Stalking is "frequently overlooked and often misunderstood."[89] According to a 2009 survey, almost 19 percent of respondents reported that law enforcement took *no* action after hearing stalking complaints. Those surveyed attributed police inaction to a lack of interest in getting involved, a sense that no legal authority existed, and incompetence.[90] Christopher Mallios, an attorney who assists law enforcement in their response to violence against women, explains, "It seems crazy, but traditional stalking laws have been on the books for only the past 20 years; before that, stalking was treated as a 'summary harassment offense,' which is the equivalent of a traffic ticket. It's still a struggle in many places to get law enforcement to take stalking seriously; cyberstalking, even more so."[91]

Inadequate Understanding of the Law: The Revenge Porn Victim's Case

Ignorance of the law was on display in law enforcement's initial fumbling of the revenge porn victim's case. When local police rebuffed her, they mischaracterized her state's criminal law. An officer said her ex had the right to publish her nude photos and video next to her name and the suggestion that she "liked cock" and "masturbated for her students" because she shared the images with him. The officer believed her ex owned the pictures, so he could do what he liked with them. Another officer told her that because she was over eighteen, nothing could be done. Florida's cyber harassment law, however, prohibits a willful online "course of conduct" causing the targeted individual substantial emotional distress. It sets no age requirement for victims and does not exclude private videos shared with another person in confidence. Although Florida law enhances the punishment for cyber harassment if the victim is not yet eighteen years old, treating it as an aggravated felony, officers failed to recognize that the harassment statute protects victims of any age.

The FBI's dismissal of the case suggests that their agents had insufficient training on federal cyber stalking laws. The agents claimed that they could do nothing because the online abuse did not involve "national security" concerns, even though the federal cyber stalking law says nothing about national security. It is true that the federal cyber stalking statute in force in 2012 only applied when a defendant targeted a victim who lived in another state. The FBI might have declined to help her for that reason because she resided in the same state as her ex, but that is not what they told her. Instead they said her case involved a "civil" matter. They made clear that cyber stalking was not sufficiently serious to warrant their getting involved.

Inadequate training explains why Florida police initially refused to help the college student Kristen Pratt. In 2008 a fellow student, Patrick Macchione, contacted Pratt via Facebook. His messages quickly turned sexual and threatening. Macchione posted dozens of YouTube videos featuring him pointing his finger in a shooting motion and vowing to kill her.[92] He appeared in one of the videos standing outside her workplace as she drove by. He sent her threatening tweets like "It's up to you to save your life."[93] Pratt contacted the Florida Department of Law

Enforcement after Macchione called her over thirty times at her workplace. Police told Pratt that nothing could be done since Macchione did not seem to know her home address. Pratt explained, "It's not the police's fault, but I learned later that there possibly was something they could do. They just didn't want to."[94] Pratt was right. Florida's cyber stalking law covered Macchione's repeated threats of violence. Officers did not have to wait until he made clear he knew where she lived. They finally arrested him after he confronted her at her workplace. In January 2012 a court sentenced him to four years in prison.

Just Boys Being Boys: The Law Student's Experience with Law Enforcement

Sometimes law enforcement officers refuse to help victims because they do not think cyber harassment is a big deal. We saw this in the New Haven Police Department's handling of the complaint filed by the law student. The first time she spoke to the police, officers told her to ignore the abuse because the posters were "just boys being boys." To pressure the police to take her case seriously, she talked to the media. But even after the *Washington Post* wrote about her experience, officers still said they could not do anything. They advised the student to "clean up her Internet search."

To be sure, the posts fell into a hazy legal area. They may not have constituted credible threats. It was not clear if any one poster was responsible for several posts to justify criminal harassment charges. But that's not what the officers told the student. They attributed their inaction to their belief that the postings were juvenile pranks.

In the case of the young actor who faced graphic threats of violence on his site, the police detective conducting the investigation on behalf of the Los Angeles Police Department determined that the "annoying and immature Internet communications did not meet the criteria for criminal prosecution."[95] A retired LAPD detective with twenty years of law enforcement experience, however, disagreed with that assessment in testimony submitted in support of the student's tort and civil rights case against the poster responsible for several threats of physical violence. In his opinion, many of the messages constituted "a clear and specific threat of death" within the meaning of California's criminal harassment statute. He understood the postings as "a group attempting to antagonize the victim . . . to work in concert to harass, annoy, and at times threaten with violence and intimidation a boy perceived to be gay."[96]

Local police declined to assist a woman after a chat room user threatened to rape her daughter. Officers urged her to "go home [and] turn off the computer" instead.[97] Kathleen Cooper experienced much the same after someone posted threatening comments on her blog and his own. The poster said that he could not be responsible for what "his minions" might do to her. Law enforcement officials laughed it off. They told Cooper, "Oh, it's not a big deal. It's just online talk. Nobody's going to come get you."[98]

Inadequate Technical Skills: The Tech Blogger's Criminal Case Hits a Dead End

Sometimes the problem stems from inadequate technical know-how and insufficient resources to hire outside help. Recall the tech blogger who faced graphic threats and frightening doctored photographs. She reported the threats to the Boulder County sheriff's office. Unlike most law enforcement faced with cyber harassment complaints, officers took the harassment seriously. They urged her to stay home until they could figure out the perpetrators' identities and assess the nature of the danger she faced. That proved a difficult task. The tech blogger explained to me that the officers "barely understood e-mail, let alone the cyber-sleuthing needed to unravel international IP addresses and anonymous comments." Even though Boulder County expressed concern about her case, local law enforcement could not track down the perpetrators.[99]

The Boulder District Attorney's Office agreed that a crime had been committed, but it had no one to bring charges against.

The Sausalito, California, Police Department refused to pursue a case involving a woman whose contact information repeatedly appeared alongside an online advertisement for deviant sex. Officers told her that they could not pursue charges because she lacked enough evidence linking the crime to the person she suspected was behind it. The woman countered, "Why should I have to find out who's doing it in the first place? Shouldn't the police be trying to find out who that someone is?"[100] I will tackle the technical hurdles accompanying legal responses later, when exploring what law can and cannot do in addressing online harassment. For now, it is crucial to note that law enforcement agencies may decline to train officers on technical matters or to seek outside assistance because cyber harassment is not a high enough priority.

Some Forward Progress

There has been some progress, at least at the state and local level. Generally speaking, data on the enforcement of cyber stalking statutes are hard to find because most states do not collect it. North Carolina is one state that has released statistics on its enforcement of cyber stalking laws. Researchers analyzing that data found that while only twenty-eight individuals were charged with cyber stalking and four convicted in 2001, four hundred individuals were charged and forty-one convicted in 2008.[101]

A number of agencies devote considerable energy to online harassment, such as the New York City Computer Investigations and Technology Unit. CITU began its work in 1995, investigating cases in which offenders use the Internet to commit a crime. Cyber stalking has been the most prevalent crime reported to and investigated by the unit, constituting almost 40 percent of complaints.

More such efforts would go a long way to combat social attitudes that prevent police officers from taking cyber stalking seriously and enforcing existing criminal laws. Reporting statistics for arrests and convictions would help apprise the public and advocacy groups of police's responsiveness to cases. Training would help law enforcement handle cyber stalking complaints. More of that is certainly needed, as I will argue in Chapter 6. The Florida state's attorney shuttered the revenge porn victim's case before it even started due to troubling social attitudes about the seriousness of her predicament. I will discuss her legal case in Chapter 5.

Charging and Sentencing Decisions

We see the influence of social attitudes on the punishment meted out to cyber harassers who are caught. Prosecutors undercharge or, worse, refuse to charge perpetrators. According to the National Institute of Justice Stalking Workshop's 2010 report, prosecutors tend to charge stalking as a misdemeanor because they think judges will not believe the charges or because they do not view stalking as being as serious as a felony even though it could be pursued as a felony.[102] Some law enforcement officers report that when they arrest stalkers, prosecutors refuse to pursue the charges, leading them to stop making arrests.[103] As the report suggested, district attorney's offices need more training about stalking.

Judges hand out light sentences because they also need additional training to appreciate the seriousness of stalking.[104] Take, for instance, a 2006 prosecution under a federal law criminalizing the anonymous use of the Internet to threaten or harass in a case where the defendant sent threatening e-mails to his ex-girlfriend and pornographic e-mails to her colleagues under her name. After pleading guilty to two counts of harassment (with up to five years of incarceration as a possible sentence), the defendant received five hundred hours of community service and five years of probation, with no jail time.[105] The National Center of Victims of Crime reports that stalking sentences longer than a few days or weeks of jail time are rare. Most stalkers spend little time in custody if and when they are arrested, prosecuted, and convicted.[106]

There are noted exceptions. Recall the man who harassed and stalked his ex-wife and children by placing fake online advertisements suggesting their interest in being raped and by threatening to kill them in e-mails. In July 2013 a Maryland jury convicted the man for stalking, harassment, reckless endangerment, and violating a protective order. The judge handed out the harshest sentence available: eighty-five years in prison.[107]

Changing social attitudes is crucial to moving forward against cyber harassment. It is a fight we know well. During the 1960s and 1970s, the women's movement had to change how society saw and responded to domestic violence and workplace sexual harassment. That struggle provides important insights for an agenda to combat cyber harassment.

Part Two

Moving Forward

four

Civil Rights Movements, Past and Present

In the past, spousal abuse and workplace harassment were dismissed as ordinary "family disputes" and workplace "flirting." Women's complaints were ignored because they "chose" to stay with abusive husbands and bosses. Domestic batterers and sexual harassers were protected because the home and workplace had special rules. While still a presence in society, these views are no longer the norm. What helped bring about that change?

In the 1960s and 1970s, the women's movement challenged social attitudes about domestic violence and sexual harassment. Feminist activists and lawyers taught judges, officers, legislators, and ordinary people about women's suffering. They debunked the reasons society protected those practices. Thanks to their advocacy, the public began to wake up to the suffering of sexually harassed employees and battered wives.

The women's movement of the twentieth century has much to teach those interested in combating cyber harassment in this century. Education and law can help us combat destructive social attitudes. Change will not be swift, but it is within reach. With these lessons in mind, antiharassment groups are engaging in advocacy work that their predecessors engaged in forty years earlier. As one might expect, we have seen some successes and some failures. In this chapter I look at what has been happening on the ground and suggest next steps in the fight against online harassment.

The History of Fighting Back

In the 1970s, the women's movement contested the social attitudes that had protected, immunized, and legitimated subordination at home and at work. Activists and lawyers exposed sexual harassment and domestic violence as illegitimate and systemic. Much headway was made through education, the courts, and politics.

The Movement against Sexual Harassment in the Workplace

The fight against sexual harassment began with efforts to raise awareness about women's suffering.[1] In 1975 Lin Farley and her colleagues at Cornell University wrote a letter to progressive lawyers around the country describing Carmita Wood's resignation from her job as an administrative assistant after being subject to repeated sexual advances at work. After receiving a promotion, Wood began working for a physician who every day pinned her between his body and a piece of furniture and made sexual gestures. Wood's supervisor told her, "A mature woman should be able to handle such situations." He advised her "not to get into these situations."[2] Farley and her colleagues wrote that Wood's situation "is one in which working women continually find themselves and that forcing a woman to make a choice between self-respect and economic security is impossible—whichever choice she makes she will [lose]." They asked for help organizing a campaign to combat this pattern of "sexual harassment."[3]

With that letter, sexual harassment acquired a name and much-needed visibility. That spring, Farley and Wood attended a feminist "speak-out" in Ithaca, where they publicly discussed sexual harassment. A few months later, the New York City Commission on Human Rights, which was chaired by Eleanor Holmes Norton, held hearings on women in the workplace featuring Farley as a speaker. The *New York Times* covered the hearings in an article entitled "Women Begin to Speak Out against Sexual Harassment at Work."[4]

Farley's letter generated a response from a Yale law student named Catharine MacKinnon, whose ideas would galvanize efforts to delegitimize sexual harassment. MacKinnon circulated a draft of her book *Sexual Harassment of Working Women*. In it she argued that far from a "natural sex phenomenon" or personal matter that women should handle on their own, sexual harassment was a problem of sex-based power. MacKinnon made the case that sexual harassment subordinated women to men in the workplace and constituted sex discrimination. Her book made the novel claim that "quid pro quo harassment"—"put out or get out"—was not the only form of sexual harassment that violated Title VII of the 1964 Civil Rights Act. She argued that subjecting women to a hostile work environment, including repeated exposure to sexually offensive or denigrating material, as a condition of employment violated Title VII. Hostile sexual environments created a barrier to sexual equality in the workplace just as racial harassment interfered with racial equality.[5] Workplace sexual harassment was far more than individual wrongs that could be remedied by tort law; it constituted the societal wrong of sex discrimination.

Lawyers, relying on MacKinnon's arguments, brought cases asking federal courts to interpret Title VII to prohibit sexual harassment.[6] Advocacy groups like the Working Women United Institute published newsletters highlighting ways for victims to fight back. In 1977 the Working Women United Institute established a service that provided information about local laws, advice on how to handle sexual harassment, and referrals to crisis counselors. Advocates spent time teaching employers about sexual harassment and urging them to adopt antiharassment policies.[7]

Lawmakers heard from the women's movement as well. Activists lobbied for state legislation that expanded unemployment compensation law to cover sexual harassment as good cause to leave one's job voluntarily. They testified in government hearings about the economic consequences of sexual coercion in the workplace and linked those consequences to discriminatory attitudes of male supervisors.[8]

Combating Domestic Violence in the Home

The battered women's movement started much like the campaign against sexual harassment by bringing spousal battering out of the shadows and into public consciousness. Advocates coined the term *domestic violence* to expose battering as a social problem rather than a private family matter.[9] In publicity campaigns, activists talked about how domestic violence impaired women's basic capabilities. They spoke about battered women's fear, terror, and physical injuries. In the national magazine *Mother Jones*, Andrea Dworkin wrote of her own experience: "I remember being hit over and over again, the blows hitting different parts of my body as I tried to get away from him. . . . If one survives without permanent injury, the physical pain dims, recedes, ends. . . . The fear does not let go. . . . It makes the legs buckle, the heart race. It locks one's jaw. One's hands tremble. . . . As years pass, the fear recedes, but it . . . never lets go."[10] Advocates talked to the press about the practical impediments faced by battered women, including their well-founded fear of being unable to support their children financially and of facing continued violence if they moved out of the home.

These efforts to reframe the discourse were bolstered by litigation and law reform efforts. Feminist activists and lawyers engaged in retail justice by helping individual women obtain housing and public benefits.

They sought system-wide change with litigation challenging the legal system's inattention to domestic violence. Class-action lawsuits claimed that law enforcement's refusal to arrest batterers violated equal protection guarantees. Activists educated court personnel about effective legal responses to domestic violence, including orders of protection requiring abusers to leave the home. The battered women's movement supported legislation, such as mandatory arrest policies, no-drop prosecution requirements, and tougher sentences for offenders.[11]

These efforts gained the public's attention. While the *New York Times* had not made even a single reference to wife beating as a social issue in the early 1970s, it devoted numerous articles to spousal abuse in the mid-1970s. The *Times* covered activists' class-action suits filed against New York City's Police Department and Family Court for failing to protect abuse victims. By 1975 television journalists had caught on. The CBS national morning news program aired an entire series on wife beating.[12]

Scholars have shown that when social movements successfully condemn and delegitimize a social practice, judges and politicians often jump on the bandwagon.[13] On two different fronts, the home and the workplace, the women's movement got the attention of lawmakers, courts, and law enforcement by discrediting the reasons behind society's protection of domestic violence and sexual harassment.[14]

To be sure, sexual harassment and domestic violence have not disappeared, not by a long shot. Because social attitudes were deeply entrenched, change has been slow. Some legal reforms have been criticized as insufficiently protective of victims.[15] Nonetheless, the treatment of women at work and in the home is far better in the twenty-first century than it was in the twentieth. The women's movement helped lay the groundwork for social change.[16]

The Next Battleground for Civil Rights: Cyberspace

The next stage of the women's rights movement should be focused on achieving equality in digital networks. A movement to delegitimize cyber harassment is in its formative stages. A first step is changing how the public sees and understands online abuse. Much like their predecessors in the women's rights movement, antiharassment groups are working to educate the public about victims' suffering, to bring court cases, and to lobby policymakers. Individual victims and their supporters have also tried to fight back against harassers. While self-help efforts have provided some relief, some have ignited even more abuse.

Changing Social Attitudes: Making Clear Cyber Harassment's Harms

To move forward in the fight against cyber harassment, we need to dispel the myths that have prevented us from taking it seriously. Just as twentieth-century advocates educated the public about sexual harassment and domestic violence, twenty-first-century activists are working hard to highlight the problem of cyber harassment. Advocates have been talking to the press, writing op-eds, and speaking to interested groups about cyber harassment's harms. As I explored in the introduction and illustrated in case studies, cyber harassment victims lose their jobs and have difficulty finding new ones. They take off time from school and withdraw from on- and offline activities to avoid further abuse. Their emotional and physical suffering can be profound.

Responding to the Blame Game

Another myth that must be dispelled is the notion that victims bring the abuse on themselves. Cyber harassment victims are not to blame for their suffering. They cannot walk away from online abuse, as the "Turn off your computer" refrain suggests.[17] Rape threats, posts suggesting their interest in sex, damaging lies, and nude photos cannot be ignored.

Employers, clients, and friends will see the harassing posts when they search victims' names whether or not the victims shut down their computers, blogs, or social network sites.

Compare the possibility of avoiding networked abuse with in-person harassment. When a stranger sexually harasses a woman on the street, she may be able to escape the abuse by leaving the area. Although others in earshot might have heard the interaction, a recording likely would not exist for the public to watch and re-watch in the future. The woman may never see the stranger again. By contrast, when cyber harassment victims turn off their computers, posts are accessible to anyone searching their names.[18] A search of the revenge porn victim's former name reveals over a hundred sites featuring her nude photos despite her dogged efforts to have them taken down.

In any event, whether cyber harassment victims could mitigate their injuries is not the issue. No one should be expected to withdraw from online activities to avoid targeted attacks, much as women should not have been told to leave their jobs to avoid supervisors' sexual demands or to leave their homes to avoid spousal abuse. One cannot abandon online platforms without great cost, just as sexually harassed workers and abused wives could not leave the workplace and home without a steep price. Networked tools are indispensable to every aspect of our lives: jobs, professional opportunities, socializing, civic engagement, and self-expression. Victims cannot just "get rid of the technology" to prevent the abuse. They cannot dispose of their laptops or cell phones, even though their abusers are harassing them with threatening e-mails, because those devices connect them to coworkers, family, friends, and, when necessary, the police.[19]

Victims of revenge porn should not be blamed when harassers post their nude photos without permission. Victims are not at fault when ex-lovers violate their confidence and trust. We do not insist that individuals have done something wrong in giving their credit cards to waiters who give their card numbers to thieves. We should not blame individuals whose ex-partners promised to keep their nude photos private and betrayed that promise by posting the photos online.

Bloggers who write about controversial topics like sex are not to blame for their harassers' abuse. Sexual double standards are at the heart of that objection. Would we say that to men writing about sex? Tucker Max earned millions from writing books and a blog about his drunken sexual experiences with hundreds of women.[20] By contrast, female sex bloggers have been attacked and told that they "asked for it."[21] A sexual double standard is alive and well.

Cyberspace = Real Space

Cyber harassment advocates must disprove the notion that cyberspace is exempt from real-space norms, much as activists in the past had to convince the public that workplaces and homes had the same rules as the rest of society. Now, as then, the notion that more aggression is tolerated in the Wild West of cyberspace than in real space is based on a false set of assumptions. It presumes that virtual spaces are cordoned off from physical ones. When we connect to the Internet via our cell phones, computers, or tablets, we do not enter a separate space. Networked interactions are embedded in real life.[22] Harassing posts are situated wherever individuals are who view them. They profoundly influence victims' on- and offline lives.[23] Just as harm in the workplace and home have profound social consequences, so too does harassment in networked spaces.

Advocacy against (Cyber) Stalking: From Earliest Days to the Present

In the 1980s, domestic violence groups lobbied lawmakers to recognize stalking as a crime deserving serious punishment. They succeeded after several high-profile cases caught the nation's attention, including the 1989 murder of the actress Rebecca Schaeffer. The first state to criminalize stalking was California, in 1990. Within four years, all fifty states had banned stalking.

State stalking laws were not uniform. California, for instance, defined stalking as a "knowing and willful course of conduct" directed at a person that "seriously alarms, annoys, torments, or terrorizes" that person, "serves no legitimate purpose," and causes the person to suffer "substantial emotional distress." By contrast, Arizona's stalking law covered a harassing "course of conduct" involving credible threats of violence.[24] Most stalking laws required proof that defendants were in close physical proximity to victims.[25] In 1996 Congress caught up with state legislators, amending the Violence against Women Act (VAWA) to criminalize interstate stalking. Federal lawmakers defined stalking as the physical crossing of state lines with intent to injure or harass another person that placed the person in reasonable fear of death or bodily injury.

In the mid- to late 1990s, emerging technologies provided stalkers with an easy way to attack victims from afar. Stalkers no longer needed to be physically near or even to communicate directly with their victims to intimidate and psychologically terrorize them. State stalking laws were not well equipped to address these changes.

Advocates sought to update these laws to keep pace with changing technology. Advocacy groups like the National Center for Victims of Crime (NCVC) urged legislators to ban stalking via the Internet and other electronic means.[26] In 1997 Jayne Hitchcock cofounded the nonprofit Working to Halt Online Abuse to support these efforts after experiencing online harassment herself. On message boards, posters claimed that Hitchcock wanted sex and listed her contact information. Readers were urged to "stop by" her house and to call "day or night." She received up to thirty phone calls a day from strangers.[27] Her e-mail inbox was flooded with spam. Her employer received e-mails claiming that Hitchcock had quit her job.[28] Local police did not intervene because her home state, Maryland, punished only in-person stalking. The FBI's Computer Crimes Unit let her file a complaint but did not follow up because it was not yet a federal crime to use networked tools to stalk another person.[29]

Hitchcock first set out to change the law in her state. She contacted a Maryland legislator, Sandy Rosenberg, who the previous year had introduced a bill prohibiting online harassment. That bill failed to pass in 1997. The following year, with Hitchcock's help, Maryland made it a misdemeanor to harass someone via e-mail.[30] Hitchcock traveled across the country, testifying in support of other efforts to amend state stalking laws. With her support, California, Maine, and New Hampshire banned different forms of abuse communicated via electronic devices.

Congress proved more of a challenge. In testimony offered in support of the Stalking and Victim Protection Act of 1999, Hitchcock argued that a federal criminal solution was essential in cases involving victims and perpetrators from different states. Extradition requests often went nowhere if stalkers' home states did not prohibit cyber stalking.[31] Without extradition, stalkers could not be tried for their crimes. Although the 1999 bill passed the House, it died in the Senate.

Over the next few years, antiharassment advocates lobbied Congress to update its interstate stalking law to keep pace with technological change. NCVC commented on proposed legislation and testified before Congress about cyber stalking. When Congress reauthorized VAWA in 2006, it expanded the reach of the interstate stalking provision to include stalking via electronic computer systems. Congress's power to amend VAWA along these lines stems from its power to regulate instrumentalities of commerce like the Internet.

Today most states and the federal government ban cyber stalking and cyber harassment to some extent.[32] As Chapter 5 demonstrates, those laws are not perfect. Many fail to punish significant harm because they cover only stalkers' direct communications with victims. In Chapter 6 I suggest reforms that would enable stalking laws to tackle all forms of terroristic and destructive abuse.

Of course, as Chapter 3 underscored, even the most effectively drafted stalking and harassment laws cannot do much if they are not enforced. Advocates are working on this problem. They are helping to educate law enforcement about the countless ways that individuals use technology to terrorize victims, destroy their ability to obtain or keep jobs, and put them at risk of physical harm. For instance, WHOA's volunteers consult with local authorities on cases to help educate officers about the impact of stalking and the relevant laws, and the NCVC has developed fifteen-minute videos about cyber stalking for distribution to police departments across the country.[33]

Recent advocacy has focused on revenge porn. In 2011 Erica Johnstone and Colette Vogele cofounded the nonprofit Without My Consent (WMC) after representing numerous individuals whose harassers had posted their nude pictures online. Johnstone and Vogele started the advocacy group to raise awareness about the struggles facing revenge porn victims. Vogele was frustrated that law enforcement generally refused to take her clients' cases seriously. Her clients feared bringing private litigation because in courts where pseudonymous litigation is disfavored, suing harassers would publicize their identities and draw further attention to their nude images posted online. WMC's website details state laws governing pseudonymous litigation. Much like their predecessors in the women's movement, Johnstone and Vogele have been talking to the press about the difficulties facing revenge porn victims in an effort to sensitize the public to their suffering.

Revenge porn victims have spearheaded similar efforts. The revenge porn victim Holly Jacobs created the End Revenge Porn website, which is devoted to educating the public about revenge porn and advocating for its criminalization. Through the site, she has collected over two thousand signatures in support of legislative efforts to criminalize revenge porn. Battling dismissive social attitudes is a key part of the site's mission. The site exposes law enforcement's refusal to help victims: "State police argue that the crime is occurring on the internet, which therefore crosses state lines and is out of their jurisdiction. The FBI claim that these cases are civil and/or do not threaten national security and should therefore be handled solely by lawyers."[34]

In 2013 a senior at New York University started a pseudonymous site describing her difficulties after her ex-boyfriend filmed them having sex and posted the video on revenge porn sites.[35] Bekah Wells, founder of the site Women against Revenge Porn, argues, "Let us stop putting the blame on the victims. Let us start putting it back where it belongs—on the perpetrators who thrive on the harassment, degradation, and humiliation of their victims. Let us amend laws to redefine cyber harassment, so that one day, Revenge porn perpetrators will suffer consequences for their actions. Then, victims can turn boldly, without fear, to their betrayer and rightfully say, 'You should've known better.'"[36]

Lawyers and academics have joined victims and supporters to lobby state legislatures. Mary Anne Franks, a law professor and criminal law scholar, the revenge porn victim Jacobs, and Charlotte Laws, whose daughter was a victim of computer hacking and revenge porn, have been advising lawmakers in seventeen states on how to ban revenge porn. Franks and I worked together on a bill to criminalize revenge porn in Maryland. These efforts are gaining traction.

Enlisting the Blogosphere

Bloggers have also tried to fight back against online abuse. After the attacks on the tech blogger gained national attention in 2007, the tech publisher Tim O'Reilly and Wikipedia's cofounder Jimmy Wales urged bloggers to take responsibility for abusive online behavior. They offered a bloggers' code of conduct that would "change what is acceptable online." Their code urged bloggers to pay attention not just to their own words but also to the words of others. In their view, bloggers needed to moderate online discussions and remove bigoted harassment if necessary. The idea was that a blogger's moderation could change the direction of online subcultures toward norms of respect, just as a community's repair of broken windows could help avert crime.

In conversations on his blog, O'Reilly underscored that the more we tolerate abusive behavior, the worse it gets. He raised concerns about "transient anonymity," that is, the ability to post under different pseudonyms and then discard them at will. Summarizing his call for a "social self-examination on the part of the blogging community," he said, "There's a strong undercurrent on the Internet that says that anything goes, and any restriction on speech is unacceptable. A lot of people feel intimidated by those who attack them as against free speech if they try to limit unpleasantness. If there's one thing I'd love to come out of this discussion, it's a greater commitment on the part of bloggers not to tolerate behavior on the Internet that they wouldn't tolerate in the physical world. It's ridiculous to accept on a blog or in a forum speech what would be seen as hooliganism or delinquency if practiced in a public space."[37]

Several renowned journalists endorsed this sentiment. Public Broadcasting Corporation's Andy Carvin organized a "Stop Bullying Day." Writers discussed a possible "safe space for women banner" that site owners could display to indicate that harassment and threats would not be tolerated on their sites.[38] The technologist Robert Scoble lamented, "It's this culture of attacking women that has especially got to stop. I really don't care if you attack me. I take those attacks in stride. But, whenever I post a video of a female technologist there invariably are snide remarks about body parts and other things that simply wouldn't happen if the interviewee were a man. . . . It's a culture that allows and, even, sort of encourages sexual attacks on women. Look at Justin.TV's chat room. The comments there are rife with sexual overtones. If it's not attacks on women, it's that someone is 'gay.'"[39]

Unfortunately a large majority of bloggers refused to support efforts such as the bloggers' code of conduct.[40] This is in part due to the social attitudes I have discussed and in part to the fact that site operators saw any move to address online harassment as an affront to free speech, a legal and ethical question that I address in Chapter 8.

Challenges of Fighting Back in Cyberspace

Some victims have tried fighting back on their own. In a National Public Radio program devoted to the online harassment of law students on AutoAdmit, the attorney for the site's former educational director told victims that if they did not "like the level of civility" online, they should "call [others] on it."[41] Nancy Miller, the editor of *Fast Company*, has urged bloggers to tweet the harassment they face, including the harassers' names and employers, with the hashtag #ThreatoftheDay attached. The blogger Alyssa Rosenberg explains, "So here's the deal. Threaten me, and I will cheerfully do my part to make sure that when employers, potential dates, and your family Google you, they will find you expressing your desire to see a celebrity assault a blogger. And then I will ban you. Or as Jay-Z puts it, via a suggested soundtrack from Spencer Ackerman, 'I put the wolves on ya' by which I mean the Wolves of Internet Disapprobation rather than actual carnivores."[42]

Handling cyber harassment on one's own can be fruitful *if* everything goes as planned. Exposing and criticizing harassers can serve as a powerful deterrent. Perpetrators might stop if they thought their actions would impact their own reputations, not just their victims'. Social stigma could convince them that the abuse is not worth their time. Site operators might follow victims' lead, warning perpetrators to stop or face sanctions, such as the revocation or suspension of their privileges.

Talking back allows victims to tell their side of the story. In explaining what happened, they might combat the assumption that they warranted the harassment. Counterspeech could also help victims gauge threats made against them. The tech blogger explained, "The main reason I went public with my story was because it was the quickest way to reduce the level of fear I had at the time. I needed to know exactly how afraid I really needed to be—and for that, I needed a lot more information about who was behind the threatening and harassing comments, posts, and graphics, and this seemed like the best way to provoke people into coming forward, and/or to get their co-authors to 'out' them. This worked, and although it is still not over for me (there is still one person responsible for the *worst* of it, who is still unidentified), I have gotten all the information I could possibly get from having made this post, and at this point, moving forward is my top priority."[43]

Crucially, fighting back could help individuals gain confidence about taking matters into their own hands.[44] As one cyber harassment victim noted, talking back to online harassers is "mentally healthy since it makes me less likely to hold onto it. In my brain, it is the equivalent of catching the snowball and throwing it right back with your best aim. And if nothing else, fighting back feels good."[45] The feminist scholar Dale Spender recalled the salutary impact of teaching female students how to program a virtual dog to bark at and scare away unwanted sexual advances in chat rooms. After the women programmed their "dogs," they felt able to log on with confidence.[46]

Naming and Shaming: Limits and Dangers

Even in ideal situations, talking back cannot repair everything. Despite the fact that counterspeech is helpful and productive for victims, it cannot return them to the position they were in before the attack. It cannot undo their mental suffering, although it might provide some psychological relief. It cannot erase false suggestions that women harbor rape fantasies from the minds of third parties who confront them offline. To prevent future injuries, site operators must remove or de-index all of the destructive posts.

Counterspeech may be unable to resolve a victim's professional problems. Even in the case of "merely" defamatory speech, it is hard to believe that all of the damage will be undone. Because so many people will see the material, some will inevitably miss the victim's response, while others will not believe it. When dealing with attacks on their character, victims often do not have an affirmative case they are trying to make; they are only seeking to dispel the harm. It is hard to present a counter-narrative to the claim that someone is interested in sex with strangers or is a lying criminal.

Naming and shaming may be impossible to achieve. It's difficult to bring social pressure to bear on individuals whose actual identities are hidden. Posting anonymously or pseudonymously can insulate people from shaming efforts. A victim's message will have little impact on posters who can easily replace pseudonyms. A discarded online identity cannot be embarrassed. Because the author no longer cares about the identity's reputation, the victim's counterspeech lacks an interested and invested audience.

What is worse, a victim's counterspeech might improve posters' standing. On some sites, destructive, hostile, and bigoted behavior generates applause. AutoAdmit users gave each other "high fives" for posting law students' e-mail addresses, pictures, and other personal information. One commented, "Really good detective work." Sites like AutoAdmit differ from those whose users enjoy success only if their online identities have trustworthy and respectful reputations. On eBay, for instance, pseudonymous sellers receive positive reputation scores for reliable service. The news site Slashdot prominently features comments from users with high scores for trustworthiness, while those with low scores are less accessible. Unlike eBay or Slashdot participants, whose online reputations might suffer from bigoted activities, cyber mob members may gain credibility for their attacks.

Even if perpetrators could be shamed under their real names, that possibility may not matter. Some victims may have no interest in talking back, and it is not hard to understand why. It may be too intimidating to respond to someone who threatened rape. Victims may fear saying anything if they have no way to assess their harassers' intentions. A survey conducted in 2011 found that nearly 60 percent of cyber harassment victims did not respond to their abusers.[47] Many victims prefer going offline or assuming identity-disguising pseudonyms to fighting back. It can be less frightening to fade into the background.

Fueling the Abuse and Worse

A far more troubling concern is that naming and shaming harassers can exacerbate the abuse. Particularly if harassers experience mental illness, a victim's response may not register embarrassment and fear of disapproval but instead fuel their delusions. Consider what happened when "Dissent Doe," a noted psychologist, fought back against her online harasser. During the late 1990s, Doe participated in an online forum that brought parents of children with mental health issues together with experts. A man began attacking her on the forum. When she asked him to stop because he was destroying the forum's discussions, he grew furious and his attacks became more intense. The man impersonated her on sex forums, sent her threatening e-mails, and continuously attacked her online. Because the man wrote under his real name, Doe could assess her attacker. She discovered that he suffered from severe mental illness and had been previously hospitalized. Trying to shame the man failed. Due to his mental illness, responding just made matters worse.[48]

These problems converged when Jill Filipovic, a law student at New York University who was attacked on the message board AutoAdmit, responded to her harassers. A well-known feminist blogger, Filipovic initially worried that writing about the attacks would make her look like a whiner. Truth be told, she was frightened, but she did not want anyone to know. Posters could be law school classmates or neighbors, as many suggested, so saying something could provoke them to confront her in real space. All of that was enough to dissuade her from fighting back.

Six months after the attacks began, she broke her silence.[49] Ignoring the harassment was not working. Posters kept at her with no sign of slowing down. The time had come for her to say something. Because she had a supportive community of feminist bloggers and readers behind her, she wrote about the attacks. Though she could not name and shame the pseudonymous posters, she denounced their actions.

Filipovic's concerns were warranted. After she blogged and talked to the media about her experience, posters attacked her with vigor. Posts appeared with titles such as "Has anybody here fucked Jill Filipovic up the ass?" and "We talk about what we'd like to do to Jill Filipovic." Posters descended on her blog with threatening comments. They put up the "Official Jill Filipovic RAPE thread" and linked to her sister's picture.[50] She received a barrage of threatening and harassing e-mails. One man claimed to have gone to New York University to meet with her professors and tell them what a "dumb cunt" she was. Even after she graduated from law school, someone sent dozens of e-mails to the partners and associates at her law firm in an effort to get her fired.[51]

Adria Richards's experience shows how perilous taking to the Internet can be. At a conference for Python coders, Richards, a technology developer, overheard two men making sexist jokes. She took their picture and tweeted it along with a statement about why their remarks made her uncomfortable. Her initial tweet might give us pause because it prematurely turned a private conversation into an act of public embarrassment. Richards did not tell the two men how she felt in real space, nor did she tweet their remarks without identifying them to see what others thought. She instead posted the men's picture, sparking an even more disturbing chain of events.

Shortly after the conference, one of the men lost his job. Someone at his workplace had seen Richards's post, and it dovetailed with other problems he was having at work. In a blog post, the man blamed Richards's tweet for his firing. His post ignited hysteria, and hordes of individuals on different platforms and websites went after Richards. Social media users lashed out at her. Websites not known to troll or to engage in abusive behavior such as Hacker News jumped into the fold. Her e-mail inbox was inundated with rape and death threats. One threat sent to Richards via Twitter included her home address next to a picture of a bloody, beheaded woman with the caption "When Im done."[52] A 4chan user released Richards's personal information. Distributed-denial-of-service attacks were launched against her site and her employer's site.[53] Her employer devoted hours to trying to restore its site and server.

What happened next is shocking. Richards's employer reversed its initial decision to support her and instead fired her, announcing her termination via Twitter, Facebook, and the company blog. The post read, "Effectively immediately, SendGrid has terminated the employment of Adria Richards. While we generally are sensitive and confidential with respect to employee matters, the situation has taken on a public nature. We have taken action that we believe is in the overall best interests of SendGrid, its employees, and our customers." Within hours, over a thousand people "liked" her firing.[54]

Harassers respond with venom against victims who fight back as well as against those who merely stay online. This suggests that the purpose of some harassment is to force victims off the Internet. Of course, not every response to online harassment provokes retaliation. But fighting back is a gamble. Its potential upside is that victims could begin an important discussion that nudges sites toward norms of respect while helping repair some of the reputational damage. Its potential downside is retaliatory harassment far in excess of the original abuse.

Calling Supporters: Mock, Identify, Manipulate

Victims' supporters have tried to join forces to strike back against the harassers. They hope to gain strength in numbers—cyber mobs certainly do.[55] After what happened to the tech blogger, the blogger Steven D argued that users should "mock and scorn" those who "spew vile abuse towards women and minorities online." In his view, abusive posts "should be the focus of intense scrutiny and nonstop criticism by the rest of the online communities who do not value hate speech."[56] Such social pressure, if sounded by enough individuals, might convince site operators to discourage harassment on their sites. Because sites often generate advertising income based on their number of visitors, the threat of losing traffic might prompt them to act. Victims would benefit from the support as well. As one victim of online harassment explained, "I need[ed] the people who thought it was wrong to speak up and say so, in public, at the time that it happened" to prevent the issue from snowballing and to help diminish the feeling of being threatened.[57]

With such support, a site's norms could shift away from destructiveness. In the aftermath of the attacks on the tech blogger, the blogger Laura Lemay captured the idea well: "What if more of us do speak up the way Kathy did. Stop deleting the comments. Start posting the e-mail. Start telling the assholes in forums and blog comments that they are being assholes, rather than just shrugging or ignoring or clicking through or (gasp) removing that person's blog feed from our newsreader (gasp). We have a zillion ways in real life of registering disapproval when someone says something idiotic, from frowning to turning away to actually saying 'boy, that was dumb.' There's not a lot like that online. Maybe in addition to just 'digg down' or '-1' we should stand up and speak up more often. Maybe through social engineering, not just web engineering, we can create a better community and a better culture online."[58]

Supporters have lent their efforts to identifying perpetrators and bringing them to justice. In August 2012 a sixteen-year-old girl was gang-raped while she was unconscious. The night of the rape, the perpetrators, members of the Steubenville, Ohio, high school football team, posted incriminating videos, tweets, and photographs, which were soon deleted. One photo featured two football players carrying the unconscious woman. Tweets' taglines for the photo were "Whore status" and "I have no sympathy for whores." Members of the collective Anonymous devoted their efforts to finding those responsible for the rape and the subsequent cyber harassment of the girl. They reposted the Instagram photos, tweets, and a video of football players laughing and cracking jokes about the rape.[59] Members of Anonymous told local police the identity of the rapists and the individuals responsible for posting the pictures of the woman being carried unconscious. They took to the streets and the web to pressure officials to arrest the perpetrators. Their efforts to help the rape victim incurred personal risks. The FBI recently executed a search warrant of the home of an Anonymous member (who goes by the handle KY Anonymous) for his alleged involvement in the hacking of the football team boosters' e-mail accounts and website.[60]

Another strategy is supporters' use of Google bombs to blunt the impact of abusive posts. Recall that Filipovic's supporters successfully forced harassing posts into obscurity with a Google bomb. Today the harassing posts do not appear anywhere in the first twenty-five pages in the results of a search of her name. What is key is that although posters continue to harass her, their postings remain obscure in searches of her name. That is not to say that the Google bombing efforts are the only reason the harassment has been relegated to obscurity. Filipovic's blogging and media commentary have been crucial to the shaping of her search results. But her supporters helped her revive her online reputation and self-confidence at a crucial time. Their support, indexed online, continues to have an impact today.

One might think that the passage of time will always take care of the problem. Why bother doing anything if destructive posts will inevitably fade away? Regrettably, that is not the case. Even now, more than six years after the cyber mob attacks began, harassing threads continue to appear at the top of searches of the law student's name. Her LinkedIn profile appears *below* AutoAdmit threads like "Beware of lying bitch coworkers."[61] This is partly due to the fact that posters have never let up in their harassment.[62] This demonstrates the potential value of a counter Google bomb *and* its rarity. It is tough to convince people to engage in activities that do not have an immediate payoff; we see that in low voter turnout and elsewhere. Filipovic was fortunate that she enjoyed the support of feminist bloggers who felt sufficiently invested in her struggle to devote their time to a counter Google bomb. Many other victims have not been as lucky.

Recruiting help is not a sure-fire strategy. Sometimes no matter how many people support victims, the harassers manage to outpace their efforts. Consider the case of a young woman who died in a horrific car crash. Gruesome photographs of the carnage appeared on the Internet. Posters urged readers to harass her family and provided her family's home and e-mail address. More than 2,500 sites, many devoted to pornography and death, featured pictures of the girl's dead body. The girl's father received e-mails with pictures of his daughter's head and the words "Woohoo Daddy!" and "Hey daddy, I'm still alive." Her family, friends, and the firm Reputation.com, then called Reputation Defender, asked sites to remove the pictures. Some sites agreed to do so but far more refused.[63] In the end, it proved impossible to contact every one of the thousands of sites.

Cyber Mobs Turn on Supporters

A troubling concern is that harassers can turn their sights on a victim's supporters. Researchers have shown that stalkers often target victims' family and friends. Recall the author of the Sex and the Ivy blog Lena Chen. People tried to wreck not only her life but also "the lives of every person close" to her, including her boyfriend, a graduate student she met during her sophomore year while he was a teaching assistant in one of her classes. At the gossip site Juicy Campus, posters "outed" her boyfriend, revealing his e-mail and home address as well as his work information. Posters spread lies about the couple, suggesting that they dated while he was her teaching assistant (they actually started dating nearly two years later); that he gave her illegal drugs; and that he sexually assaulted her. Readers were told to "protest" the college's refusal to "take action against this teacher who abused his position." They listed the contact information of her boyfriend's department chair and the director of graduate studies.[64] His professors and colleagues received anonymous e-mails calling for his expulsion.

Posters did not just go after Chen's boyfriend. Her best friends and younger sister were also attacked.[65] Posters listed her roommates' cell phone numbers. Pictures were posted of her fifteen-year-old sister underneath captions naming her and saying she is the "slut sister" of a porn star.[66] When Chen's sister went to college, posters revealed her e-mail address and linked to her college directory.[67] Her sister has received anonymous e-mails asking her if she is a whore like her sister.[68]

Posters went after the *readers* of Chen's new blog, which is devoted to women's issues. The names, schools, and e-mail addresses of hundreds of individuals who "liked" or commented on her blog have appeared online alongside the warning "Beware of the sites you surf, that's the lesson several dozen witless surfers learned the hard way, after being unmasked and punished for surfing [Chen's] blog."[69] Posts have claimed, falsely, that Chen's readers are Asian "herpes infected sluts" who have been reprimanded by their colleges and fired by their employers for reading her blog.[70] One thread provided a reader's name alongside the accusation that she "sucked dean cock to get into Harvard."[71] Another listed the names and e-mail addresses of individuals who attended Chen's talk at a university.

Posters have directly contacted Chen's readers through their Tumblr accounts. Readers were ominously asked if they wanted to get kicked out of school for reading her blog. Readers' siblings who were still in high school received similar messages. Frightened and rattled, readers worried about their safety and the impact of the online postings on their search results.[72] Chen received over fifty e-mails from readers who were "completely freaked out about how their names and e-mails and various affiliations were discovered and printed all over the Internet."[73] After seeing what was going on and hearing from readers, she posted a warning on her blog that urged readers to post comments anonymously as "guests" and to avoid logging into her comment system through a third-party account like Twitter. She advised readers to remove their identifying details from their blogs before reblogging her posts.[74]

Retaliation against victims' supporters has long been a problem. In the early 1990s, on a Usenet discussion forum devoted to alternative magazines, a young woman expressed interest in magazines devoted to punk girl bands. Some participants said that the woman should start a newsgroup called "altgrrl.dumbcunts." Stephanie Brail and her boyfriend wrote in support of the woman and challenged the sexist comments. Soon they received harassing e-mails from fake senders that included pornographic text detailing gang rapes. A participant calling himself "Mike" barraged Brail with obscene e-mails. He impersonated Brail on the alt.sex.bondage Usenet group. Brail received a menacing e-mail that warned, "I know you're in Los Angeles. Maybe I can come for a date and fix your plumbing?" Brail stopped posting on the forum. She "censored herself out of fear."[75]

One-Way Ratchet to Degradation

Naming and shaming can become a one-way ratchet to degradation. It can spiral out of control with cyber mobs on both sides and no ability to control the damage. The abuse and counterabuse often resembles an arms race. Consider what happened after a group of individuals struck back against users of the Reddit forum Creep Shots who posted revealing pictures of women without their permission. The group tracked down pseudonymous posters' identities and created a site called Predditt (in a play on *predator*) where they exposed the identities, schools, addresses, and pictures of individuals responsible for Creep Shots pictures. The Creep Shots posters faced death threats, and, according to one report, a poster was physically attacked. A countercycle of abuse then began. Anonymous posters hit Reddit with denial-of-service attacks and harassed site administrators. Destructive behavior cannot be the answer to destructive behavior unless we want a Hobbesian nightmare for our society.

Getting past social attitudes and changing online behavior are chal lenging tasks. In the past, advocacy groups joined their education efforts with legal ones. That is precisely where we find ourselves now. The next chapter introduces law's potential to combat cyber harassment. Just as the enforcement of existing criminal and civil rights laws and the adoption of new laws to combat sexual harassment and domestic violence have not destroyed the home or workplace, a cyber civil rights legal agenda will not ruin cyberspace.

five

What Law Can and Should Do Now

Talking to the media, blogging about victims' struggles, and fighting back online has taken us only so far. In this chapter I argue for the robust enforcement of law against cyber harassment. I begin with a brief overview of civil, criminal, and civil rights laws that could be brought to bear against harassers. Tort claims redress victims' damaged reputations, privacy invasions, and intentionally inflicted emotional distress. Criminal law punishes stalking, harassment, threats, extortion, solicitation, harmful impersonation, and computer crimes. Civil rights law redresses and punishes the economic, social, and psychic costs inflicted when individuals are denied the right to pursue life's crucial opportunities because of their membership in a protected group.

To explore law's potential and its limits, this chapter returns to the experiences of the tech blogger, the law student, and the revenge porn victim. To the extent that current law falls short, in Chapter 6 I suggest proposals for reform.

Components of a Legal Agenda: Civil Remedies

Victims could sue their abusers under tort and copyright law. Tort is a body of law that requires defendants to compensate plaintiffs whose injuries they have wrongfully caused. Victims can bring claims for defamation, intentional infliction of emotional distress, and invasion of privacy.

Libel, a form of defamation, is a false written statement of fact that damages someone's good name. Plaintiffs do not need to show special damages like specific economic losses if defendants' false statements injure their careers and cause them disgrace.[1] Falsely accusing someone of having a sexually transmitted infection, a criminal conviction, or an inappropriate sexual affair amounts to libel that does not require proof of special damages.

Another key tort claim is intentionally or recklessly causing severe emotional distress with "extreme and outrageous conduct." Humiliating, threatening, and persistent online cruelty amounts to "extreme and outrageous" activity because it falls outside the norms of decency.[2]

When harassers interfere with victims' privacy, they can be required to compensate for victims' emotional distress, humiliation, and reputational harm.[3] Under the public disclosure of private fact tort, a defendant may be liable for publicizing someone's private, "non-newsworthy" information if it would highly offend a reasonable person. Plaintiffs cannot sue for the disclosure of embarrassing, truthful facts if the public has a legitimate interest in learning about them. Nude photos published without subjects' consent are roundly understood as non-newsworthy and provide strong grounds for recovery.[4] Privacy tort law also remedies intentional intrusions on someone's private affairs in a manner that would be highly offensive to a reasonable person. Hacking into a person's password-protected computer counts as a tortious intrusion on seclusion.

Copyright law can provide redress if a harasser posts a victim's copyrighted photograph or video. A person who takes an image is considered its copyright owner; only that person can sue for copyright violations. Harassers can be sued for copyright infringement related to the posting of nude photos that victims took of themselves. Victims are out of luck if someone else took their nude photo. The cyber law scholar Derek Bambauer has argued for an expansive conception of joint authorship that might cover these victims, but his theory is untested.[5]

Besides the possibility of monetary damages, copyright has another advantage that I will address in Chapter 7. Federal copyright law facilitates a notice-and-takedown procedure that can result in the removal of victims' nude images. Once an image is posted online, however, getting it removed from one site does not guarantee its removal from other sites to which it has migrated.

As valuable as civil suits can be, they are not an option for everyone. Victims bear the costs of bringing tort and copyright claims, and those costs can be heavy. Having lost their jobs due to online abuse, they cannot pay their rent, let alone the fees for attorneys and computer-forensic specialists. Even if victims can afford to sue their attackers, they may be reluctant to do so if their attackers have few assets. It may not be worth spending time and resources suing someone who is effectively judgment-proof. Of course not all victims feel that way. One victim told me she intends to sue a man who secretly taped her having sex and posted the videos online even if he cannot pay her much because what he did was deeply harmful and wrong.

Another practical concern that prevents some victims from pursuing litigation is that they may be required to bring suit in their real names. Courts often deny requests to sue under pseudonyms. If victims have to file suits under their real names, the public can quickly and easily learn about the abuse if their complaints appear online, as is often the case.[6] This puts many victims in an untenable situation. They can seek justice but risk exacerbating their suffering or let injustices stand with some privacy intact. Some victims would rather give up their claims than give the harassment more publicity.

It also may be hard to find lawyers willing to take cases involving on-line abuse. Most lawyers do not know this area of law, and many are not prepared to handle the trickiness of online harassment evidence. This reduces the deterrent effect of civil litigation, as would-be perpetrators are unlikely to fear a course of action that has little chance of materializing.

Traditional Criminal Law

Given the limited availability and utility of civil remedies, criminal law has a crucial role to play. The government pays for criminal prosecutions, ensuring law's efficacy when victims cannot afford to bring suit. Criminal convictions are powerful deterrents because of their lasting collateral consequences.[7] Even if harassers are not afraid of being sued because they have no money to lose, they might fear a criminal conviction that would appear on their records forever. Criminal cases may minimize some of the publicity concerns that prevent victims from pursuing civil remedies because they are brought in the government's name. Of course the media might learn the victims' names and publish stories mentioning them, but that risk may be worth enduring to ensure that attackers are punished.

Assuming law enforcement and prosecutors take victims' complaints seriously, various criminal charges might be pursued. State and federal law punishes credible threats of violence.[8] Under state law, it is a felony generally known as assault to threaten grave bodily injury to another person if the speaker intended the statement to be taken as a threat or if a reasonable person would understand the statement as a threat. Threats must be unequivocal, unconditional, and specific.[9] Victims typically need to feel tangible, sustained, and immediate fear.

Online attackers can face criminal stalking and harassment charges.[10] Under state law, stalking is usually defined as threats made with intent to place another person in imminent fear of grave bodily injury in connection with a malicious "course of conduct" that would cause a reasonable person to suffer substantial emotional distress.[11] Harassment is typically understood as a willful and malicious "course of conduct" directed at a person that would cause a reasonable person to suffer substantial emotional distress and that does cause the person to suffer distress.

Over the past twenty years, every state has to some extent updated its laws related to stalking and harassment to keep pace with technological change. Some statutes reach abuse perpetrated via particular technologies such as e-mail. Other statutes cover only abuse directly communicated to victims.[12] Only a few states prohibit harassment communicated directly or indirectly, on- or offline. Whereas stalking is sometimes a felony with significant penalties, harassment is usually a misdemeanor with modest sentences and fines.[13]

Federal stalking and harassment laws capture a wide range of online abuse. The first, the interstate stalking statute known as Section 2261A, makes it a felony to use any "interactive computer service or electronic communication service or electronic communication system" to engage in a "course of conduct" with intent to harass or intimidate another person. The course of conduct must either place the other person in reasonable fear of serious bodily injury or death or cause or attempt to cause the person to suffer "substantial emotional distress" or be expected to cause a reasonable person to suffer substantial emotional distress.[14] Section 2261A covers "substantial emotional distress" because even when stalking victims do not fear bodily harm, "their lives are totally disrupted and they are interfered with in the most insidious and frightening ways."[15] Defendants can be punished for up to five years in prison and fined up to $250,000, with additional sentencing requirements for repeat offenders and for defendants whose offense violates a restraining order. The court will also order restitution, in which case the defendant must pay the victim for any losses the victim suffers as a proximate result of the offense.

The second relevant statute, the telecommunications harassment statute known as Section 223, prohibits harassment and threats over interstate communications networks. It punishes the knowing use of a telecommunications device without disclosing one's identity with intent to "abuse, threaten, or harass any specific person."[16] The crime is a misdemeanor, punishable by a fine and up to two years in prison.[17]

Using the Internet to solicit strangers to physically attack or stalk another person is a crime.[18] Some solicitation laws prohibit the electronic publication of a person's personally identifiable information, including digital images of the person, with intent to place the person in reasonable fear for his or her safety and for the purpose of immediately causing that person unwanted physical contact, injury, or harassment by a third party.[19] Under impersonation statutes, it is a crime to knowingly and "credibly" impersonate another person online with intent to "harm, intimidate, threaten, or defraud" the person.[20] Impersonating someone in online advertisements or social network profiles that list the person's home address and interest in sex could support criminal charges.

Harassers can be punished for computer-related crimes, such as hacking into someone's computer to steal sensitive information and using technology to shut down people's sites.[21] Most states have video voyeurism laws that prohibit the nonconsensual recording of another person in a state of undress. The federal Video Voyeurism Protection Act of 2004 makes the nonconsensual taping or disclosure of someone's nude image illegal, but it applies only to recordings taken on federal property. In most states, however, it is not a crime to publish another person's nude photos knowing that person has not consented to the publication if the photos were obtained legally.

Prosecutors can charge harassers with aiding and abetting identity theft for publishing someone's social security number. Social security numbers are keys to individuals' bank accounts; they enable criminals to take out loans, obtain health services, and get credit cards in their owners' names. Courts have upheld convictions for aiding and abetting identity theft in cases where defendants posted online social security numbers, home addresses, and driver's licenses to assist identity thieves.[22]

The Importance of Civil Rights Law

Civil remedies and traditional criminal penalties deter, redress, and punish reputational harm, emotional distress, fear of bodily harm, and other individual injuries. They send the message that it is unacceptable to engage in persistent cruelty causing severe emotional distress, privacy invasions, credible threats, malicious stalking, and solicitation of strangers to harm victims. But they cannot address all of the harm that cyber harassment inflicts. They do not tackle the injuries suffered when harassers interfere with victims' important life opportunities on the basis of their group membership.[23] They do not respond to the stigmatization and humiliation endured when victims are targeted for online abuse due to their gender, race, national origin, or sexual orientation. For instance, a libel claim redresses the harm to a person's good name but not his or her loss of work and humiliation due to unjust discrimination.

Civil rights laws make up for these deficits. They address the professional sabotage and inferiority that individuals experience when they are harassed because of their gender, sexual orientation, religion, or skin color. They respond to the harm suffered by a victim's group. When posters threatened to rape the tech blogger, other female bloggers saw themselves as vulnerable to physical attack.[24] When a cyber mob threatened to kill the author of the Ask This Black Woman blog and told her to "get back into the cotton fields, you filthy n***r," her African American readers felt intimidated and threatened.

Cyber harassment undermines group members' ability to participate in online life. The journalist Amanda Hess explained that when anonymous posters say they would like to "rape us, or cut off our heads, or scrutinize our bodies in public, or shame us for our sexual habits—they serve to remind us in ways both big and small that we can't be at ease online."[25] Group members go offline or hide their identities to avoid being subject to online harassment. A 2005 Pew Internet and American Life Project study attributed a 9 percent decline in women's use of chat rooms to menacing comments.[26] Civil rights laws remedy these psychic, economic, social, and political costs.[27]

Civil rights laws also respond to more systemic harms. Graphic sexual fantasies about what (male) posters would do to (female) victims remind victims and society of men's sexual dominance over women, further entrenching gender hierarchy. Cyber harassment reinforces gender stereotypes by casting women as sex objects that are unfit for life's important opportunities. The media scholar Lisa Nakamura argues that the default identity online is a white male; cyber harassment reinforces this assertion by driving women offline.[28] Even if that insight cannot be proven, society is the loser when victims retreat from on- and offline activities.[29]

Civil Rights Law: What They Can Do and Say

State and federal law punishes harassment and threats motivated by someone's race, national origin, or religion. Only a few states penalize online abuse based on gender or sexual orientation bias.[30] Some states punish private individuals who threaten someone in the exercise of a right or privilege guaranteed by the constitution of the state or the United States, including the right to work, education, and self-expression.[31] State attorneys and private counsel may be able to seek civil penalties for bias-motivated threats and intimidation.[32] Criminal sentences can be enhanced if defendants' crimes were motivated by a victim's perceived membership in a protected group.[33]

Despite the importance of civil rights law, it is rarely enforced in cases of online abuse. That is regrettable. Civil rights law not only could repair and deter harms that civil and criminal law cannot, but it has the potential to transform our social attitudes about cyber harassment and cyber stalking.

Consider the way that civil rights law changed our views about sexual harassment. In the late 1970s, courts ruled, for the first time, that sexual harassment was a manifestation of women's inequality in the workplace, not trivial personal matters.[34] In short order, the Equal Employment Opportunity Commission adopted the policy that sexually hostile environments constituted sex discrimination under the Civil Rights Act of 1964. The press got the point. National media began covering stories involving high-profile men who abused their power over subordinate employees.[35]

Soon enough, sexual harassment at work was seen as sex discrimination rather than business as usual. Victims spoke up about their bosses' sexual demands and filed complaints with the EEOC.[36] Increasing numbers of employers trained employees about sexual harassment and treated it as unacceptable. Even though sexual harassment in the workplace has by no means disappeared, law helped send a clear message: sexual harassment was unjust discrimination.

Civil rights law has the same potential for civil rights violations in cyberspace. Law would signal that online abuse produces corrosive harm to individuals, groups, and society, just as law helped people appreciate the social harms of sexual harassment in the workplace. Civil rights law would help show victims that they do not have to sacrifice their emotional and physical well-being to work, speak, and interact online, much as courts in the 1970s made clear that women did not need to choose between working in sexually harassing environments and earning a living.[37]

Slowly but surely, as tort, copyright, criminal, and civil rights laws are brought to bear against cyber stalking and cyber harassment, social norms might change. Rather than shutting down their blogs and retreating in isolation, victims might sue their harassers and report abuse to law enforcement. Police and prosecutors who pursue cases against cyber harassers can set an example for others to follow. Jurisdictions might devote more resources to training personnel to handle cyber harassment investigations if they see other jurisdictions bringing successful cases. The real possibility of criminal sanctions might convince some potential perpetrators that cyber harassment is not worth the trouble. Those inclined to tolerate cyber harassment might show their disapproval. More people might talk to their kids and friends about cyber harassment's harms. As a society, we might begin to understand cyber harassment and cyber stalking as tortious, criminal, and unjust discrimination.

Law could change our cultural software, what Professor Jack Balkin calls our "collectively created tools that constitute us as persons and that we use to make new tools for understanding the world around us, interacting with others, and expressing our values."[38] Revisiting our case studies illustrates the potential value of existing legal tools and their limits.

Law's Possibilities: The Tech Blogger

Let us return to the tech blogger who first was attacked in e-mail, her blog, and group blogs and then was set upon by a cyber mob. Recall the graphic threats she received via e-mail and in the comments section of her blog. Doctored photos of her being strangled and with a noose beside her neck appeared on group blogs. After she blogged about the abuse, a cyber mob spread her social security number and defamatory lies about her all over the web.

Turning to the criminal sphere accomplished little. Officers in the Boulder Sherriff's Office took the threats she faced seriously but ultimately threw up their hands due to their technical ignorance. Although they might have spent resources to identify her attackers, they declined to do so.

If her harassers had been identified, they, like other cyber stalkers, might have been prosecuted for violating criminal threat laws. For instance, a man created a website listing the personal information of a company's employees, including their social security numbers and home addresses, after the company refused to hire him. Although the company obtained a restraining order against the defendant, he posted text, voiceovers, and pictures threatening company employees. On one page, he warned a process server who had served him with a lawsuit, "Have you ever been stabbed with a knife? I have. . . . If I ever see you near my family again, and I know how to stalk too, I will kill you." On another page "Dead-icated" to the company's attorney, the lawyer's name, address, telephone number, and photograph appeared next to a map of her home. When clicking on the page, readers heard a voiceover from *Cape Fear*, a film about the stalking and attempted murder of a lawyer.[39] The defendant was convicted of making criminal threats on his site.

Vincent Johnson pleaded guilty to sending threatening e-mails to employees of five civil rights groups.[40] Under the e-mail address devilfish579@aol.com, Johnson warned, "Do you have a last will and testament? If not better get one soon"; "Our guns are ready to take you out"; "I won't waste my time with legal endeavors . . . my preference would be to buy more ammunition to deal with the growing chaos created by the pro-illegal alien groups. RIP [recipient's name]."[41] Johnson was sentenced to fifty months in prison and fined $10,000.

In the tech blogger's case, comments on her blog and in e-mails included clear and unambiguous threats. They described violating her with a machete and said she deserved to be raped and have her throat slit. She reasonably feared that the anonymous individuals would make good on their threats. Nothing about them suggested that the threats were a joke. Their hostile tone and graphic description of violence signaled their seriousness. The Boulder Sherriff's Office affirmed the reasonableness of her reaction by urging her to stay at home.

Cyber stalking charges might have been appropriate as well. Under Colorado law, stalking involves a credible threat to another person made in connection with repeated communications with that person. A threat is credible if it would cause a "reasonable person to fear for his or her safety." The law also covers repeated "forms of communication with another person" in a manner that would cause a "reasonable person to suffer serious emotional distress" and that "does cause that person to suffer serious emotional distress." Victims do not need to have sought professional treatment to show that they suffered serious emotional distress.[42]

The threats made on the tech blogger's blog and in e-mails sent directly to her would have caused a reasonable person to fear for her safety and to suffer serious emotional distress. It is, however, impossible to know if any one person engaged in "repeated" communications with her or if instead several individuals made a single threat. What is clear is that the stalking statute did not cover the abuse appearing on third-party platforms such as the group blogs. Prosecutors could not have considered the posts of the doctored photos, defamatory lies, and social security number. As a practical matter too, criminal charges might have been difficult to pursue against defendants living outside Colorado. Some prosecutors refuse to pursue even strong cyber stalking cases if suspects have to be extradited from other jurisdictions. Sometimes a defendant's home state will refuse to comply with an extradition request unless actual violence occurred.[43]

What if the tech blogger had gone to federal authorities? Charges might have been pursued under the federal interstate stalking statute, which bans use of the Internet to engage in a "course of conduct" that is intended to and that causes another person to fear bodily harm or to suffer substantial emotional distress. Unlike Colorado's cyber stalking law, the federal interstate stalking law applies to online abuse even if it is not communicated directly to victims. There would, however, need to be proof that the tech blogger's tormentors engaged in a pattern of abusive actions. The statute would apply, for instance, if the same person who uploaded the doctored photos also sent the threatening e-mails.

Federal prosecutors could have considered bringing charges for aiding and abetting identity theft against the cyber mob members who posted the tech blogger's social security number online. Federal law criminalizes the use of someone's personally identifying information with intent to aid or abet unlawful activity amounting to a felony, such as identity theft. Whoever posted her social security number could have been prosecuted for enticing others to use it for the purpose of identity theft.

Suppose that federal prosecutors had brought charges against the tech blogger's attackers. If convicted, their sentences could have been enhanced for targeting her because of her gender.[44] Of course, sentence enhancements must be requested and granted. Unfortunately, civil rights laws have been woefully underutilized in cyber stalking cases. From 2010 to 2013 federal prosecutors pursued ten cyber stalking cases.[45] In five cases, the defendants were convicted; in one case, a defendant pleaded guilty. In those cases, the defendants targeted female victims with rape threats, fake ads claiming their interest in sex, posts of their nude photos, and calls for strangers to rape them.[46] It seems that none of the prosecutors asked the court to enhance the defendants' sentences on civil rights grounds.

What about criminal penalties for violating civil rights law? Although Section 245 of federal civil rights law criminalizes discriminatory threats designed to interfere with someone's employment, a charge included in Vincent Johnson's plea bargain, it covers only threats motivated by the victim's race, national origin, or religion.[47] Under Colorado's bias intimidation law, victims can recover damages from individuals who threaten violence with intent to intimidate because of that person's actual or perceived race, color, religion, disability, or sexual orientation.[48] Neither law covers gender bias. Because the tech blogger was targeted due to her gender, as the posts and e-mails suggested, Section 245 and Colorado's bias intimidation law were inapplicable. In Chapter 6 I propose legal reforms to fill this gap and criminalize threats made due to someone's gender.

What if the tech blogger had sued her attackers to recover for her emotional suffering and reputational harm? She had a strong case for intentional infliction of emotional distress against whoever threatened to rape and beat her and whoever posted the doctored photographs of her being suffocated and featured next to a noose. Society would surely find graphic threats of violence and menacing photos beyond the bounds of decency. She could have sued for the libelous posts about her alleged domestic abuse and work as a prostitute. She had a viable claim for public disclosure of private fact against whoever posted her social security number. Courts have deemed the posting of social security numbers highly offensive to the reasonable person because such posting makes it easy to hijack someone's financial identity.

The tech blogger, however, had no interest in bringing a lawsuit. She worried that if she sued, the cyber mob would strike back even harder than it did when she simply spoke out against the abuse.

The Law Student: Modest Success in Civil Court

With the support of pro bono counsel, the law student sued thirty-nine cyber mob members for intentional infliction of emotional distress, defamation, and copyright violations, among other claims. The federal district court allowed her to file the lawsuit under a pseudonym. This meant that the posters, once she determined who they were, would know her actual identity, but court documents would not list her real name. This was fortunate and rare. Courts typically require people to sue in their real names in the interest of transparency in the judicial process.[49]

The law student would not have brought the suit if she had to list her real name in the lawsuit's caption. That is not unusual. I have talked to numerous cyber harassment victims who declined to sue their attackers not because they did not want to or because they could not afford counsel but because they feared having to include their name in court documents. As I argue in Chapter 6, law's presumption in favor of real-name litigation should not apply to cyber harassment victims.

The law student's claims for intentional infliction of emotional distress and defamation were strong. Pseudonymous posters engaged in unrelenting personal attacks, including rape threats, e-mails to her faculty and employer designed to hurt her reputation and job opportunities, and a Google bomb to ensure the prominence of their destructive threads. Courts have awarded emotional distress damages for online abuse that is targeted, repeated, cruel, and reliant on sensitive material.[50] The posters' false claims that the law student had a sexually transmitted infection, inappropriate sexual affairs, and a 152 LSAT score exemplify the sorts of lies that society recognizes as defamatory.[51]

After two years of litigation, the law student entered into a confidential settlement with seven defendants whose real names were discovered. The lawsuit was dropped against the thirty-two posters who could not be identified. Although the law student cannot divulge the details of the settlement, she can share how she felt about the lawsuit. She is glad that she sued. The suit let her take a stand against her attackers. It made clear that the cyber mob attacks were far from harmless "frat boy" nonsense but instead constituted deeply damaging abuse.

However, the litigation experience was not easy or costless. It is true that court documents did not list her name and thus did not further associate her identity with the threats, damaging lies, and privacy invasions. But suing as a Jane Doe did not insulate her from retaliatory abuse. After her lawyers posted the complaint on the message board to notify the posters about the suit so that they could come forward for proper service, she faced more abuse. The cyber harassment got worse and continued for years.[52]

What about civil rights remedies? Did the posters violate the law student's civil rights by interfering with her ability to work, attend law school, and engage with others online because of her sex? Recall that posters urged readers to contact the top law firms to dissuade them from hiring her and that sixteen firms declined to offer her a summer associate position. She withdrew from law school for a semester due to her emotional distress and anxiety. The cyber mob arguably attempted to interfere with her work opportunities and education because she is a woman. Her gender is probably all most posters knew about her, since it is unclear if more than one or two knew her personally.

Connecticut's civil rights law would not have reached the cyber mob attack. It recognizes claims against private actors who maliciously destroy another person's property or who place a noose on private property with the purpose of depriving the owner of his or her "rights, privileges, or immunities, secured or protected under state or federal law or the Constitution of the United States" because of the person's race, national origin, sex, sexual orientation, disability, or other protected characteristic.[53] The statute would not apply to the cyber mob's interference with the law student's job search and education.

Had law enforcement taken her case seriously, prosecutors might have looked to Connecticut's bias intimidation law, which punishes malicious threats to cause physical harm to another person because of that person's actual or perceived race, religion, ethnicity, sexual orientation, or gender identity or expression.[54] Recall that posts derogatorily attributed the law student's admission to law school to her perceived race and religion. Posters also claimed she had a lesbian affair to get into law school. If the person responsible for those posts also threatened "I'll force myself on her, most definitely" and "I think I will sodomize her," a case could have been made against that person for bias intimidation. The key would be connecting the threats of physical contact with bias based on race or religion. The statute does not cover threats made toward someone because of his or her sex.

Federal civil rights laws would not have applied to the law student's predicament. Antidiscrimination laws, such as Title VII and Title IX, hold employers and schools responsible for addressing discrimination based on sex and other protected characteristics. However, those laws do not extend to private actors who interfere with victims' work or educational opportunities from outside of those institutions. The Internet is not a workplace or school with clear lines of accountability. In Chapter 6 I argue for civil rights laws to address private actors who interfere with another person's ability to pursue life's crucial opportunities due to group bias.

Suppose the New Haven Police Department had not told the law student, "Boys will be boys," and had investigated her case. Punishing the cyber mob might nonetheless have been a difficult task. When the law student reported the abuse, Connecticut's stalking law required proof that the defendant "lie in wait" or appear in close physical proximity to the victim.[55] Because the cyber mob attacked the law student on message boards, blogs, and e-mails, but never in person, the law would not have been applicable.

Connecticut makes it a misdemeanor to engage in written communications with another person in a manner likely to cause "annoyance or alarm" with intent to "harass, annoy, and alarm."[56] Only one or two of the law student's attackers contacted her directly: the person who sent anonymous e-mails to her and her employer claiming that she slept with her dean and should not be hired and the person who sent her the menacing e-mail saying he or she was watching her. None of the message board posts could have been relied on as evidence because they were not communicated directly to her.

By contrast, federal prosecutors could have viewed all of the abusive posts and e-mails in assessing the viability of federal interstate stalking charges under Section 2261A(2)(A): using the Internet to engage in a harassing "course of conduct" with intent to cause a person substantial emotional distress that causes the person substantial emotional distress or that would cause a reasonable person to suffer substantial emotional distress. Nonetheless, abuse perpetrated by cyber mobs presents structural difficulties that might make it difficult to prove the harassing "course of conduct" element under the federal statute. The pseudonymous poster "STANFORDtroll" kicked off the abuse with defamatory lies about the law student, and other pseudonymous posters quickly jumped on. Countless message threads proceeded in the same manner, with one poster starting the abuse and others piling on. If each cyber mob member was responsible for only one or two isolated posts, then the cyber mob's actions may constitute a pattern of harassment, but no single person may be responsible for it.

Suppose that person A authored the defamatory e-mails, put up posts urging readers to track the law student's whereabouts, and falsely claimed that she had herpes and a 152 on her LSAT score. A case certainly could be made that person A engaged in a harassing "course of conduct" because the posts would have been part of a destructive pattern of abuse. Now instead assume that person A sent a defamatory e-mail to her employer (and did nothing else), person B urged others to discredit her with law firms, and person C falsely asserted that she had herpes.[57] Section 2261A(2)(A) would not cover their actions because *as individuals* none of them repeatedly attacked her, even though their actions as a whole did.

Prosecutors could have considered bringing conspiracy charges against posters if (and this is a big "if") they had agreed to engage in a coordinated campaign of cyber harassment. Conspiracy law requires an agreement between two or more people to engage in criminal activity, overt acts to implement the agreement, and the intent to commit the substantive crime.[58] Federal law prohibits conspiracy to commit *any* federal crime, including cyber stalking.[59]

Posters urged others to tell the "bitch" how they felt about her and to contact law firms so she would not get hired. Posts provided instructions for Google bombing and discussed the best ways to ensure that destructive posts remained at the top of a search of the law student's name. But those posts may not sufficiently prove an illicit agreement. Prosecutors would have to demonstrate beyond a reasonable doubt that members of the cyber mob had a "meeting of the minds"—an agreement to be a part of a harassment campaign. In the case of a cyber mob with no offline contact, that might be difficult to prove.

To be sure, some posts arguably suggested a coordinated agenda to harass the law student. If the posters' identities could be ascertained and a warrant issued for their online accounts, posters' private communications might suggest a "meeting of the minds." Without such proof, however, the threads arguably suggested the posters were engaged in a one-upmanship contest rather than an agreed-upon plan of abuse. Even though conspiracy law seems a natural way to address destructive cyber mobs whose abuse as a whole wreaks havoc on victims' lives, it would be tough to prove the state of mind necessary to make out a conspiracy claim.

To sum up, criminal law would not support charges against the destructive cyber mob. The state harassment statute would not have covered abuse on third-party platforms, and even if it had, the responsibility for cyber mobs is so dispersed that criminal charges would be unlikely. In the case of cyber mob attacks, criminal law may be unable to deter and punish destructive abuse.

The Revenge Porn Victim: Criminal Action and Civil Suit

The abuse of the revenge porn victim involved nude photos appearing on hundreds of sites alongside her name and work bio, impersonation (posts falsely claiming her interest in sex), phone calls to her university accusing her of sleeping with her students, and an e-mail threatening to send her nude photos to her work colleagues if she did not respond, which were sent to her colleagues after she refused to reply.[60]

In similar circumstances, prosecutors have gotten convictions for cyber stalking. Consider a case involving a woman whose ex-boyfriend threatened to distribute her nude photographs unless she resumed their relationship. After she refused, the man posted the photos and videos online. He sent her colleagues postcards with her nude image and the missive "Just a whore 4 sale." The defendant was convicted.[61] Another man has been indicted for cyber stalking his ex-girlfriend by posting sex videos of her on porn sites and putting up online ads with her contact information and supposed interest in sex.[62]

Recall that local police initially turned away the revenge porn victim because, in their words, her predicament was a "civil" matter. But that was not the case. Florida's criminal harassment law bans the use of "electronic communication services" to engage in a "course of conduct" directed at a person that causes him or her substantial emotional distress. It defines a "course of conduct" as a pattern of acts over a period of time showing a continuity of purpose.[63] Officers should have investigated the revenge porn victim's case. The extortionate threat, hundreds of posts with her nude photos, online ads impersonating her, and phone calls to her employer demonstrated a pattern of abuse that caused her substantial emotional distress.

In early 2013 the Florida state attorney's office took up the revenge porn victim's case after Senator Marco Rubio's office contacted the state's attorney on her behalf. Her ex was charged with misdemeanor harassment. Investigators successfully traced one of the porn posts to her ex's IP address, but they told the revenge porn victim that they needed a warrant to search his computer for evidence tying him to the rest of the abuse. Her ex responded to the charges by claiming that he had been hacked. He denied posting her photos.

In October 2013 the charges against her ex were dismissed. Looking at all of the evidence suggests that prosecutors had a strong case. Nonetheless, prosecutors told the revenge porn victim that they could not *justify* seeking a warrant for a misdemeanor case. Their hands were tied, they said. This was disappointing—and avoidable. "I've been hacked" is a standard defense in cyber stalking cases. The main way to disprove it is for the police to get a warrant to search a defendant's computer or home. There is no legitimate reason why prosecutors could not have obtained a warrant to investigate a misdemeanor charge. The obvious explanation is that prosecutors did not think the abuse was serious enough to be worth the effort. Criminalizing revenge porn and harassment as felonies might have made a difference in the way that Florida prosecutors handled her case. In Chapter 6 I propose reform along those lines.

What about the revenge porn victim's civil suit? When we first talked in early 2012, the revenge porn victim had serious misgivings about suing because her newly changed name would appear in court documents. If those documents were posted online, anyone searching her name would be able to connect her new identity to her real name and its ruined online reputation.

In 2013 she changed her mind about suing in her new name. Revealing her identity made sense because she wanted to talk to the media about her anti–revenge porn advocacy. Her attorney reached out to several media outlets; all were interested in talking to her. She appeared on NBC's *Today* show, CNN, and other media outlets. She knew it was a gamble to sue in her real name and to talk to the press, but in her mind it was one worth taking.

Her lawsuit, which is ongoing, seeks compensation for public disclosure of private fact, intentional infliction of emotional distress, and defamation. Her complaint does not allege copyright violations even though she took the photos herself and owns the copyright to them because copyright claims can be brought only in federal court. Her lawyer brought the case in state court.

The revenge porn victim's tort claims are strong, assuming she can show that her ex authored the posts rather than a hacker, as he claims. Turning to the public disclosure of private fact tort, the posting of her nude images constitutes an actionable privacy invasion. The public certainly has no legitimate interest in the nude photos that she sent to her ex in confidence. Their release would be "highly offensive to the reasonable person."[64] Courts have recognized privacy tort claims in cases where the plaintiff shared sensitive information with one other trusted person.[65] Because she shared her nude photos with one other person on the understanding that he would keep them to himself, she enjoyed a reasonable expectation of privacy in those photos.[66]

There is a solid case that her harasser intended to inflict severe emotional distress. There were hundreds of her nude pictures alongside her contact information; posts impersonating her on sex sites; anonymous calls to her university to discredit her. The claims that she slept with her students and had sex for money constituted false statements of fact that damaged her reputation.

Other revenge porn victims have successfully sued their tormentors. A woman brought a lawsuit against her ex-boyfriend after he posted her nude photos, contact information, and her alleged interest in a "visit or phone call" on twenty-three adult websites. The defendant created an online advertisement that said the woman wanted "no strings attached" masochistic sex. Strange men left her frightening voice mails. The woman suffered severe anxiety and stress. She worried the abuse would impact her security clearance at work. A judge awarded the woman $425,000 for intentional infliction of emotional distress, defamation, and public disclosure of private fact.[67]

The revenge porn victim did not sue only her ex; her complaint includes claims against the operators of revenge porn sites Sextingpics. com and Pinkmeth.tv, among others. It alleges that site operators encouraged users to upload women's and children's nude photographs without their permission. According to the complaint, their purpose was to cause "severe embarrassment, humiliation, and emotional distress to the victims." Those claims are important for what they are trying to accomplish, but current federal law may stand in the way.

Internet intermediaries are generally shielded from state criminal and civil liability for publishing third-party content under Section 230 of the Communications Decency Act of 1996. As I propose in Chapter 7, Congress needs to narrow the federal immunity afforded under Section 230.

six

Updating the Law: The Harassers

In this chapter I offer suggestions for legal reform to enhance the accountability of perpetrators. On the criminal law front, harassment and stalking laws should be updated to reach the totality of the abuse, and revenge porn should be banned. Civil rights law should penalize online harassers who interfere with someone's right to pursue life's crucial opportunities—work, education, and self-expression—due to group bias. Pseudonymous litigation should be permitted so that victims can pursue redress without drawing further attention to the harassment. Recent developments in the fight against revenge porn suggest that state lawmakers may be amenable to these proposals. States were at the forefront of antistalking efforts in the 1990s; they may be interested in doing so again.

We cannot pin all of our hopes on a legal reform agenda centered on the abusers. Law cannot communicate norms, deter unlawful activity, or remedy injuries if defendants cannot be found. Perpetrators can be hard to identify if they use anonymizing technologies or post on sites that do not collect IP addresses. Because the law's efficacy depends on having defendants to penalize, legal reform should include, but not focus exclusively on, harassers. Chapter 7 considers other sources of deterrence and remedy.

Updating Criminal Harassment and Stalking Laws

In 2013 Ian Barber allegedly posted his ex-girlfriend's nude photos on Twitter and e-mailed them to her employer and sister. New York prosecutors charged him with aggravated harassment. Although the court condemned his conduct as "reprehensible," the case was dismissed because he never sent the harassment, the nude photos, to the victim, as New York law required.[1]

New York is not an outlier. State harassment and stalking laws are often limited to abuse communicated directly *to* victims. When the tech blogger and the law student contacted local law enforcement, the stalking and harassment laws in their states would not have reached the threats, defamation, and privacy invasions posted on third-party platforms like the message board and group blogs, even though they were at the heart of the abuse. As our case studies show, cyber harassers generate grave fear and emotional distress without sending communications to victims—something legislators could not have fully appreciated when they adopted harassment and stalking laws.[2] Today social media, blogs, message boards, and GPS-tracking devices are used to terrorize victims. Tomorrow it may be robots or drones. Only time will tell.

States should revise their stalking and harassment laws to reflect this reality. Stalking and harassment laws should cover any means, methods, or technologies exploited by perpetrators to stalk and harass victims.[3] Prosecutors then could present the totality of the abuse; that totality is what imperils victims' safety, careers, and peace of mind. For guidance, lawmakers could look to recent amendments to the federal telecommunications harassment statute.[4] In 2013 Congress replaced the language "harass any person at the called number or who receives the communication" with "harass any specific person." Although such reform would not make it easier to prosecute cyber mobs, it would allow prosecutors to present a full view of the damage.

In amending their statutes, lawmakers should avoid overbroad or vague language that raises due process and free speech concerns. Many harassment laws cover communications likely to cause "annoyance." Those statutes are vulnerable to constitutional challenge because annoying speech is constitutionally protected. Courts have upheld harassment statutes as facially valid even though they contain overbroad words like *annoy* because other language limits the statutes' reach. Nonetheless, as states revise their laws, they ought to omit such overbroad language.

State legislators should consider treating stalking and harassment as felonies. As the revenge porn victim's case showed, prosecutors are reluctant to devote significant resources to misdemeanors. Classifying cyber harassment as a felony is warranted. The harm is serious enough to justify the punishment meted out for felonies. We have seen that cyber harassment destroys people's careers, emotional health, and physical safety. The federal cyber stalking statute treats the same abuse as a felony; states should do the same.

These reforms should be paired with mandatory training about the phenomenon of cyber harassment. Far too often, police officers fail to address cyber harassment complaints because they lack familiarity with the law and the technology. Law enforcement seemingly misunderstood the law in the law student's and the revenge porn victim's cases; the police had no idea how to find the posters in the tech blogger's case. In response to the graphic threats made to the journalist Amanda Hess, officers asked her, "What's Twitter?"

As I showed in Chapter 3, these cases are the tip of the iceberg. States should condition the receipt of funds on the establishment of programs that teach officers about the different forms of online abuse, the techniques necessary to investigate cyber harassment complaints, and the relevant laws. The Philadelphia Police Department has invested considerable resources into training officers on stalking law and investigation protocols. The department's informal research on the training program found an increased number of stalking investigations, suggesting a heightened understanding of the crime among officers and a greater ability to advise victims about the crime.[5] Prosecutors and judges should receive these lessons as well. They often have difficulty with cyber harassment cases because they do not appreciate the seriousness of the abuse or because they have trouble with all matters involving the Internet.

States should require police departments to report the number of cyber stalking and cyber harassment complaints they receive and the outcome of those cases. Publicly released statistics would allow the public to engage in a dialogue about the efficacy of training efforts. Even if state lawmakers do not amend harassment laws along the lines suggested above, they should allocate funds to training and mandatory reporting. This might encourage the enforcement of existing law, which would be better than doing nothing at all.

Criminal Invasions of Privacy: Revenge Porn and Its Ilk

"Jane" allowed her ex-boyfriend to take her nude photograph because, as he assured her, it would be for his eyes only. After their breakup, he betrayed her trust. He uploaded her nude photo and contact information to a revenge porn site. Jane received e-mails, calls, and friend requests from strangers, many of whom demanded sex.

After the frightening calls and e-mails intensified, Jane went to her local police department. Officers told her that nothing could be done because her ex had not engaged in a harassing "course of conduct." One post amounted to an isolated event, not a pattern of abusive behavior. Officers pointed out that her ex had neither threatened physical harm nor solicited others to stalk her.[6] Things might have been different had her ex secretly taken the photo. In that case, charges for "unlawful surveillance"—the secret recording of someone's nude image without consent—might have been appropriate. But it was legal to publish the nude photo taken with Jane's consent, even though her consent was premised on the promise that the photo would be kept private.[7]

The nonconsensual disclosure of someone's nude image deserves criminal punishment. In their groundbreaking article "The Right to Privacy," published in 1890, Samuel Warren and Louis Brandeis argued, "It would doubtless be desirable that the privacy of the individual should receive the added protection of the criminal law."[8] Since then, legislators have criminalized privacy invasions. The federal Privacy Act of 1974 includes criminal penalties for the disclosure of agency records containing personally identifiable information to any person or agency not entitled to receive it.[9] Federal law prohibits the wrongful disclosure of individually identifiable health information.[10] Most states ban the nonconsensual recording of someone in a state of undress without permission. New York's unlawful surveillance law, for instance, prohibits the use of an imaging device to secretly record or broadcast another person undressing or having sex for the purpose of degrading that person where that person had a reasonable expectation of privacy. In November 2013 a New York man was indicted for secretly taping his sexual encounters with different women. The man allegedly posted the recordings on password-protected online accounts.[11]

Why is it legal in many jurisdictions to disclose a person's nude image without that person's consent? A combination of factors is at work.[12] One stems from the public's ignorance about revenge porn. As brave individuals have come forward to tell their stories, we are only now beginning to understand how prevalent and damaging revenge porn can be. Another reason is that society has a poor track record addressing harms primarily suffered by women and girls. As I explored in Chapter 3, it was an uphill battle to get domestic violence and sexual harassment recognized as serious issues. Because revenge porn impacts women and girls far more frequently than men and boys and creates far more serious consequences for them, it is another harm that our society is eager to minimize, trivialize, and tolerate.

Our disregard of harms undermining women's autonomy is closely tied to idiosyncratic views about consent with regard to sex. A victim's consensual sharing of nude photos with a confidante is often regarded as wide-ranging permission to share them with the public. We saw that mentality at work in cases involving sexual harassment. Chapter 3 highlighted the once-prevalent view that female workers' appearance signaled their desire for employers' sexual advances. For years, women have had to struggle with legal and social disregard of their sexual boundaries. Although most people today would recoil at the suggestion that a woman's consent to sleep with one man can be taken as consent to sleep with his friends, this is the very logic of revenge porn apologists.

Outside of sexual practices, most people recognize that consent is context-specific. Consent to share information in one context does not serve as consent to share it in another context. When people entrust waiters with their credit cards, they neither expect nor impliedly permit them to give their cards to identity thieves. When individuals confide their HIV-positive status with support groups, they do not expect nor impliedly permit group members to tell their employers about their medical condition. What individuals share with lovers is not equivalent to what they would share with the world.[13] Common sense teaches us that consent is contextual; consent does not operate as an on/off switch.

The nonconsensual sharing of an individual's nude photo should be no different: consent within a trusted relationship does not equal consent outside of that relationship. We should no more blame individuals for trusting loved ones with intimate images than we blame someone for trusting a financial advisor, support group, or waiter not to share sensitive personal information with others.

Consent's contextual nature is a staple of information privacy law. Best practices and privacy laws make clear that permitting an entity to use personal information in one context does not confer consent to use it in another without the person's explicit permission. Lawmakers have long recognized the importance of context to the sharing of sensitive information. Congress passed the Gramm-Leach-Bliley Act to ensure that financial institutions do not share customers' financial information with third parties unless customers give their explicit permission. The Video Privacy Protection Act recognizes that individuals may be willing to share their film preferences with video providers but not with the world at large; consumers have to explicitly consent to the sharing of their film-watching habits with third parties. In a report entitled "Protecting Consumer Privacy in an Era of Rapid Change," the Federal Trade Commission advised that when personal information is collected for one purpose and then treated differently, the failure to respect the original expectation is a cognizable harm.[14]

Criminal invasion of privacy laws should reflect the contextual understanding of consent and ban nude photos published without the subject's permission. There is precedent for such legislation. The federal Video Voyeurism Prevention Act of 2004 prohibits the intentional broadcasting of an image of another person in a state of undress without that person's consent if the image was taken under circumstances in which the person enjoyed a reasonable expectation of privacy. Unfortunately it does not apply to most revenge porn cases because it covers only images taken on federal property.[15]

A few states have banned revenge porn. New Jersey was the first. In 2004 it adopted a criminal invasion of privacy statute prohibiting the disclosure of someone's sexually explicit images without that person's consent.[16] Under New Jersey law, an actor commits the crime of invasion of privacy if, "knowing that he is not licensed or privileged to do so, he discloses any photograph, film, videotape, recording or any other reproduction of the image of another person whose intimate parts are exposed or who is engaged in an act of sexual penetration or sexual contact, unless that person has consented to such disclosure." The crime carries a prison sentence of between three and five years and monetary penalties of up to $30,000.[17]

New Jersey prosecutors have pursued invasion of privacy charges in a few cases. In 2010 a Rutgers University student, Dahrun Ravi, was charged under the New Jersey statute after he secretly filmed his roommate, Tyler Clementi, having sex with a man and watched the live feed with six friends. Clementi committed suicide after discovering what had happened. The jury convicted Ravi of two counts of invasion of privacy: the first count was for the nonconsensual "observation" of Clementi having sex, and the second count was for the nonconsensual "disclosure" of the sex video. Ravi was also convicted of bias intimidation—committing the crime of invasion of privacy with the purpose to intimidate because of the victim's sexual orientation. In a more recent case, a New Jersey man was convicted of invasion of privacy for forwarding his ex-girlfriend's nude photos to her employer (a school), stating, "You have an educator there that is . . . not proper."[18]

As of the writing of this book, five other states have criminalized revenge porn: Alaska, California, Idaho, Maryland, and Utah. In 2013 California made it a misdemeanor to distribute a consensually taken sexually explicit image of a person with knowledge the person expected the image to be kept private and with intent to cause the person substantial emotional distress. The law does not cover nude images that victims take of themselves (self-shots), which limits its effectiveness. A recent study found that 80 percent of revenge porn cases involve self-shots that victims shared with intimate partners with the understanding that the images would be kept private. California lawmakers aim to fix that flaw: a recently proposed amendment would extend the law to self-shots. Adopting the amendment would be wise. Revenge porn is as harmful to the person who shared a nude photo with a trusted partner as it is to the person who permitted the partner to take the picture. In both cases, victims expected their confidantes to keep the nude photos private and their trust was betrayed.

Advocates have made headway in other states. Revenge porn bills are pending in twenty-two states.[19] State Senator Michael Hastings of Illinois submitted a bill that would make it a felony for a person to knowingly place, post, or reproduce on the Internet "a photograph, video, or digital image of a person in a state of nudity, in a state of sexual excitement, or engaged in any act of sexual conduct or sexual penetration, without the knowledge and consent of that person."[20]

Civil liberties groups worry that that if revenge porn laws "aren't narrowly focused enough, they can be interpreted too broadly."[21] Digital Media Law Project's Jeff Hermes has expressed concern that revenge porn laws might criminalize speech in which the public has a legitimate interest. Both of these concerns can be overcome with clear and narrow drafting.

Lawmakers must take steps to ensure that revenge porn laws provide clear notice about what is unlawful and include enough specifics so they do not punish innocent activity. One step is to clarify the mental state required. Revenge porn laws should apply only if a defendant disclosed another person's nude image knowing the person expected the image to be kept private and knowing the person did not consent to the disclosure. By clarifying the mental state in this way, legislation would punish only intentional betrayals of someone's privacy. Carelessly or foolishly posting someone's nude image would not constitute criminal behavior. It would not be a crime, for instance, to repost a stranger's nude photos having no idea that person intended them to be kept private. Another way to avoid criminalizing innocent activity is to require proof of harm. Speech should not be criminalized unless it has inflicted injury, such as emotional distress, reputational harm, or financial loss.

To give defendants clear notice about the conduct covered under the statute, revenge porn legislation should specifically define its terms. Defendants need to understand what is meant by the term *sexually explicit* so they understand the kind of images that are covered. Lawmakers should also make clear what they mean by the term *disclosure*. On the one hand, disclosure could mean showing the image to a single other person; on the other hand, it could refer to publication to a wide audience. Lawmakers should define disclosure in the former sense. When a perpetrator sends a victim's nude image to her employer, the victim's career can be irrevocably damaged and her emotional wellbeing destroyed. Criminal law should cover sexually explicit images that are made available to others, whether it is a single other person or the public at large.

Given the common misunderstandings about the contextual nature of consent, revenge porn legislation should make clear that giving someone permission to possess a sexually explicit image does not imply consent to disclose it to anyone else. Recall what law enforcement initially told the revenge porn victim: that because she shared her nude photos with her ex, he owned the photos and could do what he wanted with them including publish them online. Clarification about consent would help prevent outmoded social attitudes from interfering with the law's enforcement.

In addition to being clear about the activities covered by revenge porn laws, lawmakers should clarify the activities that fall outside them. Revenge porn legislation, for instance, should exclude sexually explicit images concerning matters of public importance. Consider the case of the former New York congressman Anthony Weiner, who shared sexually explicit photos of his crotch with women to whom he was not married. On one occasion, Weiner sent unsolicited images of his penis to a college student whom he did not know personally. His decision to send the images to the student sheds light on the soundness of his judgment, a matter of public interest given his desire to return to politics. The public interest exception may not arise often because most revenge porn victims are private individuals. Nonetheless, courts are well suited to address a public interest exception as it comes up in cases.

The last issue is the penalty for revenge porn convictions. If legislation treats the nonconsensual disclosure of someone's nude image as a misdemeanor, it risks sending the message that the harm caused to victims is not severe. At the same time, overly harsh penalties might generate resistance to legislation, especially among free speech advocates who generally oppose the criminalization of speech. Categorizing revenge porn legislation as a misdemeanor sends a weak message to would-be perpetrators and would be a less effective deterrent than a felony. Lesser penalties may, however, ease the passage of proposed bills.

A model state law might read:

> An actor commits criminal invasion of privacy if the actor harms another person by knowingly disclosing an image of another person whose intimate parts are exposed or who is engaged in a sexual act, when the actor knows that the other person did not consent to the disclosure and when the actor knows that the other person expected that the image would be kept private, under circumstances where the other person had a reasonable expectation that the image would be kept private. The fact that a person has consented to the possession of an image by another person does not imply consent to disclose that image more broadly.
>
> *Definitions:*
> (1) "Disclosure" or "disclosing" means to make available to another person or to the public.
> (2) "Harm" includes emotional harm, reputational harm, and financial loss.
> (3) "Image" includes a photograph, film, videotape, digital reproduction, or other reproduction.
> (4) "Intimate parts" means the naked genitals, pubic area, anus, or female adult nipple of the person.
> (5) "Sexual act" includes contact, whether using a body part or object, with a person's genitals, anus, or a female adult nipple for the purpose of sexual gratification.
>
> *The statute does not apply to the following:*
> (1) Lawful and common practices of law enforcement, criminal reporting, legal proceedings; or medical treatment; or
> (2) The reporting of unlawful conduct; or

(3) Images of voluntary exposure by the individual in public or commercial settings; or

(4) Disclosures that relate to the public interest.[22]

It is not unrealistic to urge Congress to play a role here as well. Professor Mary Anne Franks is working with Congresswoman Jackie Speier on crafting a federal revenge porn statute. A federal criminal law would be a crucial companion to state efforts. It would provide legal protection against revenge porn in cases where the states either failed to pass legislation or state law enforcement refused to act.

The federal cyber stalking law, Section 2261A, could be amended along the same lines as the model state law.[23] A key innovation would be the inclusion of a takedown remedy. If cyber stalking convictions were accompanied by court orders to remove nude photos posted without subjects' consent, the law would respond directly to victims' continued harms rather than acting as just a tool of deterrence and punishment. Because takedown orders would stem from federal criminal law, Section 230 of the federal Communications Decency Act would not bar them. For these suggested reforms to be meaningful, they should be paired with better training of law enforcement on revenge porn specifically and cyber stalking more generally as well as reporting requirements that permit the public to assess the enforcement of these laws.[24]

Amending Civil Rights Laws to Reach Harassers

After the media critic Anita Sarkeesian announced she was raising money on Kickstarter to produce a series on sexism in video games in the summer of 2012, a cyber mob descended upon her. Posters tried to hijack her fundraising effort.[25] A campaign was organized to mass-report her Kickstarter project as fraud to get it canceled.[26] Posters tried to shut down her Twitter and Facebook profiles by reporting them as "terrorism," "hate speech," and spam.[27] Her e-mail and social media accounts were hacked.[28] After her Wikipedia page was continually vandalized with explicit sexual images and sexist commentary, Wikipedia reverted the text and locked it down so no further edits could be made.

The cyber mob engaged in tactics designed to terrify her. Hundreds of tweets threatened rape. Anonymous e-mails said she should watch her back because they were coming for her. Someone created an online game whose goal was to batter an image of her face. Users of the game were invited to "beat the bitch up" and punch a digital version of her face until it appeared bloodied and bruised.[29] Images of her being ejaculated on and raped spread all over the web.[30] As of March 2014, the attacks had not stopped. Her website Feminist Frequency continues to be hit with denial-of-service attacks.[31]

The media critic lives in California, a state with robust civil rights laws. Under California law, state attorneys can seek civil penalties of up to $25,000 from individuals who interfere with another person's "right to be free" from "intimidation by threat of violence" because of their race, religion, sex, or sexual orientation. They can seek civil penalties for bias-motivated threats or intimidation interfering with someone's state or federal statutory or constitutional rights, including education, employment, contracts, and speech.[32] Private attorneys can bring suit as well; attorney's fees can be awarded. The young actor attacked on his fan site with homophobic, graphic threats brought claims against his attackers under these civil rights laws.

California's civil rights laws might have addressed the abuse that the media critic faced. The cyber mob tried to intimidate her from pursuing her work. The threats and images of her being battered and raped sent the insidious message that she would be harmed if she did not stop working on her project. The cyber mob tried to shut down her fundraising effort with denial-of-service attacks and false abuse complaints.[33] Because posters could not have known much more about her than that she was a woman working to expose sexism in video games, it was clear that she was attacked because of her gender. The sexualized and gendered nature of the abuse further attested to the bias motivation.

The media critic, however, never went to the authorities or filed a private suit. She had toyed with the idea because it might wake up authorities to the fact that cyber mob abuse is a "serious problem." Ultimately she did not reach out to the police because she did not know what to say to them: "I figured if I brought some tweets and message board posts they'd just look at me like I was nuts, we didn't know where these people lived, and there was SO much of it, thousands and thousands."[34]

Building on California's Lead: State Reform

California's civil rights laws should serve as a model for other states. Recall that the civil rights laws in the states where the tech blogger, the law student, and the revenge porn victim lived—Colorado, Connecticut, and Florida—did not protect against cyber stalking designed to sabotage a person's right to work, obtain education, and expression because of the person's gender or sexual orientation. Only racially or religiously motivated threats were prohibited.

States should prohibit cyber stalking that interferes with victims' civil rights, including employment, contracts, education, and expression, due to their race, national origin, religion, sex, sexual orientation, gender identity or expression, or disability. Cyber stalking should be defined along the lines of the federal interstate stalking statute: intentional "course of conduct" designed to harass and intimidate that causes victims to fear bodily harm or to suffer substantial emotional distress (or that would cause a reasonable person to suffer substantial emotional distress) whether conducted offline, online, or via other technologies.

Much like California law, states should permit their attorneys general and district attorneys to seek civil penalties against perpetrators. Such actions would help secure deterrence in cases where victims cannot afford counsel or fear bringing suits in their own names. Of course, state budgets are limited, and government enforcement would drain precious resources. But enforcement costs should be considered along with their potential benefits. Deterring bigoted cyber harassment has the potential to generate positive returns: as online abuse falls, so will its cost to victims' work earnings, ad revenues, and job opportunities, and victims will have the ability to contribute to innovation rather than being silenced. Failing to recognize those benefits discounts the important upside to the adoption of civil rights laws.

Civil rights law could then protect against bias-motivated cyber stalking that interferes with someone's equal opportunity to pursue education. The law student took a leave of absence from school during the cyber mob attack. The noted social media expert danah boyd left college for a semester after being targeted on a "rumor" forum run by her colleagues in her computer science department. Posters directed rape threats at her and her female classmates. Someone hacked into her computer and posted her private e-mail messages on the forum. She received abusive phone calls. When she returned to campus, she refused to take certain classes and avoided working in her department because she did not want to be surrounded by her online attackers.[35]

To be sure, there may still be problems finding perpetrators and victims may still be reluctant to come forward, as the media critic was. But amending state civil rights laws would send a powerful message to victims that bigoted cyber mob attacks are unacceptable and illegal. Victims might internalize this message and seek the help of state attorneys, district attorneys, or private counsel. The more civil rights laws are enforced, the more bigoted abuse would be remedied and deterred.

State lawmakers might be amenable to these proposals given their early responsiveness to the stalking phenomenon. Recall that states were the first to move against stalking, in the 1990s. Some responded to advocates' calls to update stalking laws to reach emerging technologies. Here again, state lawmakers are working with advocates to criminalize revenge porn. Now that advocates have the attention of state lawmakers, they should press reform along all of these lines.

The Tough Realities of Federal Reform and Proposals

Although Congress should protect against bias-motivated cyber stalking that sabotages victims' crucial life opportunities, reform is unlikely to happen any time soon. Federal lawmakers have been unable to pass a budget, let alone civil rights protections. The political challenges would be significant, as shown by recent efforts to address discriminatory conduct far beyond the realm of expression. The federal Hate Crimes Prevention Act, which criminalizes bias-motivated crimes of violence, took years of lobbying and public relations campaigning to pass. Along the same lines, legislation to prohibit job discrimination on the basis of sexual orientation has been introduced in Congress in various forms since 1975 but has yet to be enacted.

Despite these practical concerns, we should not give up on Congress. The following proposals are offered to be ready at hand if and when lawmakers take up the issue.

Civil rights laws from another era can help us understand what is at stake for the protection of civil rights in this era. Section 1981 of the Civil Rights Act of 1866 guarantees to racial minorities the right to make and enforce contracts, a guarantee that is enforceable against private actors.[36] Under that statute, Ku Klux Klan members were ordered to provide compensation to Vietnamese fishermen whom they tried to intimidate to prevent them from fishing in Gulf waters.[37] Of course, Section 1981 is not a perfect fit for today's problems. It was passed to address the Klan's campaigns of terror, which often involved physical violence. Although Section 1981 grew out of a particular time and ignominious history, it resonates with the harm that cyber harassers inflict.

Today's cyber harassers try to hinder victims' job prospects because of their gender, much as Klan members tried to intimidate former slaves and immigrants from pursuing work due to their race or nationality. Recall the cyber mob attack on the law student. Posters e-mailed damaging statements to her summer employer to prevent her from receiving a permanent offer; the entire Yale Law faculty, who would serve as future job recommenders, received e-mails with defamatory lies about her; readers were urged to contact law firms to talk them out of hiring her.

Civil rights laws should ban cyber stalking that interferes with someone's equal right to pursue professional opportunities. Congress could pass a statute along the lines of Section 1981 that protects women and sexual minorities who are harassed online. Alternatively, it could amend Title VII, which currently prohibits discrimination only by employers and their agents.[38] Title VII could permit discrimination claims against individuals who do not employ victims but who nonetheless interfere with their ability to pursue work due to discriminatory animus.[39] Just after Congress passed Title VII, courts upheld discrimination claims against individuals whose intimidation prevented racial and ethnic minorities from pursuing their chosen careers.[40] Prohibiting cyber harassers from engaging in activities that impede victims' success in the job market would honor Title VII's statutory purpose: eliminating discrimination in employment opportunities.

Might cyber harassers bear some responsibility for interfering with victims' ability to pursue their educations? Title IX bans discrimination in public education and applies to educational institutions receiving federal funds. Under Title IX, sexual harassment is understood as unwelcome conduct of a sexual nature, which can include spreading sexual rumors, rating students on sexual activity or performance, and calling students sexually charged names. Schools violate Title IX if they fail to investigate or remedy sexual harassment.[41] Title IX could be amended to recognize claims against cyber harassers who interfere with victims' ability to pursue education, whether private or public, due to their membership in a traditionally subordinated group.

Another potential avenue for reform is Section 245 of the federal Civil Rights Act of 1968, which punishes threats of force designed to interfere with someone's private employment, application for work, or public education due to his or her race, religion, or national origin.[42] Vincent Johnson pled guilty under that statute for threatening to kill employees working for a Latino civil rights organization.[43] In 2006 a man sent threatening e-mails to a Jewish woman who blogged about Arab American and Muslim affairs. The e mails stated, "Hey White Bitch Jew . . . We're going to blow you up" and "You will soon be raped and will die." The defendant pleaded guilty to interfering with the woman's work with threats of violence due to her religion under Section 245.[44] The protections of Section 245 should be extended to protect against threats intended to interfere with a person's work prospects or employment because of his or her gender or sexual orientation. That would update the law to accord with this century's problems because the majority of cyber harassment victims, who often face threats of violence, are female or LGBT.

Congress could also look to VAWA. Although the Supreme Court struck down VAWA's civil remedy for victims of gender-motivated violence because the conduct the law targeted did not have a substantial enough effect on economic activities to warrant congressional action under the Commerce Clause, Congress could amend VAWA pursuant to its power to regulate the Internet, an instrumentality of commerce. Section 2261A, a provision of VAWA, could punish posters whose threats interfere with individuals' ability to pursue work because of their gender or sexual orientation. This is in line with the Department of Justice's policy statement urging federal prosecutors to seek hate crime penalty enhancements for defendants who electronically harass victims because of their race, gender, sexual orientation, or religion.[45]

Civil rights law should protect against anonymous cyber mobs whose goal is to deny individuals' right to free expression. Nineteenth-century civil rights laws recognized the dangers that anonymous mobs pose to equality. During Reconstruction, civil rights law adapted to conditions like anonymity that exacerbated extreme mob behavior. The Ku Klux Klan Act of 1871 prohibited private conspiracies to deprive individuals of their basic rights under the cloak of anonymity. Section 2 of the 1871 Act, known today as Section 1985(3), allows damage suits against two or more people who conspire or go in disguise on the highway to deprive any person of the equal protection of the laws.[46] Section 241 established criminal penalties for "two or more persons [who] go in disguise on the highway" to hinder a person's "free exercise or enjoyment of any right or privilege" secured by the Constitution or federal law.[47]

Cyber mobs go in disguise on the Internet to deprive women and minorities of their right to engage in online discourse. Victims are forced offline with cyber mobs' technological attacks. To avoid further abuse, victims shut down their social network profiles and blogs.[48] They limit their websites' connectivity by password-protecting their sites.[49] They close the comments on their blog posts, foreclosing positive conversations along with abusive ones.[50] A cyber mob's interference with victims' free expression produces tangible economic harms. Closing down one's blog or website can mean a loss of advertising income.[51] The absence of an online presence can prevent victims from getting jobs.[52] Victims' low social media influence scores can impair their ability to obtain employment.[53]

Unfortunately we cannot pursue this era's cyber mobs with the prior era's civil rights laws. In 1875 the Supreme Court narrowed the reach of the Ku Klux Klan Act of 1871 to conspiracies involving governmental actors.[54] In a more recent decision, the Court held that Sections 1985(3) and 241 covered conspiracies of purely private actors only if their aim was to interfere with rights protected against both private and public infringement. The Court explained that although freedom of speech is not such a right, Congress is free to pass a statute that proscribes private efforts to deny rights secured only against official interference, such as free speech, under its power to regulate interstate commerce or the instrumentalities of interstate commerce.

Federal lawmakers could ban anonymous cyber mob conspiracies that interfere with targeted individuals' free speech. The federal electronic harassment statute prohibits a defendant's use of the Internet without disclosing his or her identity to harass a specific individual.[55] It could be amended to criminalize private conspiracies to deprive individuals of their basic rights, including their right to free speech, perpetrated under the cloak of anonymity. A parallel civil remedy could accompany the criminal penalty, much as Section 1985(3) supplements Section 241.

Some cyber harassment cases seem well suited for such reforms. In 2008 anonymous posters maintained a list of sites and blogs devoted to women's issues that they claimed to have forced offline. The list included the names of shuttered sites with a line crossed through them and the accompanying message. "Down due to excessive bandwidth great success!" When a site reappeared online, the post was updated to inform members of the cyber mob, "It's back! Show no mercy." The group took credit for closing over a hundred feminist sites and blogs. Targeted bloggers and site operators confirmed the cyber mob's claims. They described the denial-of-service attacks that shut down their sites. One site operator said, "Being silenced for over two weeks felt infuriating, stifling, imprisoned by gang just waiting for me to try to get up from underneath their weight so they could stomp me down again."[56] Individuals should be able to express themselves online free from anonymous cyber mobs bent on silencing them because of their gender, sexual orientation, gender identity, race, or other protected characteristic.

Pseudonymous Litigation

In 2006 a business owner discovered that her ex-boyfriend had posted her nude photographs, work address, and name on a revenge porn site. Her photos appeared under the caption "Jap Slut." Strangers inundated her with phone calls and e-mails. After being turned away by the police, she hired counsel to file a lawsuit against her ex.

The businesswoman's attorneys asked the court to permit her to sue as a Jane Doe.[57] As her lawyers explained to the judge, suing under her real name would raise the visibility of the posts. The posts were fairly obscured in a search of her name, but that would likely change if the complaint or other court documents with her name appeared online. The businesswoman was afraid that her clients would stop working with her if they found out about the nude photos. After the court refused to permit her to sue under a pseudonym, she felt she had no choice but to dismiss the lawsuit.[58] This should not have happened.

Victims should be able to bring civil claims without having to risk further invasions of their privacy. Nonetheless, courts generally disfavor pseudonymous litigation because it is assumed to interfere with the transparency of the judicial process, deny a defendant's constitutional right to confront his or her accuser, and encourage frivolous claims being asserted by those whose names would not be on the line. Arguments in favor of Jane Doe lawsuits are considered against the presumption of public openness, a heavy presumption that often works against plaintiffs asserting privacy invasions.[59]

The assumptions underlying the presumption against pseudonymous litigation are faulty. Allowing plaintiffs to sue as Jane Doe would not render the entire proceedings secret. Only the plaintiff's actual name would be kept from the public; the rest of the case would proceed in the public eye. Pleadings, motions, and other court documents would be available to interested parties, albeit without the plaintiff's real name in the caption. Hearings and trial would be open for observation. The defendant would know the plaintiff's identity and could confront his or her accuser. Defendants would have every opportunity to mount an effective defense.

What about the possibility that plaintiffs could misuse pseudonymous litigation to bring frivolous claims against defendants? Without question, plaintiffs could seek the shelter of pseudonymous suits to prevent their real names from being associated with frivolous claims. A court's sanction rules would go a long way to deter abuses of pseudonymous litigation. As an illustration, consider the Federal Rule of Civil Procedure 11. Much like state court sanction rules, Rule 11 requires that written requests of the court must not be presented for an improper purpose, such as to harass, cause unnecessary delay, or needlessly increase the cost of litigation. If a litigant moved for leave to sue pseudonymously to protect his or her reputation while pressing baseless claims, the court could order the litigant to pay for defense counsel's fees and costs. The court could revoke the litigant's permission to sue pseudonymously and use his or her name in the caption of its sanctions order.[60] The potential for such sanctions would go a long way to preventing abusive pseudonymous litigation.

The privacy law scholar Daniel Solove contends that the presumption in favor of real-name litigation should disappear in cases where the nature of the allegations would prevent victims from asserting their rights.[61] State legislatures and the drafters of the Federal Rules of Civil Procedure should create a presumption in favor of pseudonymous litigation in cyber harassment and invasion of privacy cases. Limits could be placed on that presumption to ensure the transparency of court processes. One possibility would be to place an expiration date on the use of pseudonyms, such as five years after the close of the case. Another possibility would be to permit courts to reassess the presumption if knowledge of the plaintiff's name would shed light on an issue of public concern.[62]

To be sure, such legislation would not necessarily insulate cyber harassment victims from subsequent abuse at the hands of attackers. The law student sued as a Jane Doe, yet she still faced retaliatory abuse. Nonetheless, a presumption in favor of pseudonymous litigation could benefit individuals who would otherwise decline to bring suit for fear of subsequent privacy invasions.

There is some good news to report. Although the businesswoman dropped her lawsuit, she went on to lobby Hawaii legislators to pass a bill sanctioning pseudonymous litigation to protect the privacy of plaintiffs in cases involving cyber harassment and domestic violence. With her guidance and support, lawmakers submitted a bill supporting pseudonymous litigation. Academics, myself included, offered written testimony in support of the legislation. In 2011 the state legislature adopted the bill and the governor signed it into law.[63] States should follow Hawaii's lead in endorsing pseudonymous litigation in cases involving online abuse.

Limits of a Regulatory Agenda Aimed at Harassers

When the law student sued her harassers, she could identify only seven posters. The identities of thirty-two posters and the authors of the e-mails attempting to sabotage her job remained elusive. That included the pseudonymous poster "STANFORDTroll," whose initial post, "Stanford bitch to attend Yale law," initiated the cyber mob attack against her.

As the law student's experience demonstrates, a legal strategy focused on harassers has important limits. Victims cannot sue, and prosecutors cannot pursue, individuals whose real names cannot be ascertained. Law cannot communicate norms or exact costs without identifiable defendants.

Identifying posters can be challenging. Computers connected to the Internet have or share IP addresses. Although the United States has not adopted mandatory data retention rules (as in the European Union), most major Internet service providers keep records of IP addresses assigned to particular computers from six months to a year.[64] With court orders and subpoenas, plaintiffs and law enforcement can secure the name and account information for the user of an IP address from the ISP that assigned it or possibly from sites that have been accessed while using the IP address.[65]

Tracing posters through their computers, however, is not a straightforward task. Harassers can use public computers in libraries or Internet cafés that do not require registration, preventing their traceability through the IP address assigned to a computer. They can employ technologies that mask the IP address assigned to their computers. Free software like Tor establishes anonymous Internet connections by funneling web traffic through encrypted virtual tunnels.[66] If harassers use anonymizing technologies like Tor, the IP address connected to their posts may be impossible to find.

Even if harassers do not try to mask their online activity, their computers may be connected to a network, often true for workplaces and universities, which makes it look like the same IP address as other computers on the network. If someone uses a workplace computer, the assigned IP address may belong to the employer's local network rather than any particular computer on the network.[67] That would make it hard to connect harassing posts to a defendant's computer. Some site operators refuse to collect IP addresses. The law student could not identify most of her attackers because the message board had a "no track" policy.

Ultimately, as the cyber law scholar Jonathan Zittrain explains, "it's a cat and mouse game of forensics." But if people do not try to stay anonymous, it is often possible to figure out who they are.[68] According to the computer scientist Harlan Yu and the legal scholar David Robinson, plaintiffs who have difficulty identifying online attackers could subpoena data held by third-party web service providers whose information could help identify posters.[69] Online comments could also be linked to a poster's web-browsing history, which could provide clues about the person's identity.[70]

No matter the circumstance, time is of the essence. Victims and law enforcement need to act quickly to ensure that third-party sites and ISPs have not deleted identifying information. Identifying data often disappear long before the time expires for plaintiffs to bring suit.[71] The hard truth confronted by many of the victims I interviewed is that they could not find their attackers.

Given these problems, laws targeting harassers can be an illusory source of deterrence and remedy. Chapter 7 turns to legal reforms centered on website operators and employers.

seven

Legal Reform for
Site Operators and Employers

Website operators and employers are important sources of deterrence and remedy. Congress should narrowly amend the federal law that currently immunizes online platforms from liability related to user-generated content. Site operators who encourage cyber stalking and make a profit from its removal or whose sites are principally used for that purpose should not enjoy immunity from liability. Extending immunity to the worst actors makes a mockery of the federal law designed to encourage self-monitoring by online service providers. Legal reform should also extend to employers who should give potential employees a chance to address online abuse before it can be held against them.

The Role of Website Operators

What about law's ability to shape the behavior of sites hosting online abuse? Site operators are in an optimal position to lower the costs of cyber harassment and cyber stalking. Because site operators control content appearing on their sites, they can minimize the harm by removing or de-indexing abuse before it spreads all over the Internet. They can moderate discussions, adopt clear guidelines for users, and suspend users' privileges if they harass others. They are free to do all of these things unrestrained by the First Amendment because they are not state actors.

Some platforms go to great lengths to assist cyber harassment victims and to inculcate norms of respect on their sites. Others do nothing about online abuse. For some sites, it is a matter of principle to let users say what they want. For others, their scale makes it challenging to respond in a cost-effective manner. Worst of all, some sites encourage online abuse. After all, it is their business model. In some cases, they earn money from the removal of destructive content that they have solicited.

Revenge porn site operators often boast that they cannot be sued for ruining people's lives because federal law immunizes them from liability for user-generated content. In their view, they are simply giving users the opportunity to shame others; what users do is on them.[1] A revenge porn site operator told Hollie Toups that she could either pay him $75 to remove her photo or "live and learn."[2] He told her that federal law makes him untouchable from liability for others' postings. Unfortunately, he might be right.

One might ask, as many cyber harassment victims do, how this is possible. What set of events led Congress to immunize site operators from liability? How far does that liability extend? To appreciate the forces that led to the immunity enjoyed by site operators as well as other online service providers, we need to return to two cases decided in the early years of the commercial Internet.

Liability and Early Internet Providers
The first case involved the Internet service provider CompuServe. In 1990 CompuServe hosted hundreds of forums operated by third parties, including "Rumorville." The plaintiff claimed that a user of the

"Rumorville" forum posted defamatory material about its business and sued CompuServe. The plaintiff had good reason to sue because, under the common law of libel, someone who republishes defamatory content is as responsible for the defamation as the person who originally published it. The common law presumes that republishers know what they are publishing.

Rather than viewing CompuServe as a publisher, the federal district court analogized the online service provider to a distributor like a bookstore or newsstand.[3] The court held that CompuServe enjoyed the protections of a distributor, meaning it could not be held liable unless it actually knew about the defamatory content or reasonably could have known about it. The court's decision matched the reality of running an ISP. Much like bookstores and newsstands, ISPs could not realistically preapprove all of the content hosted on their services.[4]

The second case involved Prodigy, an ISP that filtered profanity to make its services more attractive to families. On one of its financial bulletin boards called "Money Talks," an anonymous user posted defamatory comments about the securities firm Stratton Oakmont and its president, Jordan Belfort.[5] The firm sued Prodigy, arguing that because the provider used screening software to filter certain kinds of content, it exercised editorial control over the message board and thus was liable for the defamation as a publisher. Prodigy responded by arguing that it could not possibly edit the sixty thousand messages posted to its bulletin boards each day. The state trial court sided with the firm, holding Prodigy liable to the tune of $200 million. For the court, any exercise of editorial control by an online service provider would eliminate its First Amendment protection as a distributor and render it liable as a publisher.[6]

The early Internet providers got the message. If they tried to screen material on their networks but did an incomplete job, as in the *Prodigy* case, they could incur liability as publishers of defamatory content.[7] On the other hand, if they did not actively monitor content, as in the *CompuServe* case, they would face only limited distributor liability. So ISPs acted rationally: they stopped monitoring for defamatory content to avoid publisher liability (and its presumption of knowledge).

That online service providers sat on their hands was an anathema to lawmakers who wanted to encourage private actors to remove offensive content. Federal lawmakers set out to create a safe harbor from liability for online providers that attempted to regulate objectionable content provided by third parties, so long as they had not contributed to the development of the content themselves.

The Passage of Section 230

In 1995 Senators J. James Exon and Slade Gorton introduced the Communications Decency Act (CDA) to extend existing protections against harassing and obscene phone calls to other communications media and to tighten the regulation of obscenity on radio and cable television.[8] Incorporating much of the CDA into the Telecommunications Act of 1996, a Senate committee said it hoped to "encourage telecommunications and information service providers to deploy new technologies and policies" to block offensive material.[9]

Representatives Christopher Cox and Ron Wyden echoed these concerns, offering their own amendment, entitled "Protection for Private Blocking and Screening of Offensive Material."[10] The Cox-Wyden amendment "provided 'Good Samaritan' protections from civil liability for providers or users of an interactive computer service for actions to restrict or to enable restriction of access to objectionable online material."[11] The amendment eventually was incorporated into Section 230 of the CDA.[12]

In passing Section 230, Congress sought to spur investment in Internet services while incentivizing online intermediaries to restrict access to objectionable material. Section 230 shields interactive computer services, including ISPs, search engines, and websites, from liability by stating, "No provider or user of interactive computer services shall be treated as the publisher or speaker of any information provided by another information content provider."[13] With regard to civil liability, the provision guarantees that "no provider or user of an interactive computer service shall be held liable on account of any action voluntarily taken in good faith to restrict access to or availability of material that the provider or user considers to be obscene, lewd, lascivious, filthy, excessively violent, harassing, or otherwise objectionable, whether or not such material is constitutionally protected." State laws to the contrary are preempted: "No cause of action may be brought and no liability may be imposed under any State or local law that is inconsistent with this section."

Providing a safe harbor for ISPs, search engines, and massive social networks has its virtues. If communication conduits like ISPs did not enjoy Section 230 immunity, they would surely censor much valuable online content to avoid publisher liability. The same is true of search engines that index the vast universe of online content and produce relevant information to users in seconds and, for that matter, social media providers that host millions, even billions of users.

Supporters of Section 230 argue that without immunity, search engines like Google, Yahoo!, and Bing and social media providers like Facebook, YouTube, and Twitter might not exist. The point is well taken. The fear of publisher liability surely would have inhibited their growth. For that reason, Congress reaffirmed Section 230's importance in the SPEECH Act of 2010, which requires U.S. courts to apply the First Amendment and Section 230 in assessing foreign defamation judgments.

Under the prevailing interpretation of Section 230, websites enjoy immunity both from publisher and distributor liability for user-generated content. Courts have roundly immunized site operators from liability even though they knew or should have known that user-generated content contained defamation, privacy invasions, intentional infliction of emotional distress, and civil rights violations.[14] That helps explain why cyber cesspool operators have boldly defended their business models. Even if victims notify site operators about the harassment, as the law student and the revenge porn victim did, operators can ignore their requests to do something about it.

Broad but Not Absolute

Although Section 230 immunity is broad, it is not absolute. It exempts from its reach federal criminal law, intellectual property law, and the Electronic Communications Privacy Act. As Section 230(e) provides, the statute has "no effect" on "any Federal criminal statute" and does not "limit or expand any law pertaining to intellectual property." If Congress amends the federal cyber stalking statute to include a takedown remedy for revenge porn posts, Section 230 would not stand in its way.

As I was finishing this book, federal prosecutors indicted the notorious revenge porn operator Hunter Moore for conspiring to hack into people's computers to steal their nude images. According to the indictment, Moore paid a computer hacker to access women's password-protected computers and e-mail accounts in order to steal their nude photos for financial gain—profits for his revenge porn site Is Anyone Up.[15] Moore arguably could have faced charges for aiding and abetting cyber stalking under Section 2261A(2)(A) because he called for the posting of individuals' nude photos and posted (on his own) the screen shots of their Facebook profiles, sometimes including their locations, which enabled strangers to stalk them.[16] Moore's indictment shows that Section 230's immunity is not boundless. Site operators may be held accountable for violating federal criminal law.

Section 230 does not immunize site operators from copyright claims. Cyber harassment victims can file a notice-and-takedown request after registering the copyright of self-shots. The site operator would have to take down the allegedly infringing content promptly or lose its immunity under federal copyright law.[17] Many revenge porn sites ignore requests to remove infringing material because they are not worried about being sued. They know that most victims cannot afford to hire a lawyer to file copyright claims.

By No Means "Good Samaritans": Sites Devoted to
Revenge Porn and Other Abuse

Sites that are principally designed to host cyber stalking and revenge porn may not be violating federal criminal law or intellectual property law, but they certainly are not the "Good Samaritans" envisioned by Section 230's drafters. Hollie Toups and twenty others contend that Section 230 should not shelter the revenge porn site Texxxan.com from liability because the site was conceived for the purpose of causing the plaintiffs and others to suffer severe embarrassment, humiliation, and emotional distress.[18] The revenge porn victim sued several revenge porn sites hosting her nude photos on a similar legal theory.[19]

These plaintiffs may be fighting an uphill battle. Courts have repeatedly found that generalized knowledge of criminal activity on a site does not suffice to transform a site operator into a co-developer or co-creator of the illegal content.[20] If plaintiffs succeed in showing that defendant site operators helped create or develop the revenge porn, then Section 230's immunity would not apply. Section 230 protects site operators from liability only for content created by others, but not for content that they helped create or develop.

Courts are unlikely to find revenge porn operators ineligible for Section 230 immunity based solely on their encouragement of users to post illicit content. Take, for example, a lawsuit against Roommates.com, a classified advertisement service designed to help people find suitable roommates. To sign up for the service, subscribers had to fill out questionnaires about their gender, race, and sexual orientation. One question asked subscribers to choose a roommate preference, such as "Straight or gay males," "only Gay males," or "No males." Fair housing advocates filed suit, arguing that the site's questionnaires violated state and federal antidiscrimination laws.

Section 230 did not immunize the site from liability because it was partially responsible for the development of the allegedly discriminatory content. As the Ninth Circuit held, the site crafted the questions

and possible responses that "materially contributed" to the development
of the allegedly discriminatory content.[21] Crucial was the fact that the
defendant website required users to disclose certain illicit preferences.
The court distinguished the defendant's site from search engines that do
not "use unlawful criteria to limit the scope of searches" or play a role in
the development of unlawful searches.[22] The court remanded the case for
a trial to determine whether Roommates.com had violated fair housing
laws. Ultimately the site was found not liable.[23]

In another case, the Federal Trade Commission brought an action to
enjoin the web service Accusearch from selling confidential telephone
records. Although the defendant itself did not obtain the confidential
phone records, it paid researchers to do so on its behalf. The Tenth Circuit refused to extend Section 230 immunity to the defendant because it
was "responsible" for the development of the confidential phone records.
According to the court, the site contributed "mightily" to the researchers' unlawful conduct by actively soliciting and paying for confidential
phone records and charging for the resale of those records. Key to the
court's finding was the defendant's payment of researchers to obtain records that they knew were obtained illegally and its sale of those records.

What does this mean for revenge porn sites and other cyber cesspools?
Although cyber cesspool operators encourage users to post revenge
porn and other private information, they do not pay them for it, unlike
the defendant in the *Accusearch* case. After the *Roommates.com* ruling,
revenge porn operators have deleted drop-down screens that allowed
users to upload their exes' nude photos. Without screens that facilitate
the posting of specific content—nude photos, for instance—courts may
find that they did not "require," and hence help develop, such content.

Whether such strategies will help site operators avoid a finding that
they materially contributed to the development of illegal content is not
settled. Although a few trial courts have held that encouraging illicit
content eliminates Section 230 immunity, it is fairly safe to predict that

appellate courts will not go that far without additional proof that site operators materially contributed to the development of the allegedly illicit content. That helps explain why dozens upon dozens of revenge porn sites are up and running.[24]

Section 230 and Extortion Sites

Now to the question of Section 230 immunity for sites that encourage users to post content like revenge porn and make a profit from its removal.[25] The revenge porn site ObamaNudes.com advertises its content removal service for $300.[26] WinByState, a private forum that allows users to view and submit "your ex-girlfriend, your current girlfriend, or any other girl that you might know," advertises a takedown service that charges $250.[27] MyEx.com removes people's nude photos within forty-eight hours after people pay them $400.[28] Revenge porn site operators are not the only ones in this business. Sites like Campus Gossip promise to remove unwanted gossip for individuals willing to pay a monthly fee. There are also sites showing people's mug shots and charging for their removal.

It is unclear whether Section 230's immunity extends to sites that effectively engage in extortion by encouraging the posting of sensitive private information and profiting from its removal. In December 2013 California's attorney general Kamala Harris brought the first case to press the issue. Her office indicted Kevin Bollaert, operator of the revenge porn site UGotPosted, for extortion, conspiracy, and identity theft. His site featured the nude photos, Facebook screen shots, and contact information of more than ten thousand individuals, including "Jane" who I discussed in Chapter 6. The indictment alleged that Bollaert ran the site with a companion takedown site, Change My Reputation. According to the indictment, when Bollaert received complaints from individuals, he would send them e-mails directing them to the takedown site, which charged up to $350 for the removal of photos.

Attorney general Harris argued that Bollaert "published intimate photos of unsuspecting victims and turned their public humiliation and betrayal into a commodity with the potential to devastate lives."[29]

Bollaert will surely challenge the state's criminal law charges on Section 230 grounds. His strongest argument is that charging for the removal of user-generated photos is not tantamount to co-developing them. Said another way, removing content for a fee is not the same as paying for or helping develop it. The state's identity theft charges will surely be dismissed because Bollaert never personally passed himself off as the subjects depicted in the photos.[30] By contrast, the state has a strong argument that the extortion charges should stand because they hinge on what Bollaert himself did and said, not on what his users posted. Only time will tell if that sort of argument will prevail. No matter the outcome of this case, these sorts of extortion sites are undeniably gaming the CDA.

If Bollaert's state criminal charges are dismissed on Section 230 grounds, federal prosecutors could charge him with federal criminal extortion. Sites that encourage cyber harassment and charge for its removal or have a financial arrangement with removal services are engaging in extortion. At the least, they are actively and knowingly conspiring in a scheme of extortion. Of course, this possibility depends on the enforcement of federal criminal law vis-à-vis cyber stalking, which, as we have seen, is stymied by social attitudes and insufficient training. Opening another avenue for victims to protect themselves against such sites is indispensable.

The Perversity of Section 230

Although Section 230 has secured crucial breathing space for the development of online services, it has produced unjust results. Citizen Media Law Project's Sam Bayard explains that a site operator can enjoy the protection of Section 230 while "building a whole business around people saying nasty things about others, and . . . affirmatively choosing not to track user information that would make it possible for an injured person to go after the person directly responsible."[31]

Partly for that reason, the National Association of Attorneys General (NAAG) has pressured Congress to amend Section 230 to exempt state criminal laws. At a NAAG meeting in June 2013, several state attorneys general argued that Section 230 should exempt from its safe harbor not only federal criminal law but state criminal law as well. This proposal stems from concerns about advertisements of child-sex traffickers.[32]

Although attention to the issue is encouraging, the NAAG proposal is too broad. It would require online providers to shoulder burdensome legal compliance with countless state criminal laws that have nothing to do with the most troubling uses of online platforms, such as child-sex trafficking and revenge porn. Rather than addressing the unjust results of Section 230 with the sweeping elimination of the immunity for state criminal law, a more narrow revision is in order.

Proposal: Excluding the Worst Actors from Section 230's Immunity

Congress should amend Section 230's safe harbor provision to exclude the very worst actors: sites that encourage cyber stalking or nonconsensual pornography and make money from its removal *or* that principally host cyber stalking or nonconsensual pornography.[33] Mirroring Section 230's current exemption of federal criminal law and intellectual property, the amendment could state, "Nothing in Section 230 shall be construed to limit or expand the application of civil or criminal liability for any website or other content host that purposefully encourages cyber stalking or nonconsensual pornography and seeks financial remuneration from its removal *or* that principally hosts cyber stalking or nonconsensual pornography."

In amending Section 230, Congress could import the definition of cyber stalking from Section 2261A(2)(A): an intentional "course of conduct" designed to harass that causes another person to fear bodily harm or to suffer substantial emotional distress.[34] The amendment could define nonconsensual pornography along the lines of the revenge porn proposal detailed in Chapter 6. If Congress adopted this proposal, an escape hatch could be included that would secure a safe harbor for covered sites that promptly removed harassing content after receiving notice of its presence.

A few examples can help demonstrate the modest though important reach of this proposal. Campus Gossip is just the sort of extortion site that would not enjoy immunity. It purposefully encourages the targeting of individuals and offers a removal subscription service. Many revenge porn sites similarly solicit the posting of nude photos and make money from their removal. Other revenge porn sites do not have takedown services but would be covered by the proposed amendment because they principally host nonconsensual pornography. Such sites could not evade a finding that they principally hosted cyber stalking or nonconsensual pornography by including pages of spam.[35]

What about the message board AutoAdmit, where posters targeted the law student? At the time of the attack, countless threads on the board were devoted to attacking individual students. The cyber law scholar Brian Leiter conducted an informal study of the board, finding that hundreds of threads had racist, misogynist, homophobic, and anti-Semitic themes. But did the site principally host cyber stalking or encourage its posting and make money from its removal? The answer is no. Let me explain why.

Having spent hours looking at the site, it seems difficult to suggest that the site was *principally* used for cyber stalking. Many used the site for its stated purpose: to discuss colleges and graduate schools. As the commenter "Jimmy" said, "I used autoadmit . . . for years to help me navigate everything [about] law school," including the "decision to go to law school, how to prepare for law school, [and] how to get a job. . . . Granted there are some poor, poor threads and comments on the board, but it's the first place I turn to after a rough final or for the latest financial aid tips."[36] The board's operators never received money from the removal of threads. To the contrary, they steadfastly refused to remove any of the harassing posts targeting the law student. As dissatisfying as this assessment might be, the board generated enough speech that has nothing to do with cyber stalking and it never charged for the removal of threads, so it would not be covered by my proposed amendment.

What about 4chan, discussed in Chapter 1? 4chan is not principally used to facilitate cyber stalking, even though one of its hubs, the /b/ forum, hosts trolling activity, including attacks on individuals. Most of 4chan's forums have nothing to do with cyber stalking. Some are de voted to Japanese animation and videos; others concern weapons and video games.

What if 4chan's /b/ forum had its own site operator? The question would be whether the operator's forum was principally used to facilitate cyber stalking. Because the /b/ forum is used for many different purposes aside from targeting individuals, it would not fall outside my proposed exemption to Section 230 immunity. If, however, the /b/ forum was principally used to host cyber stalking, then the person operating it would not enjoy Section 230 immunity.

Why remove the safe harbor immunity only for a narrow category of sites and otherwise leave it intact? Why not eliminate the safe harbor for all sites that know or should know about destructive abuse and do nothing about it? Is the better course to reinstate distributor liability?

It is not. Distributor liability entails a far greater risk of self-censorship than the amendment I proposed. To be sure, distributor liability would be an attractive option if sites *only* received complaints, and then removed, harmful, unprotected expression. But regrettably, that would not be the case. Under the phenomenon known as the "heckler's veto," people complain about speech because they dislike the speakers or object to their views, not because they have suffered actual harm, such as defamation and credible threats. If site operators do not gain much from any given post, they will filter, block, or remove posts if their continued display risks expensive litigation.[37] It is foolish to keep up speech that adds little to a site's bottom line and risks liability, even if the person's objection is clearly frivolous, as in the heckler veto.

Take the popular news-gathering site Reddit. Given the site's crowd-sourcing goal, it lacks a vested interest in any particular post. If the site could incur liability as a distributor, it would be inclined to remove speech reported as defamation, for instance, rather than hire people to assess the validity of complaints. The smarter choice would be to remove reported speech rather than spend time trying to figure out what is going on.

By contrast, excessive self-censorship is far less likely for sites that have an incentive to keep up complained-about content. That is true for sites whose business model is to host cyber stalking or revenge porn. Campus Gossip and MyEx.com, for instance, benefit financially from hosting harassing material. It is in their economic interest to keep up destructive material that attracts viewers and in turn advertising fees. As the *Slate* reporter and cyber bullying expert Emily Bazelon has remarked, concerns about the heckler's veto get more deference than they should in the context of revenge porn sites.[38]

Dispensing with the immunity for a narrow set of site operators would *not* mean that they would be strictly liable for user-generated content. Much like offline newspapers, such sites could incur publisher liability for defamatory content to the extent the First Amendment allows. They could face tort liability for having enabled torts and crimes on their sites. Tort law recognizes claims against parties who engage in conduct generating risks and causing harm that arise from third-party intervention. Courts permit recovery because the defendant paved the way for a third party to injure another. Enablement claims are premised on the notion that negligence's deterrence rationale would be defeated if those enabling wrongdoing could escape judgment by shifting liability to individuals who cannot be caught and deterred.[39]

Enablement liability has been recognized against those who gather or communicate information on the theory that their actions facilitated criminal conduct. A stalker killed a woman after obtaining her work address from the defendant, a data broker. A court ruled that the data broker had a duty to exercise reasonable care in releasing personal information to third parties due to the risk of criminal misconduct. Information brokers should know that stalkers often use their services to obtain personal information about victims and that identity theft is a common risk associated with the disclosure of personal information like social security numbers.[40] As I explain in Chapter 8, the First Amendment would permit enablement liability against site operators who intentionally facilitate crimes like cyber stalking but not for those who do so negligently.

The above proposal endeavors to strike a balance in addressing the needs of the harassed while maintaining the vibrancy of the Internet. It may not satisfy everyone. It may meet with disapproval from those who oppose intermediary liability and from those who do not think intermediaries should enjoy immunity at all. Nonetheless, it ensures that cyber harassment victims have some leverage against the worst online actors, even though they could not sue many news-gathering sites, search engines, and social media providers when abuse appears on their services.

Employers

Cyber harassment victims have difficulty finding and keeping jobs because searches of their names prominently display the abuse wrought by cyber mobs or individual stalkers. Employers admittedly rely on social media information in making hiring and firing decisions. They have little reason to think that consulting search results in employment matters would violate the law. No one has sued an employer on the theory that online searches have a disparate impact on certain groups such that reliance on them amounts to employment discrimination. This is not surprising given that employers have no obligation to tell applicants or employees that search results were the reason for their employment difficulties.[41] We need a change in course if we want to give victims a fair chance to develop their careers in our networked age.

Some countries ban employers from considering search results in their hiring and firing decisions. Finland, for instance, prohibits employers from using the Internet to research potential or current employees without first getting their approval.[42] It adopted that rule after an employer refused to hire an applicant because an online search yielded information that the individual had attended a mental health conference. The employer assumed that the applicant had mental health problems; as it turned out, the applicant attended the conference as a patient's representative. The Finnish government adopted a bright-line rule to prevent employers from jumping to conclusions based on incomplete or false information appearing in search results.[43]

U.S. policymakers are unlikely to adopt such a sweeping ban because search results yield both unreliable *and* reliable information. With such a prohibition, employers would lose access to a cheap way to verify applicants' claims on their résumés. Some states ban employers from asking applicants for their social media passwords,[44] though this provides no help to victims who are harassed on third-party sites.

An alternative approach is to adopt policies that mitigate the possibility that cyber harassment would unfairly impact women and minorities in their careers. Consider the EEOC's approach to the use of arrest records in hiring matters.[45] The EEOC has interpreted Title VII to ban employers from using arrest records as the sole basis for rejecting job applicants. As discussed in Chapter 5, Title VII of the Civil Rights Act of 1964 prohibits employment discrimination on the basis of race, national origin, sex, or religion.[46] Under the theory of disparate impact, Title VII bans neutral employment practices that have a disproportionate adverse impact on protected groups when those practices cannot be justified as "job related for the position in question and consistent with business necessity."[47] For this reason, the EEOC has instructed that employers can learn about individuals' arrest records, but they cannot use them as an automatic disqualifier except in narrow circumstances. The policy is designed to offset the potential for discrimination because racial minorities disproportionately face arrest.[48]

The EEOC could and should interpret Title VII to ban employers from using search engine results as the basis for denying individuals' employment opportunities. Employers' reliance on searches to research candidates has a disparate impact on women given the gendered nature of cyber harassment. Cyber harassment victims often have difficulty obtaining and keeping jobs because searches of their names prominently display the abuse.

If the EEOC adopts this policy, employers facing lawsuits on this theory would surely contend that anonymous postings have little weight on employment decisions because they are unreliable. Saying so, however, would not necessarily bar such suits. Evidence increasingly supports the argument that employers are unlikely to ignore cyber harassment. As behavioral economists have shown, we tend to credit what we first learn about someone; our initial knowledge gets anchored in our memories, making it hard to shake first impressions.[49] Recent studies suggest that information's prominence in searches is often used as a proxy for reliability, which is terrible news for cyber harassment victims.[50] Researchers have also found that people are more inclined to credit negative online information than positive online data even if the positive information is more current than the negative.[51] Plaintiffs' counsel can argue that employers have a hard time ignoring destructive posts, no matter how improbable or stale.

Without legal reform, cyber harassment victims cannot combat these cognitive biases because they do not get the chance to explain their side of the story. In the law student's case, if law firms relied on search engine results in assessing and rejecting her candidacy, they never told her. She was not given the opportunity to explain that she did not actually have sex with her dean, score 152 on her LSAT, or have herpes. Because cyber harassers disproportionately target women, the negative impact on the use of search engines to make decisions in hiring matters falls unequally on them, in violation of Title VII's guarantee against sex discrimination.

Federal legislators might consider adopting legislation that prohibits employers from rejecting candidates based solely or primarily on search results because of the likelihood that such results will more often disadvantage women and minorities. Such a policy should be coupled with training about the phenomenon of cyber harassment, in much the way that Title VII has been interpreted to provide certain immunities to employers if they teach employees about antiharassment policies. Employers who receive such training would be more likely to scrutinize negative information appearing online and to appreciate its potential peril to traditionally subordinated groups. Training has been effective in combating our tendency to believe the judgments of automated systems. According to recent studies, individuals who receive training on the fallibility of automated decision making are more likely to scrutinize a computer system's suggestions.[52] But training cannot be a one-time affair. In the context of Title VII, antiharassment training has had limited impact on workplace norms because employers treat it as a box to check rather than as part of their daily culture. The most effective training programs repeat their lessons early and often.

Additional protections could mirror what I have called "technological due process"—ensuring that de facto adjudications made by software programs live up to some standard of review and revision. Fair credit reporting laws are a helpful illustration. The Fair Credit Reporting Act (FCRA) was passed in 1970 to protect the privacy and accuracy of information included in credit reports. Under the FCRA, employers are required to inform individuals that they intend to take an adverse action against them due to their credit report.[53] This gives individuals a chance to explain inaccurate or incomplete information and to contact credit-reporting agencies to dispute the information in the hopes of getting it corrected.[54] Professor Frank Pasquale has proposed a fair reputation reporting act, which would require employers to reveal online sources that they use in evaluating applicants. The act would give job applicants a chance to review the digital dossiers compiled about them. Under the aegis of the Federal Trade Commission, the approach would give victims a chance to address cyber harassers' anonymous allegations before it costs them jobs.

If employers use third parties to compile information on prospective employees, including data culled online, they may already be required to comply with the FCRA. The Federal Trade Commission recently decreed that social media intelligence companies constitute consumer-reporting agencies subject to the FCRA because they assemble information used by third parties in determining a consumer's eligibility for employment. Data brokers and social media intelligence companies compile and sell profiles on consumers to human resource professionals, job recruiters, and businesses as employment screening tools. If an employer obtains an Internet background check on a cyber harassment victim from such companies, it must let that person know before it makes an adverse decision based on such digital dossiers. Under the current regulatory regime, employers do not have to give candidates a chance to respond to online abuse if *they* use the Internet to research candidates rather than hiring someone else to do so, to the detriment of cyber harassment victims.[55]

Should We Worry about Having Too Much Law?

Law can admittedly breed problems. Some resist new laws because, in their view, our society is already prone to overcriminalization. That concern is pressing in the so-called war on drugs. In the United States, the prison population has exploded: the increase is attributable to the incarceration of drug dealers and drug users who are disproportionately African American, even though people of all races sell and use drugs at similar rates. The civil rights scholar Michelle Alexander has powerfully argued that the mass incarceration of black men is this century's Jim Crow.[56]

Overcriminalization is a problem for drug crimes but not for crimes predominantly impacting women and girls like cyber stalking. Law enforcement has not taken stalking seriously, and cyber stalking even less so. For now, the hard work is convincing police and prosecutors to enforce cyber stalking laws at all rather than to back off from doing too much.

Commentators also worry about the criminalization of revenge porn because they fear that prosecutors will use their discretion to investigate and charge defendants in arbitrary and objectionable ways. Although this can be said about existing and future laws, it is a valid concern.

Examples abound of prosecutors pursuing individuals who, by all societal accounts, are either trying to help others or are victims themselves. Recall that the computer hacker KY Anonymous in the Steubenville case used legal and illegal means to find out the rapists' names to put pressure on local law enforcement to arrest the perpetrators. Even before local law enforcement charged the alleged rapists, KY Anonymous was indicted for criminal computer hacking. KY Anonymous may have hacked a private computer, but his motive was to help the police identify the victim's attackers. That is not to say that he did not break the law, but law enforcement's resources should have been devoted to pursuing the real criminals: the individuals who raped the young girl.

In another troubling case, a man secretly taped women having sex with him. One of the women (with whom he was in a relationship) suspected him of taping their intimate moments. To figure out what was going on, she went into his e-mail account without his permission. What she found was horrifying. The man had countless sex videos not only of her but also of other women. She took screenshots of the videos and went to law enforcement with the proof. Rather than looking at the screenshots, the police arrested her for gaining "unlawful access" to the man's e-mail account and for harassing him. Eight months later, prosecutors dropped the charges against her. The man was indicted for several counts of unlawful surveillance. But considerable damage had already been done to her professional and social life. The prosecutor should not have gone after the victim, who did what she could to get proof of the invasion of her privacy and, as it turns out, that of other women.[57]

In another case, someone uploaded nude photos of a married teacher on The Dirty and MyEx.com. The posts caused her considerable emotional anguish, and she lost her job.[58] When the woman went to the police, she told officers that she had lost her phone and had never shared the photos with anyone except her husband. After some investigation, officers figured out that the teacher did e-mail her nude photos to another person, who was not her husband. The police charged the woman with obstructing justice by lying to them.[59] The woman admitted that she covered up the fact that she had shared her photos with someone who betrayed her trust. That was wrong, but far worse was the fact that police charged her with a crime and seemingly gave up on investigating the person who posted her nude photos on the gossip site and other revenge porn sites, which might have amounted to criminal harassment.

Is the possibility of prosecutorial overreaching or poor judgment a good reason not to adopt the proposals I have outlined? New laws, no more and no less than existing laws, can be inappropriately invoked. The potential for prosecutorial abuse is always present, no matter the crime. Rather than giving up on law's potential to deter and punish wrongdoing, the indictment of KY Anonymous and the others discussed above should engage the public in a conversation about prosecutorial missteps. Something good could come of those conversations. The more the public expresses their disapproval, the more prosecutors (whose bosses are elected) may think twice about pursuing cases that do not serve the broader goals of justice. Having those public conversations can help combat inappropriate prosecutions. As a society, we should not abandon legal reform because some prosecutors may abuse their power.

Another related concern is that prosecutors can manipulate vaguely drafted laws to troubling ends. An example of this involved the suicide of a Missouri teenager, Megan Meier. Lori Drew, the mother of one of Meier's classmates, impersonated a teenage boy named "Josh" on MySpace. After Meier was duped into believing that Josh liked her, the fictitious Josh dumped her with the missive that the "world would be better off without her." Meier, who had a history of depression, committed suicide. Federal prosecutors wanted to do something, so they charged Drew with various computer crimes, none of which captured her behavior. Their strained interpretation of vague language in the Computer Fraud and Abuse Act (CFAA) had everything to do with the public's outcry over the teen's suicide and very little to do with computer hacking that the law covered.

Lawmakers can curtail some prosecutorial overreaching by drafting clear and narrowly tailored laws. The revenge porn bill proposed in Chapter 6, for instance, is drafted with enough specificity to forestall these concerns. By contrast, CFAA's broad language made it easy for prosecutors to indict Drew. That lawmakers *can* draft broad and vague laws is a good reason for those laws to be challenged and struck down as unconstitutional. But that is not a good reason to prevent the adoption of well-crafted laws that prevent and punish grave harms. The harms to cyber harassment victims and society are too grave to ignore. Society has previously combated activity that incurs grave costs while dealing with concerns about overreaching; it can do the same now.

Lawmakers are also urged to proceed cautiously for other reasons. They are advised to avoid turning so-called repugnant behavior into crimes. That is the theme of some objections to proposals to criminalize revenge porn. Of California's prosecution of the revenge porn site operator Kevin Bollaert, the law professor Eric Goldman remarked, "Let's start with the premise that it's not a crime to be despicable. There are crimes on the books and we need to find the crimes that apply to the facts. If we can't do that, we may have a hole in the law, but we don't have criminal behavior."[60]

Calls for caution seem to stem from the notion that "distasteful" behavior is not sufficiently harmful to warrant criminalization. Suppose a state did not criminalize theft. Would the public question legislative proposals to ban stealing? The answer is probably not, given our shared understanding that stealing exacts unacceptable societal costs. Revenge porn is no different. Indeed, it inflicts financial, emotional, and physical harms far graver than many thefts. The overcriminalization objection is another way that online harassment is trivialized.

We still need to address whether a cyber civil rights legal agenda can survive First Amendment challenges. Would a robust legal campaign compromise free speech values? As I argue in Chapter 8, a legal agenda comports with First Amendment doctrine and does not meaningfully undermine the concerns underlying why we protect free speech in the first place.

eight

"Don't Break the Internet" and Other Free Speech Challenges

People often bristle at the prospect of a regulatory response to cyber harassment. In their view, people should be allowed to say anything they want online because it is "free speech."[1] Commentators warn that the Internet would cease to foster expression if law intervened. Regulation should be avoided because online expression would be chilled, end of story. But First Amendment protections and free speech values are far more nuanced than that. They do not work as absolutes. And there are speech interests beyond that of the harassers to consider.

A legal agenda would not undermine our commitment to free speech. Instead, it would secure the necessary preconditions for free expression while safeguarding the equality of opportunity in our digital age. The proposals offered in this book do not seek to expand the categories of unprotected speech. Rather, they work within the framework of existing First Amendment doctrine that permits the regulation of certain categories of "low-value speech" and accords less rigorous constitutional protection to other speech as a historical matter, including defamation, true threats, crime-facilitating speech, certain cruelty rising to the level of intentional infliction of emotional distress, and privacy invasions involving purely private matters.

As history has demonstrated in other contexts, civil rights can be balanced with the values of free speech. Now to apply those lessons to a cyber civil rights legal agenda.

Would Law Wreck the Internet?

Many resist the regulation of online speech as antithetical to our commitment to public discourse because the Internet is the "equivalent of the public square."[2] The message to lawmakers is "Don't wreck our virtual town meetings."[3]

Underlying this concern are two faulty assumptions. The first has to do with the way online platforms are conceptualized. Without question, online platforms are indispensible to public dialogue. They enable ordinary people to reach a national and even global audience.[4] With networked tools, citizens can communicate with government officials and staffers as never before. On social network sites, government agencies engage with citizen-experts on policy matters.[5] As President Obama enthused at a town hall meeting held at Facebook's Palo Alto headquarters in April 2011, "Historically, part of what makes for a healthy democracy, what is good politics, is when you've got citizens who are informed, who are engaged. And what Facebook allows us to do is make sure this isn't just a one-way conversation; makes sure that not only am I speaking to you but you're speaking back and we're in a conversation, we're in a dialogue."[6]

But public conversation is not the only thing happening online. Online platforms host a dizzying array of activities. Some sites are hybrid workplaces, schools, social clubs, and town squares. Some are password-protected; others are not. Recall the different roles that the tech blogger's site played. Her blog Creating Passionate Users established her professional expertise and attracted clients while hosting a public conversation about software development and marketing. Networked spaces serve as crucial speech platforms, but they are not one-dimensional speech platforms.

The second faulty assumption is connected to the first. It presumes that if networked platforms serve as public forums like public parks and streets, then special protections for free speech are in order. The concern is that regulation would endanger indispensible channels of public discourse. Although online sites facilitate expression (after all, they are all made up of 1s and 0s), they do not warrant special treatment, certainly no more and no less than speech in other platforms with diverse opportunities for work, play, and expression. Workplaces, schools, homes, professional conferences, and coffee shops are all zones of conversation, but they are not exempted from legal norms. Civil rights, criminal, and tort laws have not destroyed workplaces, homes, and social venues. Requiring free speech concerns to accommodate civil rights will not ruin networked spaces.

Another concern is that any regulation will embark us on a slippery slope to a profoundly worse-off society. This is a familiar refrain of absolutists. When twentieth-century civil rights movements came into conflict with entrenched societal values, supporters of those values insisted that the greater good demanded that they be upheld absolutely lest they lose their force by a thousand cuts. That was said of civil rights protections in the workplace. As judicial decisions and EEOC regulations recognized claims for hostile sexual environments in the 1980s, many argued that they would suffocate workplace expression and impair worker camaraderie.[7]

On the fiftieth anniversary of Title VII, we can say with confidence that accommodating equality and speech interests of all workers (including sexually harassed employees) did not ruin the workplace. Although antidiscrimination law chills some persistent sexually harassing expression that would create a hostile work environment, it protects other workers' ability to interact, speak, and work on equal terms. As we now recognize, civil rights did not destroy expression in the workplace but reinforced it on more equal terms.[8] A legal agenda against cyber harassment and cyber stalking can balance civil rights and civil liberties for the good of each.

Self-Governance and the Digital Citizen

In her senior year at college, Zoe Yang applied for and got a position as the sex columnist for her school newspaper. It was an exciting opportunity to engage in a public dialogue about issues she had been talking about with her friends. She paired her column with a personal blog, Zoe Has Sex, where she discussed sex, race, and family relationships. After she blogged about her sexual fantasies, anonymous posters attacked her on her blog and on message boards. After graduation, she closed her blog, and the online attacks faded.

In 2008 Yang moved to New York City to work at a management-consulting firm. In her spare time, she maintained a blog about restaurants. Posters found out about her food blog and started attacking her again. They called for readers to tell her work colleagues about her "fuckie-suckie past" and listed their e-mail addresses. Posters spread false rumors that she had been fired from her job. Attack blogs were set up in her name, such as Zoe Yang Skank and Zoe Yang Is Whoring It Up Again.

Yang decided to give up her online pursuits. Her blogging was "an incredible learning experience," but it was far too costly to continue.[9] Yang told me that her anonymous attackers intimidated her from participating as a "citizen" in our digital age.[10] She has stayed offline for the past five years because the attacks are still ongoing.[11]

Having the opportunity to engage as a citizen and to participate in the creation of culture is one of the central reasons why we protect speech. As Professor Neil Richards argues in his book *Intellectual Privacy: Civil*

Liberties and Information in the Digital Age, "we need free speech if we are to govern ourselves."[12] Much inspiration for the "self-governance" theory of the First Amendment comes from Supreme Court Justice Louis Brandeis. In his concurrence in *Whitney v. California,* Justice Brandeis argued that "the freedom to think as you will and to speak as you think are means indispensable to the discovery and spread of political truth; that, without free speech and assembly, discussion would be futile; that, with them, discussion affords ordinarily adequate protection against the dissemination of noxious doctrine."[13] Citizens, not the government, must determine what is a fit subject for public debate.[14]

The "self-governance theory" is based on the idea that individuals who can speak freely and listen to others who speak freely make more informed decisions about the kind of society they want to live in.[15] Civic virtue comes from "discussion and education, not by lazy and impatient reliance on the coercive authority of the state."[16] Building on these ideas, Professor Jack Balkin powerfully argues that free speech promotes "democracy in the widest possible sense, not merely at the level of governance, or at the level of deliberation, but at the level of culture, where we interact, create, build communities, and build ourselves."[17]

Online speech is crucial for self-government and cultural engagement. Networked spaces host expression that is explicitly political and speech that is less so but that nonetheless is key to civic and cultural engagement.[18] Blogs about food, software design, body image, and sex may explore political issues, or they may not; in either case, they contribute to the exchange of ideas and the building of online communities. They reinforce the skills of discourse, just as Justice Brandeis contemplated. The Internet holds great promise for *digital citizenship,* by which I mean the various ways online activities deepen civic engagement, political and cultural participation, and public conversation.[19]

Cyber harassment does little to enhance self-governance and does much to destroy it. Its contribution to public conversation is slight. Cyber mobs and individual harassers are not engaged in political, cultural, or social discourse. The posters who spread lies about Yang's job and called for readers to contact her work colleagues were not criticizing her ideas about food or sex. The rape threats on the tech blogger's site and the doctored photos of her being suffocated and with a noose beside her neck had no connection to social issues. Lies about the law student's herpes and LSAT score did not shed light on cultural concerns. The revenge porn victim's nude photos contributed nothing to conversations about issues of broad societal interest. The cruel harassment of private individuals does not advance public discussion. Listeners learn nothing of value from it.

We gain little and lose much from online abuse. Cyber harassment destroys victims' ability to interact in ways that are essential to self-governance. As Yang remarked, online abuse prevents targeted individuals from realizing their full potential as digital citizens. Victims cannot participate in online networks if they are under assault. Rape threats, defamatory lies, the nonconsensual disclosure of nude photos, and technological attacks destroy victims' ability to interact with others. They sever a victim's connections with people engaged in similar pursuits.

Robust democratic discourse cannot be achieved if cyber mobs and individual harassers drive victims from it. As Yang's case and that of so many others show, victims are unable to engage in dialogue that is essential to a healthy democracy if they are under assault. Defeating online aggressions that deny victims their ability to engage with others as citizens outweighs the negligible contribution that cyber harassment makes to cultural interaction and expression.

Expressive Autonomy and the Cyber Mob

Commentators argue that concerns about victims' "hurt feelings" do not justify impeding harassers' self-expression. They contend that denying cyber stalkers and cyber harassers' ability to say what they want, even if it harms others, interferes with their basic capacity to express themselves. The argument draws on a crucial theory of why free speech matters: its ability to facilitate individual autonomy.[20] As Justice Lewis Powell Jr. remarked, the First Amendment serves "the human spirit—a spirit that demands self-expression."[21]

Regulation will admittedly chill some self-expression. Cyber harassers use words and images to attack victims. But to understand the risks to expression inherent in efforts to regulate online abuse, we need to account for the full breadth of expression imperiled. Some expression can make it impossible for others to participate in conversation. Cyber harassment perfectly illustrates how expression can deny others' "full and equal opportunity to engage in public debate."[22]

Professor Steven Heymann argues that when a person's self-expression is designed for the purpose of extinguishing another person's speech, it should receive no protection.[23] Sometimes, as Professor Owen Fiss contends, we must lower the voices of some to permit the self-expression of others.[24] Along these lines, Professor Cass Sunstein contends that threats, libel, and sexual and racial harassment constitute low-value speech of little First Amendment consequence.[25] As one court put it, the Internet can "never achieve its potential" as a facilitator of discussion unless "it is subject to . . . the law like all other social discourse. Some curb on abusive speech is necessary for meaningful discussion."[26] Rarely is that more true than when one group of voices consciously exploits the Internet to silence others.

We should be less troubled about limiting the expressive autonomy of cyber harassers who use their voices to extinguish victims' expression. Silencing is what many harassers are after. The cyber mob spread the tech blogger's social security number and defamatory lies about her all over the web because she spoke out against the threats on her blog and the photos on the group blogs. Recall that one of her attackers said he "doxed" her because he did not like her "whining" about the abuse she faced. The cyber mob achieved its goal: the tech blogger shut down her blog to prevent further reprisal. The law student had a similar experience. The message board posters exploited expression—a Google bombing campaign—to drown out her writing with their own destructive posts. While the law student was working in South Korea, she shut down her cooking blog, which helped her stay in touch with her family, because it provoked destructive responses from her harassers. Another cyber harassment victim confided to me that she felt she was left with no choice but to withdraw from online life because whenever she engaged online, harassers went after her, and whenever she stopped, so did they.

Restraining a cyber mob's destructive attacks is essential to defending the expressive autonomy of its victims. The revenge porn victim would not have closed her social media accounts and extinguished her former identity had she not faced online abuse. The law student would not have shut down her blog if the attacks had not resumed. The tech blogger surely would be blogging today if the cyber mob had not targeted her.

Free from online attacks, victims might blog, join online discussions, share videos, engage in social networks, and express themselves on issues large and small. Protecting victims from defamation, threats, privacy invasions, and technological attacks would allow them to be candid about their ideas.[27] Preventing harassers from driving people offline would "advance the reasons why we protect free speech in the first place," even though it would inevitably chill some speech of cyber harassers.

The Marketplace of Ideas in Cyberspace

Some may argue that a legal agenda will undermine the ability to discover truths in our networked age. After all, if cyber harassers cannot speak their minds, certain "truths" about victims will not come to light. The public may be unable to learn that people so dislike a blogger that they are inspired to threaten to rape and beat her. Employers may not be given the chance to assess claims that a prospective employee supposedly wanted to sleep with strangers. Potential mates may not be able to learn that a date shared nude photos with an ex-lover in confidence. The argument is that readers will be able to figure out what is going on: if posts are obviously false, they will be ignored.

Justice Oliver Wendell Holmes drew on similar notions about truths and falsehoods when he articulated his theory of the "marketplace of ideas": "The best test of truth is the power of the thought to get itself accepted in the competition of the market."[28] The marketplace metaphor suggests that truth can be determined by subjecting one's ideas to strenuous challenge. Hateful views should be aired so that they can be refuted. As John Stuart Mill argued in *On Liberty*, the best protection against prejudice is open debate and strong counterarguments.[29] According to Mill, citizens should work to persuade others of the truth.

An extreme version of the truth-seeking theory might insist that listeners sort out cyber harassers' deceptions and assaults. To do so, however, the theory has to assume that we could have an open, rigorous, and rational discourse about rape threats, social security numbers, nude photos posted without the subject's consent, technological attacks, and impersonations suggesting someone's interest in sex. A more plausible vision of the truth-seeking theory suggests that no truths are contested in these cases. Threats, for instance, tell us nothing about victims. They do not constitute ideas that can be refuted unless responding that someone should not be raped amounts to a meaningful counterpoint. Individuals' social security numbers and technological attacks are not truths or half-truths to be tested in the marketplace of ideas.

Posts with a woman's nude photo, home address, and supposed interest in sex are not facts or ideas to be debated in the service of truth. When dealing with falsehoods impugning someone's character, the victim does not have an affirmative case she is trying to convey—she is only seeking to dispel the harm from anonymous posters' attacks. Even if victims could respond, their replies may never be seen. The truth may be unable to emerge from a battle of posts.

Then too, images of a private person's naked body have little value to the general public and can destroy that person's career. They ensure that victims are undateable, unemployable, and unable to partake in online activities. Importantly, as Professor Daniel Solove aptly notes, "Truth isn't the only value at stake."[30]

What First Amendment Doctrine Has to Say

Even if cyber harassment contributes little to free speech values, its regulation must comport with First Amendment doctrine. A quick reading of the First Amendment to the U.S. Constitution appears to prohibit any effort by government to censor or punish what we say. "Congress shall make no law . . . abridging the freedom of speech, or of the press." But rather than an absolute prohibition on speech, the First Amendment has been interpreted as an instruction to treat rules limiting speech with a high level of suspicion. As the Supreme Court has declared, our society has a "profound national commitment to the principle that debate on public issues should be uninhibited, robust, and wide open."[31]

A bedrock principle underlying the First Amendment is that government cannot censor the expression of an idea because society finds the idea itself offensive or distasteful.[32] Hateful words thus enjoy presumptive constitutional protection.[33] The antidote to speech we do not like is counterspeech. As the Court instructs, our right and civic duty is to engage in "open, dynamic, and rational discourse."[34]

Ordinarily, government regulation of the content of speech—what speech is about—is permissible only in a narrow set of circumstances. Content regulations, such as forbidding the public from disclosing classified government secrets or banning antiabortion protests, have to serve a compelling interest that cannot be promoted through less restrictive means. We call that "strict scrutiny review," and it is difficult to satisfy because we distrust government to pick winners and losers in the realm of ideas. Much like Pascal's gamble on faith, the better bet for us is to allow more speech, even if that means living with some of its undesirable consequences.

Nonetheless, not all forms of speech are worthy of being protected with strict scrutiny. Certain categories of low-value speech can be regulated due to their propensity to bring about serious harms and slight contribution to free speech values. They include true threats, speech integral to criminal conduct, defamation, fraud, obscenity, and imminent and likely incitement of violence.[35] First Amendment protections are less rigorous for public disclosures of certain private facts, including nude photos and intentional cruelty about purely private matters causing severe emotional distress.

The legal agenda proposed in this book comports with the First Amendment because it regulates only speech that receives less rigorous protection or no protection. Let me explain how.

True Threats

A woman receives an anonymous e-mail warning: "One day soon, when you least expect it, I will get you. I will smash your head with a bat and leave you in the gutter." While the sender made the threat with words, that fact would not provide a defense to liability. The First Amendment does not protect "true threats"—speech intended to convey a serious intent to hurt another person or that a reasonable person would interpret as expressing a serious intent to cause bodily harm.[36] True threats do not cover political argument, idle talk, and jest.[37]

To figure out if speech constitutes a true threat, the expression is viewed in context in light of the principle that debate on public issues should be uninhibited.[38] This helps us distinguish a political candidate's e-mail message that in an upcoming debate, she will "beat her opponents with a bat."[39] The former amounts to true threat given the likelihood that it would instill fear in a reasonable person; the latter generally would be accepted as political hyperbole.

The First Amendment does not protect true threats because of their minimal contribution to public debate and their infliction of serious harm. True threats generate profound fear of physical harm that disrupts victims' daily lives. Because victims know they cannot protect themselves at all times, they experience extreme emotional disturbance. Victims try to engage in self-protection, which is a formidable challenge when the origin of the threat is unknown. When faced with credible threats, victims change their routines for their own physical safety. In this way, credible threats are tantamount to coercion. As Professor Kenneth Karst explains, legal limits on someone's liberty to threaten another person ultimately defend the victim's liberty.[40]

True threats can take a variety of forms. Is the burning of a cross, a symbol closely associated with the Ku Klux Klan's ideology and its history of facilitating violence, best characterized as an expression of a point of view or as a true threat? In *Virginia v. Black,* the Court addressed that question. In that case, two men burned a cross on an African American family's lawn in the middle of the night. They were convicted under a state law banning cross burning.

The Court held that cross burning is a constitutionally unprotected "virulent form of intimidation" if it is targeted at particular individuals and done with intent to instill fear of physical harm. The Court underscored that speakers need not intend to carry out the threat because the true threats exception protects individuals from the fear of violence, the disruption that such fear engenders, and the possibility that violence will occur. The Court contrasted cross burning done to convey a hateful ideology at a Klan rally, where specific individuals are not targeted. In that context, cross burning constitutes protected expression. As the Court emphasized, individuals have the right to express hateful views but not to make true threats.[41]

Online expression can rise to the level of unprotected true threats even if they are not sent directly to targeted individuals. In the mid-1990s a militant antiabortion group circulated "Wanted" posters proclaiming named abortion providers "GUILTY of Crimes Against Humanity." The group sponsored the Nuremberg Files website. The names and addresses of two hundred "abortionists" appeared on the site, and the site operator regularly updated readers on the fate of those abortion providers. When a doctor was killed, the site crossed out the person's name. Working doctors' names appeared in black, while wounded doctors' names appeared in gray. On the FBI's advice, doctors listed on the site wore bulletproof vests to work and installed alarm systems in their homes.[42]

A majority of the judges on the Ninth Circuit Court of Appeals found that the site constituted a true threat even though its operator did not explicitly say that he would kill the doctors.[43] The majority held that the site sent the implied message "You're Wanted or You're Guilty; You'll be shot or killed." The site amounted to a true threat because of the context—the murder of doctors and defendants' knowledge that doctors had stopped performing abortions because they feared for their lives.[44]

The tech blogger's case involved unprotected true threats as well. Anonymous e-mails and blog comments promised to "shove a machete" up her "cunt," to "beat" her "with a bat," and to rape her. The threats were unequivocal and graphic. The tech blogger took the threats as serious and clear expressions of the speakers' intent to inflict bodily harm, as any reasonable person would. She had no reason to doubt the speakers' seriousness—she knew nothing about them. She could not rule out the possibility that the authors were responsible for other menacing posts, like the doctored photograph depicting her with a noose beside her neck.

The posts devoted to the revenge porn victim were not true threats even though they certainly caused her to fear physical harm at the hands of strangers. One post included her nude photo, contact information, the time and location of her next speaking engagement, and her supposed interest in sex for money. The post terrified her because strangers could read it and confront her offline. Nonetheless, the post never said or implied that she would be physically attacked. Although the post would not amount to a true threat, other grounds support its proscription.

Crime-Facilitating Speech

That post might fall under another categorical exclusion to the First Amendment: crime-facilitating speech. Speech integral to criminal activity is not protected, even if the crime is not set to take place imminently.[45] Criminal solicitation, a statement that intentionally urges others to unlawfully harm another person, does not enjoy First Amendment protection.[46] Extortion and "aiding and abetting" speech do not enjoy constitutional protection for the same reason.[47]

Consider a case involving the book *Hit Man* that purported to instruct would-be assassins. The book's publisher was sued for aiding and abetting murder after a reader killed three people following the book's instructions. An appellate court upheld the civil judgment against the publisher because the book amounted to unprotected instructional speech, not protected abstract advocacy of lawlessness. The court reasoned that the book's expression could not be separated from criminal activity because it directly assisted the assassin. The writing was an integral part of a crime sufficient to find the author liable.

To prevent the punishment of lawful speech, however, the court imposed a heightened intent requirement. Mere foreseeability or knowledge that information could be misused for an impermissible purpose is not enough, only individuals who intentionally assist and encourage crime can face liability. The court hypothesized that the First Amendment would not protect a person's online publication of the "necessary plans and instructions for assassinating the President" with the specific purpose of assisting the murder of the president.[48]

In the revenge porn victim's case, several posts arguably constituted crime-facilitating speech. Consider the prosecution of the defendant

Shawn Sayer, who allegedly posted online advertisements with his ex-girlfriend's contact information and her supposed desire for sex. On porn sites, he uploaded sex videos featuring the woman alongside her contact information. Posing as his ex-girlfriend, the defendant engaged in chats with prospective sexual partners. Because strange men began appearing at her home demanding sex, the woman changed her name and moved to another state. The defendant discovered the woman's new name and address, posting them on porn sites. The cycle repeated itself, with strange men coming to her new house demanding sex. The court found the defendant's speech constitutionally unprotected because his solicitation of strangers was integral to the crime of cyber stalking.[49]

Cyber stalking convictions also have been upheld where the defendant's online activity included extortionate threats. In another case, after a woman broke off her relationship with the defendant, the defendant threatened to post her embarrassing texts and nude photographs unless she resumed their relationship. After she refused to get back together with him, the defendant sent postcards depicting her in a scanty outfit and providing links to a site that displayed her nude photos to her coworkers, family members, and business associates.[50] The court upheld the constitutionality of the defendant's conviction for cyber stalking because his speech was integral to the crime of extortion. The court pointed to the defendant's promise to destroy the victim's reputation by releasing the photos and texts unless she resumed the relationship when the victim failed to comply.

In the revenge porn victim's case, the poster arguably engaged in criminal solicitation and extortion. The post with her nude photos, location, and alleged interest in sex was designed to solicit strangers to confront her for sex.[51] As the revenge porn victim feared, she received graphic e-mails from strangers demanding sex. The anonymous e-mail threatening to send her nude photos to her colleagues unless she responded in an hour's time amounted to unprotected extortion. After she refused to write back as the person demanded, her colleagues received e-mails with her nude photos. Whoever was responsible for the posting and the e-mail cannot use expression to engage in criminal solicitation and extortion and then seek refuge in the First Amendment.

The categorical exclusion of crime-facilitating speech helps us understand the constitutionality of my proposal to amend Section 230. If Congress adopts the suggested changes, lawsuits against site operators for encouraging cyber stalking would comport with First Amendment doctrine. As the *Hit Man* case illustrates, the intentional enablement of crime is not constitutionally protected. The First Amendment does not relieve from liability those who would, for profit or other motive, intentionally assist or encourage crime.[52] Along these lines, courts have found that newspapers do not have a First Amendment right to publish a witness's name if they know the publication would facilitate crimes against the witness.[53] The First Amendment, however, would likely bar enablement liability based on a defendant's mere foreseeability or recklessness.

Lies in Cyberspace

Online as offline, people are free to share their negative opinions about individuals. Calling someone untrustworthy or ugly constitutes protected speech. But what about false claims that someone has rape fantasies or had sex with her students? Some falsehoods can be regulated without transgressing the First Amendment.

Defamation has been historically recognized as a category of speech that can be prohibited due to its serious damage to people's reputations.[54] To secure breathing room for public debate, the First Amendment limits certain aspects of defamation law depending upon the status of the person defamed and the subject matter of the speech at issue.

Beginning with *New York Times v. Sullivan*, defamation law has been reconciled with the First Amendment by adjusting the level of fault required to establish a claim. Public officials can recover for falsehoods related to their official duties only if it can be shown with convincing clarity that the speaker made the false statement with actual malice—with knowledge of its falsity or in "reckless disregard" of its truth or falsity.[55] Suppose an anonymous poster claimed a married congressman slept with one of his staffers. To recover, the congressman would have to prove that the speaker intentionally lied about the affair with the staffer or did not care whether the rumor was true or false. The actual malice standard also applies to defamation claims brought by *public figures*, a term that refers to celebrities and individuals who thrust themselves into the limelight on public controversies.[56] Actual malice is hard to establish, and most plaintiffs who have to prove it lose their cases.[57]

The First Amendment accords less rigorous protection to falsehoods about private individuals because they lack effective means to rebut false statements and because they never assumed the risk of reputational harm, unlike public figures and public officials.[58] Defamation about highly personal matters has reduced First Amendment protection as well.[59] For instance, falsehoods about the marital difficulties of a wealthy couple constituted private matters, even though society had some interest in their divorce.[60] Only a showing of negligence is required to support defamation claims involving private individuals and highly personal matters.[61]

Most cyber harassment victims are private individuals who would need to prove only defendants' negligence in support of defamation claims. As someone with minimal public influence, the law student could not easily capture the attention of the media to counter the lies about her alleged sexual relationship with her dean, sexually transmitted infection, and low LSAT score. The law student never did anything to suggest that she assumed the risk of public life as a celebrity or official. If, however, the tech blogger had sued the cyber mob members for defamation, she might have been treated as a public figure and required to prove actual malice. With a top-ranked blog and high-profile speaking schedule, she had access to mainstream media outlets to rebut the cyber mob's lies.

Unprotected defamation can support tort remedies and criminal convictions. Generally speaking, the First Amendment rules for tort remedies and criminal prosecutions are the same. The Court has refused invitations to treat civil liability differently from criminal liability for First Amendment purposes.[62] In *New York Times v. Sullivan,* the Court explained, "What a State may not constitutionally bring about by means of a criminal statute is likewise beyond the reach of its civil law." As the Court recognized, the treatment is the same though the threat of civil damage awards can be more inhibiting than the fear of criminal prosecution and civil defendants do not enjoy special protections that are available to criminal defendants, such as the requirement of proof beyond a reasonable doubt.[63]

Criminal libel laws that punish intentionally or recklessly false statements are constitutional.[64] Although cyber stalking and cyber harassment statutes do not specifically regulate lies, cyber stalking convictions have been upheld in cases where defendants' online abuse involved unprotected defamation. In a recent case, the defendant's defamatory statements about the victim—that she wanted to sleep with strangers—provided additional support for upholding the constitutionality of the defendant's federal cyber stalking conviction.[65] If defamatory statements about the law student, the revenge porn victim, and the tech blogger were posted with knowledge that they were false or with recklessness as to their truth or falsity, they would support the constitutionality of criminal stalking or harassment charges.

The Nonconsensual Disclosure of Nude Images

My proposed revenge porn statute should withstand constitutional challenge. Disclosures of private communications involving nude images do not enjoy rigorous First Amendment protection. They involve the narrow set of circumstances when the publication of truthful information can be punished.[66]

In *Smith v. Daily Mail*, a 1979 case about the constitutionality of a newspaper's criminal conviction for publishing the name of a juvenile accused of murder, the Court laid down the now well-established rule that "if a newspaper lawfully obtains truthful information about a matter of public significance then state officials may not constitutionally punish the publication of the information, absent a need to further a state interest of the highest order."[67] The Court has consistently refused to adopt a bright-line rule precluding civil or criminal liability for truthful publications "invading 'an area of privacy' defined by the State." Instead the Court has issued narrow decisions that acknowledge that press freedom and privacy rights are both "'plainly rooted in the traditions and significant concerns of the society'."[68]

In *Bartnicki v. Vopper*, for instance, an unidentified person intercepted and recorded a cell phone call between the president of a local teacher's union and the union's chief negotiator concerning negotiations about teachers' salaries. During the call, one of the parties mentioned "go[ing] to the homes" of school board members to "blow off their front porches." A radio commentator, who received a copy of the intercepted call in his mailbox, broadcast the tape. The radio personality incurred civil penalties for publishing the cell phone conversation in violation of the Wiretap Act.

The Court characterized the wiretapping case as presenting a "conflict between interests of the highest order—on the one hand, the interest in the full and free dissemination of information concerning public issues, and, on the other hand, the interest in individual privacy and, more specifically, in fostering private speech." According to the Court, free speech interests appeared on both sides of the calculus. The "fear of public disclosure of private conversations might well have a chilling effect on private speech." The Court recognized that "the disclosure of the contents of a private conversation can be an even greater intrusion on privacy than the interception itself."[69]

The Court struck down the penalties assessed against the radio commentator because the private cell phone conversation about the union negotiations "unquestionably" involved a "matter of public concern." The Court underscored that the private call did not involve "trade secrets or domestic gossip or other information of purely private concern." As a result, the privacy concerns vindicated by the Wiretap Act had to "give way" to "the interest in publishing matters of public importance." The Court emphasized the narrowness of its holding, explaining that "the sensitivity and significance of the interests presented in clashes between [the] First Amendment and privacy rights counsel relying on limited principles that sweep no more broadly than the appropriate context of the instant case."[70]

As the Court suggested, the state interest in protecting the privacy of communications may be "strong enough to justify" regulation if the communications involve "purely private" matters. Built into the Court's decision was an exception: a lower level of First Amendment scrutiny applies to the nonconsensual publication of "domestic gossip or other information of purely private concern."[71] Relying on that language, appellate courts have affirmed the constitutionality of civil penalties under the wiretapping statute for the unwanted disclosures of private communications involving "purely private matters."[72]

Along similar lines, lower courts have upheld claims for public disclosure of private fact in cases involving the nonconsensual publication of sex videos.[73] In *Michaels v. Internet Entertainment Group, Inc.*, an adult entertainment company obtained a copy of a sex video made by a celebrity couple, Bret Michaels and Pamela Anderson Lee. The court enjoined the publication of the sex tape because the public had no legitimate interest in graphic depictions of the "most intimate aspects of" a celebrity couple's relationship. As the court explained, "Sexual relations are among the most private of private affairs"; a video recording of two individuals engaged in sexual relations "represents the deepest possible intrusion into private affairs."[74]

These decisions support the constitutionality of efforts to criminalize revenge porn and to remedy public disclosure of private facts. Nude photos and sex tapes are among the most private and intimate facts; the public has no legitimate interest in seeing someone's nude images without that person's consent.[75] A prurient interest in viewing someone's private sexual activity does not change the nature of the public's interest.

Protecting against the nonconsensual disclosure of private communications, notably the sharing of nude images among intimates, would inhibit a negligible amount of expression that the public legitimately cares about, and it would foster private expression. Maintaining the confidentiality of someone's sexually explicit images has little impact on a poster's expression of ideas. Revenge porn does not promote civic character or educate us about cultural, religious, or political issues. On the other hand, the nonconsensual disclosure of a person's nude images would assuredly chill private expression. Without any expectation of privacy, victims would not share their naked images. With an expectation of privacy, victims would be more inclined to engage in communications of a sexual nature. Such sharing may enhance intimacy among couples and the willingness to be forthright in other aspects of relationships.

In his concurring opinion in *Bartnicki*, Justice Breyer remarked that although nondisclosure laws place "direct restrictions on speech, the Federal Constitution must tolerate laws of this kind because of the importance of privacy and speech-related objectives" such as "fostering private speech." He continued, "the Constitution permits legislatures to respond flexibly to the challenges future technology may pose to the individual's interest in basic personal privacy."[76] My proposed statute in Chapter 6 responds to the increasingly prevalent use of technology to expose individuals' most intimate affairs.

When would victims' privacy concerns have to cede to society's interest in learning about matters of public importance? Recall that women revealed to the press that former Congressman Anthony Weiner had sent them sexually explicit photographs of himself via Twitter messages.[77] His decision to send such messages sheds light on the soundness of his judgment. Unlike the typical revenge porn scenario involving private individuals whose affairs are not of broad public interest, the photos of Weiner are a matter of public import, and so their publication would be constitutionally protected.[78]

Another way to understand the constitutionality of revenge porn statutes is through the lens of confidentiality law. Confidentiality regulations are less troubling from a First Amendment perspective because they penalize the breach of an assumed or implied duty rather than the injury caused by the publication of words. Instead of prohibiting a certain kind of speech, confidentiality law enforces express or implied promises and shared expectations.[79]

Courts might also uphold the constitutionality of revenge porn statutes on the grounds that revenge porn amounts to unprotected obscenity. Professor Eugene Volokh argues that sexually intimate images disclosed without the subjects' consent belongs to the category of obscenity that the Supreme Court has determined does not receive First Amendment protection. In his view, nonconsensual pornography lacks First Amendment value as a historical matter and should be understood as unprotected obscenity.[80] Although the Court's obscenity doctrine has developed along different lines with distinct justifications, nonconsensual pornography can be seen as part of obscenity's long tradition of proscription.

Some argue that revenge porn cannot be prohibited because it does not fall within an explicitly recognized category of unprotected speech like defamation, incitement, or true threats. In *United States v. Stevens,* the Court considered the constitutionality of a statute criminalizing depictions of animal cruelty distributed for commercial gain. The Court rejected the government's argument that depictions of animal cruelty amounted to a new category of unprotected speech. It held that the

First Amendment does not permit the government to prohibit speech just because it lacks value or because the "ad hoc calculus of costs and benefits tilts in a statute's favor." The Court explained that it lacks "free-wheeling authority to declare new categories of speech outside the scope of the First Amendment."[81]

In *Stevens*, the Court did not suggest that the only speech that can be proscribed is speech that falls within explicitly recognized categories like defamation and true threats. To the contrary, the Court recognized that some speech has enjoyed less rigorous protection as a historical matter, even though it has not been recognized as such explicitly.[82] Publication of private communications about purely private matters has long enjoyed less rigorous protection because the individual's interest in privacy is "rooted in the traditions and significant concerns of our society."[83] Revenge porn legislation does not trample on the First Amendment because it protects a narrow category of private communications on especially private matters whose protection would foster private speech.

In the next section, I will discuss *Snyder v. Phelps*, a case decided after *Stevens*, which affirmed that speech with historically less rigorous protection continues to enjoy less protection, including claims for intentional infliction of emotional distress involving purely private matters.

Intentional Infliction of Emotional Distress

The Supreme Court first addressed the First Amendment's limits on intentional infliction of emotional distress claims in a case involving a televangelist parodied in an adult magazine. Reverend Jerry Falwell was a prominent advocate for "moral values" when the publisher Larry Flynt, his ideological adversary, ran a faux advertisement in his magazine *Hustler* suggesting that Falwell lost his virginity in a drunken encounter with his mother in an outhouse. Falwell sued the magazine for defamation, invasion of privacy, and intentional infliction of emotional distress. Although the jury rejected the defamation claim and the court directed a verdict against Falwell on the privacy claim, it awarded him damages for emotional distress.

On appeal, a unanimous Supreme Court vacated the award for damages, finding that Falwell's public stature altered the constitutional calculus for his claim of intentional infliction of emotional distress. Rather than finding such claims incompatible with the First Amendment, the Court limited a public figure's ability to recover for emotional distress over falsehoods made with actual malice. The Court adopted the actual malice standard to ensure that First Amendment limits on public figure defamation could not be evaded by recasting grievances as emotional distress claims.

The Court held that the fake advertisement amounted to a parody that could not be understood as stating actual falsehoods about Falwell's relationship with his mother. In its opinion, the Court emphasized the importance of providing breathing room for political and cultural satire that exploits a public figure's embarrassing features or unfortunate physical traits to make its point. Because parodies of public personalities are indispensible to political discourse, the Court heightened the proof required when public figures sue for intentional infliction of emotional distress.[84]

Fast-forward nearly thirty years for the Court's next review of an emotional distress claim in a case also involving a religious leader engaged in the culture wars. Over the past two decades, Pastor Fred Phelps and congregants in the Westboro Baptist Church have picketed the funerals of more than six hundred fallen soldiers with signs suggesting that the soldiers' deaths are God's way of punishing the United States for its tolerance of homosexuality. In 2006 Phelps obtained police approval to protest on public land one thousand feet from the church where the funeral of Matthew Snyder, a Marine killed in Iraq, would be held. The protestors' signs read, "God Hates the USA," "America Is Doomed," "God Hates You," "You're Going to Hell," and "Thank God for Dead Soldiers." A few weeks after the protest, a post on Westboro's website discussed the picketing of Snyder's funeral and claimed that his father, Albert Snyder, taught his son to defy his creator and raised him for the devil. Albert Snyder sued Phelps and members of his church for intentional infliction of emotional distress. The jury award was in the millions.

The Supreme Court overruled the award in favor of the Westboro Baptist Church. Chief Justice Roberts, writing for the majority, explained that the constitutional inquiry depended on whether the funeral protest concerned broad public issues or private matters. The majority began with the long-standing view that central to the First Amendment is speech on public matters, defined as speech whose content, context, and form bear on political, social, or other legitimate societal concerns. Speech on public matters is rigorously protected to prevent the stifling of debate essential to democratic self-governance. In contrast, speech about "purely private matters" receives "less stringent" protection because the threat of liability would not risk chilling the "meaningful exchange of ideas." As an illustration of a "purely private matter," the majority pointed to a government employer's firing of a man who posted videos showing him engaged in sexual activity. The employee's loss of public employment was constitutionally permissible because the videos shed no light on the employer's operation or functionality but rather concerned speech on purely private matters in which the public lacked a legitimate interest.

On this basis, the majority's decision is easy to understand. As the chief justice wrote, Snyder's emotional distress claim transgressed the First Amendment because the funeral protest constituted speech of the highest importance. As to the content of the speech, the Court found that the protest signs spoke to broad public issues: the political and moral conduct of the United States, homosexuality in the military, and scandals involving the Catholic Church. The protest's context further convinced the majority that the picketers wanted to engage in a public debate because they chose to protest next to a public street, which enjoys special protection as a forum of public assembly and debate.[85] The majority rejected Snyder's argument that the defendants sought to immunize a personal attack on his family by characterizing it as a debate about U.S. policy. The church's twenty-year history of protesting funerals with the same views and its lack of a preexisting conflict with the Snyder family demonstrated that the protests amounted to speech on public affairs, not a personal, private attack.

Although the jury considered the church's posts about Snyder as evidence supporting his emotional distress claim, the majority refused to address it because Snyder did not raise the issue in his papers to the Court. In passing, the majority suggested that the online speech in that case might present a "distinct issue" from the offline picketing. We cannot know precisely what the Court meant, but a potential difference includes the fact that unlike the protest's focus on U.S. policy, the post centered on Snyder's relationship with his son, which might have supported a finding that the online speech concerned private matters deserving less rigorous constitutional protection.

Civil remedies for emotional distress involving speech on purely private matters have long passed constitutional muster. As far as the lower courts are concerned, *Snyder* does not change that result. Although the Court has not explicitly recognized intentional infliction of emotional distress as a category of unprotected speech, it has assumed that claims to redress such cruelty are constitutional if they involve purely private matters. In *Snyder*, the Court refused to strike down the tort as unconstitutional, much as the Court refused to do so in *Falwell*.[86] In *Falwell*, the Court noted that in cases that do not involve public issues, it is understandable that the law does not regard the intent to inflict emotional distress as deserving "much solicitude."[87]

Liability for most cyber harassers' intentional infliction of emotional distress would comport with the First Amendment. In the law student's and the revenge porn victim's cases, anonymous posters did not address broad public matters. They were not engaged in debates about social, cultural, or political issues. The posts involved highly intimate, personal matters of private individuals: nude photos (the revenge porn victim), alleged sexually transmitted infection (the law student), claimed interest in sex (the revenge porn victim), and sexual threats (the law student). In both cases, the cyber harassment amounted to constitutionally proscribable cruelty.

Commentators have questioned whether emotional distress claims can be reconciled with the First Amendment when emotionally distressing expression appears in the "domain of public discourse"—that is, the Internet.[88] Recall that *Falwell* turned on the faux advertisement's focus on a public figure's views on sexual morality. As the unanimous Court made clear, if the advertisement had included malicious lies about Falwell that were presented as actual historical facts rather than as a parody, the emotional distress claim would have been constitutional, even though *Hustler* magazine was published in the domain of public discourse.

What about harassment and stalking laws that criminalize the intentional infliction of emotional distress? Harassment and stalking statutes have generally withstood facial challenges on First Amendment grounds, including Section 2261A and other laws that prohibit a harassing course of conduct that is intended to, and does in fact, inflict substantial emotional distress.[89] In many of those challenges, courts have rejected claims of vagueness and overbreadth because the guidelines surrounding terms like *harassment, course of conduct,* and *substantial emotional distress* provide precise enough instructions so the public knows the sorts of activities that constitute a crime.[90]

In the main, courts have not attributed the constitutionality of cyber stalking and cyber harassment convictions to the defendant's intentional infliction of emotional distress. Instead convictions have been upheld because the harassing speech either fell within recognized First Amendment exceptions or involved speech that has enjoyed less rigorous protection, such as true threats, libel, criminal solicitation, extortion, and the nonconsensual disclosure of private communications on purely private matters.[91]

If presented with the question, the Court might not permit the criminalization of intentional infliction of emotional distress if the law included terms like *extreme* and *outrageous* behavior, which arguably are too vague to prevent the chilling of protected speech. We need not have a definitive answer to that question to say assuredly that criminal harassment charges could have been brought against those attacking the tech blogger, the law student, and the revenge porn victim. Their attacks involved unprotected crime-facilitating speech, defamation, true threats, and privacy invasions on purely private matters.

Cyber stalking convictions have been overturned on First Amendment grounds when the abuse involved protected speech on political, religious, or social matters. For instance, in *United States v. Cassidy*, federal prosecutors pursued federal cyber stalking charges against a man who attacked a leading American Tibetan Buddhist religious figure, Alyce Zeoli, on Twitter. After the defendant was fired from Zeoli's religious organization, he posted eight thousand tweets about Zeoli over the span of several months. Most of the tweets were criticisms of her religious leadership and teaching, for instance, accusing her of being a "demonic force who tries to destroy Buddhism." A few tweets could be seen as potentially threatening, such as "Ya like haiku? Here's one for ya: 'Long, Limb, Sharp Saw, Hard Drop' ROFLMAO."[92] The court dismissed the defendant's cyber stalking indictment because the emotionally distressing harassment involved protected speech about religious matters, not any of the categories of unprotected speech or speech deserving less rigorous protection. By contrast, the cyber stalking experienced by the tech blogger, the law student, and the revenge porn victim—and much of the abuse featured in this book—did not involve political, social, or religious matters but rather constitutionally unprotected speech.

Criminal harassment convictions could include injunctive relief without offending the First Amendment in cases where the court determined that the defendant engaged in constitutionally unprotected speech to accomplish the harassment. Professor Volokh suggests that after trial, courts could issue an injunction in a criminal cyber harassment case if the order would do "no more than prohibit the defendant from repeating the defamation."[93] This supports the constitutionality of my proposal to include a takedown remedy in the federal cyber stalking statute, Section 2261A. If a court has determined that the takedown order accompanying a cyber stalking conviction covers constitutionally unprotected speech such as defamation and true threats, courts could issue orders demanding that perpetrators or host sites take down posts consistent with the First Amendment.

Civil Rights Actions

Civil rights violations have a dual character: on the one hand, they single out people from traditionally subordinated groups for abuse that wreaks special harm on victims and their communities; on the other hand, they explicitly or implicitly communicate a bigoted viewpoint. The Supreme Court has rejected attempts to ban abusive expressions because their content may be more offensive to certain groups. But, as the Court has made clear, the First Amendment poses no obstacle to civil rights claims, including the ones at the heart of a cyber civil rights legal agenda, because they proscribe defendants' unequal treatment of individuals and the unique harm that such discrimination inflicts, not the offensive messages that harassers express.

The leading cases in this area are *Wisconsin v. Mitchell* and *R.A.V. v. City of St. Paul*.[94] In *Wisconsin v. Mitchell*, the Court considered a First Amendment challenge to a Wisconsin hate crimes statute enhancing the penalty of certain crimes if the perpetrator selected the victim because of race, religion, color, disability, sexual orientation, national origin, or ancestry. After Todd Mitchell and his friends watched *Mississippi Burning,* a film featuring scenes of violence against blacks during the civil rights movement, Mitchell encouraged the group to beat up a white boy who crossed their path. After Mitchell was convicted of aggravated battery, his sentence was enhanced under the Wisconsin hate crimes law. The Court unanimously rejected the defendant's claim that the statute punished him for his racist views, saying that the statute did not transgress the First Amendment because it penalized the defendant's discriminatory motive for his conduct, not his bigoted ideas, and the great harm that results when victims are targeted for crimes because of their membership in a protected group.

The Court analogized the Wisconsin statute to federal and state antidiscrimination laws, which, it explained, were immune from First Amendment challenge. It specifically pointed to Title VII and Section 1981 as civil rights laws that do not infringe upon defendants' First Amendment rights because they proscribe defendants' unequal treatment of individuals in tangible ways, such as choosing whom to target for violence or on-the-job harassment, not the defendants' expression of offensive ideas. The Court wrote that Title VII's prohibition of sexual harassment is aimed at bias-inspired conduct that alters the terms and conditions of employment, which is not protected by the First Amendment. The Court deemed both Title VII and Section 1981 "permissible content-neutral regulation[s] of conduct." It emphasized that the state was justified in singling out bias-inspired conduct due to the great individual and societal harm it inflicts.

The *Mitchell* Court specifically distinguished *R.A.V. v. City of St. Paul,* a case involving a city ordinance that criminalized "placing on public or private property a symbol . . . including, but not limited to, a burning cross or Nazi swastika" that an individual "knows or has reasonable grounds to know arouses anger, alarm, or resentment in others on the basis of race, color, creed, religion, or gender." Late one night, R.A.V. and several other white teenagers burned a wooden cross in the yard of an African American family. R.A.V. was arrested under the city ordinance. *R.A.V.* found the ordinance unconstitutional because it discriminated on the basis of the expression's content and indeed its viewpoint; certain bigoted expressions were proscribed by the ordinance, yet the statute did not forbid those that gave offense in other ways. The *Mitchell* Court ruled, "Whereas the ordinance stuck down in *R.A.V.* was explicitly directed at expression (i.e., speech or messages), the [Wisconsin] statute in this case is aimed at conduct unprotected by the First Amendment." It concluded that Wisconsin's desire to address bias-inspired conduct "provides an adequate explanation for its penalty-enhancement provision over and above mere disagreement with offenders' beliefs or biases." In short, the *Mitchell* Court made clear that the First Amendment erects no barrier to the enforcement of antidiscrimination laws that regulate bias-inspired conduct and the special harm that it inflicts, whereas it prohibits laws that simply punish ideas like the one addressed in *R.A.V.*

Applying existing civil rights statutes, as Chapter 5 does, and amending current civil rights laws, as Chapter 6 suggests, fall on the *Mitchell* side of this line. Their proscriptions turn on harassers' discriminatory singling out of victims for abuse and the distinct harms that a defendant's abuse produces rather than on the opinions that either victims or attackers express. The harms produced by sexual harassment in networked spaces are tangible in the same way as the harms inflicted by sexual harassment in the workplace. Cyber harassment victims struggle to obtain or keep jobs when searches of their names are saturated with defamatory lies, compromising photographs, and threats of violence. They withdraw from school when anonymous posters threaten to rape them and suggest their interest in sex with strangers. They lose advertising income and miss professional opportunities when they go offline to avoid abuse. Much like the disadvantages created by sexual and racial harassment that civil rights statutes prohibit, cyber harassment deprives victims of crucial life opportunities.

As sexual harassment law developed in the mid- to late 1990s, some argued that holding employers liable for harassing speech violated the First Amendment. But courts, including the conservative jurist Antonin Scalia writing for five justices in *R.A.V.* and the unanimous Court in *Mitchell,* came to hold that regulating on-the-job sexual harassment that has the intent or effect of changing the terms or conditions of employment amounts to constitutionally proscribable conduct, not protected speech. Although cyber harassment occurs in networked spaces and not the physical workplace or school, it has the intent and effect of making it impossible for targeted individuals to keep their jobs, earn advertising income, get work, and attend school. This was true for racial harassment by anonymous mobs that prevented minorities from earning a living. Then as now, we can regulate cyber harassment that interferes with crucial professional and educational opportunities.

Civil rights protections do not turn on the opinions that either cyber harassment victims or their attackers express. Intimidating a female blogger with rape threats so that she shuts down her income-generating blog is equally offensive, and equally proscribed, no matter the anonymous perpetrators' specific views. This is true for cyber attacks that prevent women from securing gainful employment or from attending graduate school. When law punishes online attackers due to their singling out victims for online abuse due to their gender, race, sexual orientation, or other protected characteristic and the special severity of the harm produced, and not due to the particular opinions that the attackers or victims express, its application does not transgress the First Amendment.

Anonymity

Perpetrators cannot be sued or indicted if they cannot be identified. Does a legal agenda impermissibly infringe upon the right to anonymous expression in our digital age? Can we preserve communicative anonymity as a general matter even as anonymity is upended in specific cases? We can, though some explanation is in order.

Anonymous speech has played a prominent role in American political life. *The Federalist Papers,* written by James Madison, Alexander Hamilton, and John Jay, were published under the pseudonym "Publius." The Supreme Court has recognized that speech is constitutionally protected even when it is anonymous. Online speech enjoys the same constitutional footing as speech made offline, imbuing anonymous online speech with constitutional protection.[95]

As the Supreme Court has held, the First Amendment protects the right to anonymous religious and political speech. Maggie McIntyre was convicted under an Ohio statute forbidding anonymous, election-related writings after she distributed anonymous pamphlets expressing her opposition to a school tax levy. The Court struck down the conviction, finding that McIntyre had a First Amendment interest in anonymity. The Court agreed that the state's interest in preventing electoral fraud was legitimate, but determined that the specific laws against fraud served that interest and could be enforced without mandating speaker identification. Anonymity was seen as central to a speaker's autonomy, especially for individuals with modest resources who have a legitimate fear of official reprisal or social ostracism for political and religious speech.[96] Anonymous speech is protected because the speaker's identity constitutes an aspect of the message.[97]

Another aspect of anonymity involves the privacy of group associations, a crucial protection for members of threatened minorities and unpopular organizations. During the 1950s and 1960s, officials in the South sought the names and addresses of NAACP members as part of a broader strategy to chill participation in the civil rights movement. The Court struck down an Alabama court order requiring the NAACP to produce a list of its members on the ground that privacy for group associations is indispensable to preserving the freedom to associate.[98]

Although the Court has firmly rejected demands for political groups' membership lists and state mandates for identification in political and religious speech, it has never suggested that law enforcement or private litigants may not obtain the identities of people reasonably suspected of unlawful activities.[99] Free expression has never depended on speakers' absolute ability to prevent themselves from being identified and held responsible for illegal activities. The veil of anonymity can be lifted for speech that amounts to true threats, defamation, speech integral to criminal conduct, nonconsensual disclosure of sexually explicit images, and cruelty amounting to intentional infliction of emotional distress on purely private matters.

In civil matters, cyber harassment victims can pierce the anonymity of their anonymous attackers only by obtaining a John Doe subpoena issued by a judge. Courts protect the identity of anonymous posters from frivolous lawsuits by setting forth a series of requirements before granting these subpoenas. Courts increasingly insist upon proof that the claims would survive a motion for summary judgment—a heavy burden of proof indeed.[100] This assures the safety of posters' anonymity in the face of baseless allegations. So, too, law enforcement would need either a warrant or a court order to obtain information from ISPs that would allow it to trace the identity of cyber harassers. Before cable providers turn over identifying data, they are required to notify users, who could then object to the revelation of their identities.

Individuals could bring frivolous civil suits merely to identify speakers. But practical realities and procedural rules provide some prophylactic protection against attempts at baseless unmasking. Filing lawsuits is expensive, and frivolous complaints and motions to unmask can garner sanctions against attorneys and clients.[101] Since the Internet's earliest days, networked speech has been subject to libel suits. Needless to say, we have not seen an overdeterrence of anonymous defamatory comments online.

Of course, it is important to recognize that we are having this conversation amid the contemporary reality of our surveillance age. Massive reservoirs of personal data are gathered by private and public entities. Companies track and analyze our online activities to assess our attractiveness as potential customers and far more. Government is collecting, analyzing, and sharing information about us, including our online communications, providing agents with contemporary and perpetual access to details about everywhere we go and everything we do, say, and write while using or in the company of networked technologies.[102] In June 2013 documents leaked by a government contractor, Edward Snowden, revealed details of expansive surveillance programs operated by the FBI and the Department of Defense through the National Security Agency.[103] These revelations confirmed previous reports about a comprehensive domestic surveillance program under way in the post-9/11 period.[104] Apparently most major communications providers have provided government access to callers' metadata for the past several years. Our communicative anonymity from the U.S. government is either vanishing or gone, at great cost to what Professor Neil Richards has astutely conceptualized as "intellectual privacy."[105]

Such surveillance programs are as suspect as they are breathtaking. They offer the government powerful tools in their ongoing efforts to detect, prevent, and prosecute terrorism and crimes, but they endanger individual and collective expectations of privacy guaranteed by the Fourth Amendment.[106] The legal agenda at the heart of this book neither supports nor advances this state of affairs.[107] It is not ideologically or practically aligned with the mass exploitation of people's privacy by governmental surveillance programs.

Might our surveillance state help victims find perpetrators? If the government collects data about our on- and offline activities even as private entities delete them, could it help victims find perpetrators? It is certainly possible, but recent reports suggest the answer is no. The NSA refuses to talk about its data reservoirs, let alone publicly share its information with individuals pursuing civil claims. Thus, as to our shadowy surveillance state, communicative anonymity is fleeting, but it is robust when ordinary crime victims try to figure out the identities of their attackers. Even with a properly granted John Doe subpoena, perpetrators remain difficult to find.

To be sure, the NSA could share information with prosecutors interested in finding harassers and any other criminals, but government officials claim it would do so only if it first obtained a warrant. If that is true—and we have no guarantee that is the case given the secrecy of these surveillance programs—then the government would have struck a proper balance between privacy interests and its interest in fighting crime.

Beyond the legal realm, some Internet intermediaries insist that posters reveal their true identities, which makes it difficult to engage anonymously. Intermediaries' choices about their user community (and many others) are theirs to make, and the First Amendment plays no role in constraining their private actions. In Chapter 9 I explore in detail the ways that Internet intermediaries, parents, and schools can help in the fight against cyber harassment.

nine

Silicon Valley, Parents, and Schools

A legal agenda will take time. Cyber harassment and stalking, however, are problems with life-changing consequences for victims right now. What can be done today to protect victims and shift online norms while we engage in a society-wide recalibration of our response to online abuse?

Besides legal actors, there are other potential partners in the fight against cyber harassment. Internet companies are already engaged in efforts to combat destructive online activity. Some companies closest to the abuse, content hosts, prohibit cyber harassment and cyber stalking. Facebook, Blogger, and YouTube, to name a few, do not view free expression as a license to harass, stalk, or threaten. For business and ethical reasons, they are working to prevent abuse from happening and to diminish its impact when it occurs. Through user agreements and software design, these Internet companies are encouraging norms of equality and respect.

These norms have a greater chance of taking hold if parents and schools reinforce them. Teenagers need guidance navigating the challenges of having an online presence. Parents should not tune out because they feel outpaced by modern technology. They are ideally suited to teach children about respectful online engagement. School districts across the country are helping parents and students learn about online safety and digital responsibility. Their civic lessons increasingly cover the fundamentals of digital citizenship.

In this chapter I highlight some successful efforts and offer potential improvements. The combined work of Silicon Valley, parents, and schools should be applauded and nurtured. They can help all of us, young, old, and in between, become responsible digital citizens.

Silicon Valley: Digital Gatekeepers

For months, a man sent a woman threatening letters and packages of pornography. The man's letters warned that he would "cut the sin" out of the woman with God's scalpel.[1] The postal service could have stopped delivering suspicious mail if the woman asked. But what if the man had used Facebook, YouTube, and Blogger to stalk her? Unlike the postal service's single point of control, the Internet has many different digital gatekeepers. ISPs gave the man access to the Internet; search engines connected readers to his posts; and content providers like Facebook, YouTube, and Blogger hosted them.

Digital gatekeepers have substantial freedom to decide whether and when to tackle cyber stalking and harassment. The First Amendment binds governmental actors, not companies. Internet intermediaries aim to maximize the interests of their users and shareholders; they are not designed to serve public ends. As the media scholar Clay Shirky puts it, the "Internet is not a public sphere. It is a private sphere that tolerates public speech."[2] If corporate entities address cyber harassment, they are free from constitutional restraint and from most liability.

Although digital gatekeepers are not state actors and do not operate primarily to benefit the public, they exercise power that some describe as tantamount to governmental power. In her book *Consent of the Networked: The Worldwide Struggle for Internet Freedom*, Rebecca MacKinnon argues that ISPs, search engines, and social media providers "have far too much power over citizens' lives, in ways that are insufficiently transparent or accountable to the public interest."[3]

Internet intermediaries undeniably wield enormous control over online expression. Their products and services shape the content that we see and do not see. They manipulate our tastes and preferences by highlighting some forms of expression and downgrading others. MacKinnon calls for greater transparency of intermediaries' choices and more opportunities for users to have a say in corporate practices. She is right. Indeed, efforts to combat cyber harassment can be enhanced with these goals in mind: increased transparency, accountability, and user engagement in corporate decisions about harassing speech, as I will explore in detail.

Before I address what Internet intermediaries should do, consider their current practices. Internet intermediaries have different responses to online abuse. Search engines generally refuse to mediate harassing speech, though they may block speech to comply with foreign laws. ISPs do not address harassing content because they see themselves as mere conduits.

Entities hosting user-generated content are different. They often have a hand in influencing behavior on their platforms. Some encourage destructive abuse, as we have seen. Recall the message board AutoAdmit. The site's administrators not only refused to remove or denounce the destructive threads about the law student, but they also provided cover for posters. They altered the site's software design to ensure that posters' identifying information was not collected. As the site administrator Jarret Cohen told the *Washington Post*, the collection of IP addresses would "encourage lawsuits and drive traffic away. . . . People would not have as much fun, frankly, if they had to worry about employers pulling up information on them."[4]

Thankfully other companies try to prevent their platforms from being used to attack individuals. For some companies, combating abusive speech is key to their bottom line. In its heyday, the social network site MySpace aggressively removed harassment, bullying, and hate speech to secure online advertising for its customer base. As MySpace's former chief safety officer Hemanshu Nigam explained to me, the company's approach came from its sense of "what the company stood for and what would attract advertising and revenue."[5] Because kids and adults used MySpace, the company wanted to ensure a "family-friendly" site, which could be accomplished only by taking down content that "attacked an individual or group because they are in that group and . . . made people feel bad." According to Nigam, these voluntary efforts served his company's bottom line by creating market niches and contributing to consumer goodwill.

Sometimes content hosts get involved at the request of advertisers. In 2011 Facebook users began an online campaign protesting pro-rape pages like "You know she's playing hard to get when you [are] chasing her down the hallway," which accumulated 130,000 likes. Facebook refused to take those pages down even though its terms-of-service agreement banned hate speech.[6] The company did not view the pro-rape pages as hate speech because they could be seen as humor. In May 2013 Facebook changed its position after fifteen companies, including Nissan, threatened to pull their ads unless Facebook removed profiles that glorified or trivialized violence against women.[7]

Companies often attribute their policies concerning harassment, threats, bullying, and hate speech to their sense of corporate social responsibility. Facebook conveyed that message after it took down a page called "Kill a Jew Day." Spokesperson Andrew Noyes explained, "Unfortunately ignorant people exist and we absolutely feel a social responsibility to silence them" if their statements involve calls for violence against individuals and groups.[8] The social network Black Planet says that its power to communicate with millions of members "comes with great responsibility," including helping educate teenagers and adults about cyber bullying.[9] At MySpace, Nigam says, "we wanted to inspire digital citizenship and positive dialogue. . . . You can call it corporate social responsibility if you like, but I would call it the right thing to do."[10]

Companies employ various tactics to protect against attacks on individuals. Their strategies include clear policies with robust enforcement mechanisms, user empowerment, real-name requirements, architectural cues, and counterspeech. I am going to explore the efficacy of those strategies, offer critiques, and suggest improvements.[11]

Making Expectations Clear(er) for Users Who Cross the Line
Content hosts communicate their expectations in their terms-of-service agreements and community guidelines. Consider Facebook's policy: "Facebook does not tolerate bullying or harassment. We allow users to speak freely on matters and people of public interest, but take action on all reports of abusive behavior directed at private individuals." As Facebook explains to users, cyber bullying and harassment involve the repeated targeting of private individuals that inflicts emotional distress.[12] In its community guidelines, YouTube advises users, "We want you to use YouTube without fear of being subjected to malicious harassment. In cases where harassment crosses the line into a malicious attack it can be reported and will be removed. In other cases, users may be mildly annoying or petty and should simply be ignored." Tumblr, the blogging site, says that it is not meant for impersonation, stalking, or harassment. "Treat the community the way you'd like to be treated. Do not attempt to circumvent the Block feature. If you want to parody or ridicule a public figure (and who doesn't?), do not try to trick readers into thinking you are *actually* that public figure."[13]

Although these companies clearly signal their position on certain forms of online abuse, they could do a better job explaining what terms like *harassment* and *bullying* mean and the reasons for banning these practices. The more clearly and specifically companies explain those terms and the harms that they want to prevent, the better their users will understand what is expected of them. Providing users with examples of speech that violates community guidelines would help foster learning and dialogue. Concerned users would get the sense that content policies are more than platitudes, and they would better grasp the concrete implications for certain behavior.

Consider, as a modest step in that direction, Belief.net's approach to hate speech, which it defines as "speech that may cause violence toward someone (even if unintentionally) because of age, disability, gender, ethnicity, race, nationality, religion, or sexual orientation." The site gives examples of hate speech: "Hate speech sets up conditions for violence against one or more people, because they are a member of a protected group, in one of these ways: advocating violence (i.e. kill them); saying that violence would be acceptable (i.e. they ought to die); saying that violence is deserved (i.e. they had it coming); dehumanizing or degrading them, perhaps by characterizing them as guilty of a heinous crime, perversion, or illness, such that violence may seem allowable or inconsequential; making analogies or comparisons suggesting any of the above (i.e. they are like murderers)."[14]

Some companies may be hesitant to provide detailed explanations of their policies for fear that people would try to game the system. But rather than fearing those attempts, companies could leverage them in furtherance of their goals. They could call out efforts to defeat the spirit of the rules, explaining why users violated them. The YouTube community guidelines address this concern by saying, "Do not try to look for loopholes or try to lawyer your way around the guidelines." Microsoft's former chief privacy officer Chuck Cosson remarked that YouTube's instruction was a helpful way of reducing litigious exchanges with users who break the rules while allowing the company to make decisions about violations of its policies.[15] The YouTube approach is commendable; it allows companies to educate their users without sacrificing their flexibility to address harassing speech.

Leading social media providers have signaled an interest in being more transparent about their content policies. In May 2012 the Inter-Parliamentary Task Force on Internet Hate (of which I am a member) passed a formal resolution establishing the Anti-Cyberhate Working Group, made up of industry representatives, nongovernmental organizations, academics, and others to "build best practices for understanding, reporting upon and responding to Internet hate." The group regularly meets in the hopes of developing guidelines that will help users better understand terms-of-service requirements. The group's efforts aim to strike the right balance between protecting individuals from hateful speech and harassment and a respect for free expression.[16]

Safety Enforcement

Given the scale of most major social media providers, how can they implement their policies without running out of resources to fund the effort? Although some companies proactively look for harassment and other prohibited content, most rely on users to identify policy violations. User-friendly reporting mechanisms help facilitate the process. YouTube's system, for instance, asks individuals to indicate a reason for their complaints with specific follow-up questions. If users indicate that they are reporting cyber harassment or cyber bullying, they are asked if the alleged rule breakers stole their videos, revealed their personal information on the site, harassed them, or attacked or belittled another YouTube user.

Staff members typically review reported content rather than leaving it to computers, which cannot approximate the contextual judgments of human intelligence, at least not yet. As the head of Facebook's Content Policy Team Dave Willner explained to me, "Automation is better with spam than with issues about what something means."[17] MySpace's Customer Care Team engages in "labor intensive reviews of these issues to determine if the complaints are factual and then to determine the proper response."[18] Facebook has hundreds of people reviewing content in four offices across the globe.[19]

As straightforward as reporting seems, getting results can be frustrating at times. Staff members may not have adequate training to deal with cyber harassment and cyber stalking. When the revenge porn victim reported to Facebook that someone had created an account imper sonating her, a content policy team member told her that she needed to verify her identity to justify taking down the account. The staffer asked her to e-mail him a copy of her license. The revenge porn victim, however, feared doing so because she worried that her attacker might hack her account; her attacker could wreak havoc on her finances if he had a copy of her license. The staffer did not give her another means to verify her identity.

With better training about cyber harassment, including victims' concerns about the privacy of their computers or accounts, the staffer might have given the revenge porn victim an alternative way to verify her identity. Facebook ultimately was responsive to her dilemma. As soon as she alerted the staffer that someone had posted her nude photos on the Facebook page, the profile was taken down. She was grateful for Facebook's help, having had so many other content hosts ignore her requests and, worse, demand that she pay money to take down her nude photos.

Abuse complaints can languish for days or weeks if companies lack the staff to handle them.[20] When Facebook had only 100 million active users, its safety team responded to harassment and bullying complaints within twenty-four hours.[21] Five years and 1.2 billion users later, Facebook can no longer make such assurances. The company attributes delays to the overwhelming volume of complaints it receives: at least two million per week (though it is unclear how many relate to harassment, bullying, or threats).[22] YouTube's staff has difficulty keeping up with complaints because over seventy-two hours of videos are uploaded every minute.

Companies could improve their enforcement process by prompting users to provide more information that would help identify complaints requiring immediate attention. Staff would surely benefit from having the bigger picture of the harassment, including its appearance on other sites. In her book *Sticks and Stones: Defeating the Culture of Bullying and Rediscovering the Power of Character and Empathy,* the cyber bullying expert and journalist Emily Bazelon argues that social media providers should make it easier for teachers to contact their safety teams about kids who are facing destructive bullying.[23] Facebook is paying attention to that advice. In 2013 it started working with Ireland's National Association of School Principals to provide channels for school leaders to communicate with the company about their concerns.[24]

"Kill Them Quickly and Have No Regrets"

In 2010 Facebook users created a Spirit Day page devoted to gay youth like Tyler Clementi whose cyber bullying experience played a role in their suicides. In short order, individuals using fake names inundated the page with antigay messages threatening violence. Facebook's Hate and Harassment Safety Team tracked down the accounts of the offenders and shut them down. Over a ten-day period, the team closed over seven thousand profiles.[25]

When users violate a company's policies, their content may be removed. "If the content is about you and you're not famous, we don't try to decide whether it's actually mean. . . . We just take it down," explains Facebook.[26] Some social network providers temporarily restrict a user's privileges in the hopes that the user will have learned a lesson upon his or her return. If users continually abuse the site's policies, they may be kicked off permanently.

Theresa Nielsen-Hayden, a blogger and comments moderator, endorses this approach: "You can let one jeering, unpleasant jerk hang around for a while, but the minute you get two or more of them egging each other on, they both have to go, and all their recent messages with them. There are others like them prowling the net, looking for just that kind of situation. More of them will turn up, and they'll encourage each other to behave more and more outrageously. Kill them quickly and have no regrets."[27]

Depending on the circumstances, users may receive a warning that gives them a chance to adjust their behavior. Wikipedia, for instance, often places users on probation, followed by permanent banning if the abuse continues.[28] When content violates YouTube's harassment policy, users receive a strike against their accounts and can lose their privileges if reported again.

Whether companies remove content or suspend a user's privileges, they should explain their reasons. That would help users understand a site's expectations. When Facebook staffers remove content deemed to constitute cyber bullying, they send an automated message stating, "We have removed the following content you posted because it violates Facebook's Statement of Rights and Responsibilities." The message includes a link to these standards, which users have to click on before they can post new content.[29] Companies could go even further by letting users know exactly why they violated their policies. They could provide information to the user community about abuse reports that have been filed and what happened to them.

Another valuable tool involves giving users an opportunity to object to decisions made about their content or site privileges.[30] Facebook has an appeals process that enables safety team staffers to reinstate content or a user's privileges if prior decisions were not accurate. YouTube users can appeal community flags on their videos and the resulting strikes on their accounts.[31] YouTube reinstates videos that it agrees do not violate its policies. If it finds that a user's objection is without merit, the user cannot appeal other flagged videos for sixty days, which deters abuses of the reporting system.

Of course, companies have no obligation to entertain objections to their enforcement decisions. Only government actors owe individuals any "due process," which secures notice of, and a chance to object to, government's important decisions about individuals' life, liberty, or property.[32] If it is not required, why should companies bother with an appeals process?

Hearing users' objections would accomplish much. It would reinforce companies' efforts to shape community norms. When people perceive a process to be fair, they are more inclined to accept its results and internalize the reasons supporting a decision. Additional review would combat abuses of the reporting process itself. Harassers have turned reporting systems against victims. Recall that a cyber mob tried to shut down media critic Anita Sarkeesian's YouTube account by spamming the company with fake complaints about her profile. People have attempted to silence political opponents with erroneous complaints.[33] Depending on the circumstance, "killing off" users or content, as Nielsen-Hayden puts it, may be the best strategy, but it should be paired with a means of review.

Users as Norm Enforcers

Considerable internal resources are required to enforce terms-of-service agreements and community guidelines. It is true that innovation could be sacrificed to pay and train more safety staff. To defray these costs, some companies have recruited their users to help them enforce community norms. This approach has promise. According to Professor Clay Shirky, when users share a site's norms and are given the opportunity to police them, they can do as good or better a job addressing infractions as official decision makers.[34]

The open-source encyclopedia Wikipedia is an exemplar of self-governance. Through informal apprenticeships, Wikipedia editors work on pages with new users to help them understand the site's values. Once new users have shown their compliance with community norms, they can apply to become administrators with the power to create locks to prevent misbehaving users from editing.[35]

Individual users have helped the multiplayer online game League of Legends address players' abusive behavior, notably harassment and bigoted epithets. The game's creators, Brandon Beck and Marc Merrill, devised a court system called "the Tribunal." The Tribunal's defendants are players who have reports filed against them; its jurors, also players, evaluate the reports and recommend punishments. All players can view the chat logs that allegedly violated the game's policies and the juries' reasons for meting out punishment. Beck and Merrill found that not only were player-jurors willing to devote their free time to enforcing community norms, but they mostly got the decisions right. To see how well the system worked, staff members independently assessed cases considered by the jurors. More than 80 percent of the time, players' verdicts aligned with staffers' decisions. Behavior in the game also improved. Gamers who had been suspended for three days had 13 percent fewer reports going forward; those who had been suspended for fourteen days had 11 percent fewer reports. Beck and Merrill attributed the reduction in bad behavior to the fact that players knew why they had been punished. To keep the program going, player jurors received special recognition for their efforts. According to a member of the company's behavior team, "We're at a point in the Tribunal's lifespan where we are confident with the accuracy and rate of false positives and trust our players to make the right decisions in the vast majority of cases."[36]

Other companies are similarly turning over the enforcement of community norms to their users. Mozilla, the developer of the web browser Firefox, lets users personalize their browsers with artwork using an application called Personas. If approved, the artwork is made available for others to use. Mozilla has given the task of reviewing Persona submissions to trusted community members. Those individuals review submissions to make sure that they accord with Mozilla's guidelines, including its prohibition against harassing and hateful speech. Mozilla gets involved in the approval process if and only if users contest the decisions.[37]

These sorts of strategies will not work for every content host, nor do they eliminate internal costs because some oversight will surely be needed. Of course, users may not be interested in getting involved, but sites could incentivize participation with privileges or reputational endorsements. The success stories of Wikipedia, League of Legends, and Mozilla certainly show that user enforcement initiatives are worth pursuing.

Accountability: You Own Your Own Words

Limiting anonymity is a strategy being pursued to combat abusive behavior. Some blogs and discussion boards give preference to nonanonymous commenters by including their remarks at the top, while comments of unidentified users fall to the bottom. Other content hosts insist that participants identify themselves. Facebook, to name a prominent example, requires users setting up profiles to register under their real names and to provide e-mail addresses to verify their identities.

The idea is intuitive. If users have to own their words, they may be less inclined to engage in abusive behavior. As the technologist Jaron Lanier notes, the Internet's anonymity was neither an inevitable feature of its design nor necessarily a salutary one.[38] Facebook adopted its real-name approach because it believes that people behave better when they are not using fake names and hidden identities. "When users are allowed to misrepresent themselves, trust and accountability break down," Facebook notes. "Bad actors are emboldened because there is little chance of serious consequence. . . . Most of the systems and processes we have developed are intended to solve this root problem."[39]

Should digital gatekeepers require real names? Chris Wolf, an expert on hate speech and privacy, argues that the benefits of anonymity are often outweighed by its costs to civility.[40] His point is that anonymity is not an unalloyed good; it is valuable when it enables speakers to avoid retaliation but not when it simply allows them to avoid responsibility for destructive speech.

There are, however, strong reasons to push back against real-name policies. Determined harassers can easily work around them. That means bad actors will not be deterred from speaking, but others will be silenced, especially those for whom anonymity is essential to protect them from abuse. Without anonymity, domestic violence and sexual assault victims might not join online survivors' groups for fear that their abusers might discover them. LGBT teenagers might not seek advice from on-line support groups about coping with bullying if they had to worry about their peers learning of their sexual orientation. People might not discuss their medical conditions or engage in political dissent without the protection of anonymity. With inflexible real-name policies, society may lose a lot and gain too little.

Rather than real-name policies, hosts could adopt anonymity as their default setting; that is, anonymity would be a privilege that can be lost. Users who violate terms-of-service agreements could be required to authenticate their identities in order to continue their site privileges. Facebook recently adopted measures to ensure greater accountability for group pages that do not require administrators to disclose their identities. When a group page displays "cruel and insensitive" content, the group's administrators may keep up the content so long as they are willing to stand behind their words. They have to reveal their actual identities if they want their content to remain on the site. In Facebook's view, users should be accountable for their cruelty and insensitivity.[41] Facebook does not ban such content, but instead requires authors to own it. A rebuttable presumption of anonymity is wise because it preserves anonymity's upside potential and potentially forestalls its downside.[42]

Designing for Our Better Selves

Content hosts could employ design strategies to counteract destructive impulses. Just as the anonymity of networked interactions can influence our behavior, so can a site's environment. Online spaces can be designed to signal the presence of human beings, which can nudge users to treat others as deserving of respect rather than as objects that can be mistreated.[43] Virtual worlds generate images called avatars that look human.[44] Visually rich avatars help people experience other users as human beings.[45] The media studies scholar B. Coleman explores in her book *Hello Avatar* that our networked personas, often tied to our real-world identities, can imbue online interactions with a sense of human connectedness.[46]

Content hosts could include these sorts of cues to bring our humanity to the fore. An avatar's disapproving body language could remind users that their behavior is unacceptable. But a caution is in order. As in real space, so in virtual spaces: female avatars are more often sexually harassed than male avatars; openly gay avatars get gay-bashed; non-white avatars are treated in stereotypically racist ways.[47] Although avatars can help us see users as people, they can generate bigoted treatment if they are identified as belonging to a traditionally subordinated group.[48] Content hosts need to be mindful that an avatar's gender, race, and sexual orientation can shape online interactions.[49]

Another design strategy is having virtual spaces resemble physical places with prosocial norms. When primed by visual cues, users import the norms of appropriate behavior from physical places into their digital counterparts. In a study of the virtual world The Sims Online, researchers found that the social rules governing digital homes came from the players' previous experience in the game and from their experiences in offline homes. Sims users were inclined toward politeness when visiting virtual homes in part because the spatial presence of a home primed them to do so.[50] The site's design cues invited certain behavior, which the virtual homeowners reinforced with their behavior.[51] Sites might include pages designed to look like living rooms; primed with those images, posters might be more inclined to hear comments such as "Haven't you bashed that girl enough?"

Professor Nancy Kim has proposed other design strategies. For instance, companies could nudge users to think about others' humanity by slowing down the posting process in the hopes that posters would use the time to think more carefully about what they say. They could require a waiting or cooling-off period before a post is published; during that period a poster may choose to edit or remove the message.

Altering site design is one way of shaping norms. Alone, it may do little, especially if the site condones or encourages cyber harassment. However, combined with clear policies prohibiting cyber harassment and robust enforcement, such architectural cues might help remind users to treat others with respect.

The Potential for Counterspeech

What if companies rebutted harassing speech with speech of their own? That option seems the most realistic if it involves hate speech about a group rather than harassing speech targeting an individual. Companies would lack the personal knowledge necessary to rebut defamatory lies about specific people. By contrast, a company could counter demeaning messages about groups or lies propagated to inspire hatred, such as Holocaust denial. This counterspeech could make a difference in people's views because when respected companies talk, people listen.

Consider Google's response to Jew Watch, a site featuring virulently anti-Semitic content. In 2004 the number-one Google result for a search of "Jew" was Jew Watch. After the site drew considerable media response and interest-group attention, Google inserted its own advertisement, entitled "Offensive Search Results," on top of its page where the link to Jew Watch appeared in its search results. Google admitted that the Jew Watch site may be offensive and "apologize[d] for the upsetting nature of the experience you had using Google"; it assured readers that it did not endorse the views expressed by Jew Watch and provided links to additional information posted by the Anti-Defamation League. Jew Watch continues to appear prominently in searches of the word "Jew,"[52] but Google's rebuttal of bigoted falsehoods and stereotypes helped pierce the insularity of hateful messages that can lead to even more extreme views.

Google similarly posted an explanatory advertisement after images of First Lady Michelle Obama, altered to resemble a monkey, prominently appeared among the results of Google image searches of her name.[53] Of course, a company's ability to engage in counterspeech depends on its available resources. The ability to automate functions like searching for key terms and inserting prepared responses could help cut down the costs.

There is another strategy for countering harassing speech: Internet companies could enhance the visibility of victims' responses. Following the model of Google's placement of "Offensive Search Results" ads, search engines could provide discounted advertising rates to cyber harassment victims so they can respond directly to harassment generated by the search engine's results. The ability to reply might help combat defamatory lies. Professor Frank Pasquale has insightfully argued for such a "right to reply."[54] Some victims, however, do not want to engage with their harassers; some have nothing to say in response to the appearance of their nude photos or threats. These limitations aside, giving victims the option to respond could be an additional strategy to combat cyber harassment.

Getting Parents Involved

In a passionate Facebook post, the video game developer Ernest Adams called on parents to help combat misogynistic threats and demeaning comments in multiplayer online games. Not only should offenders be told to knock it off in the game, but they should also face punishment at home. "If you're the father of a boy who behaves like this online, make it abundantly clear to him that it is unmanly and unacceptable, then deny him the opportunity to do it further. We do not let nine-year-olds misuse tools to hurt other people. Take away his cell phone, his console, and his computer. He can learn to behave like a man, or he can turn in his homework in longhand like a child."[55]

Yet, all too often, parents do not heed Adams's advice because they are not involved in what their kids are doing online. According to a 2013 McAfee study, most parents shy away from overseeing their kids' networked activities. More than 75 percent of parents say that they do not have the time or energy to monitor their kids' Internet use. They cede responsibility because they feel outpaced by modern technology. Parents throw up their hands and hope for the best.[56]

According to Russel Sabella, the former president of the American School Counselor Association, parents are not trying to become more cyber literate: "They're not taking the time and effort to educate themselves." When the cyber bullying expert Parry Aftab asked a group of middle school students if they had been bullied online, sixty-eight of the 150 students raised their hands. Aftab asked them, "How many of your parents know how to help you?" Only four students raised their hands.[57]

Internet intermediaries have echoed these concerns. Despite AOL's efforts to provide parents with tools and controls to help them protect their children online, the company has said, "there are still a large number of parents who neglect to participate in the online experience of their children."[58] MySpace's Safety Team often counseled parents who did not know how to approach their kids about their Internet use. Nigam often felt that parents did not realize that they could ask their kids to shut down their social network profiles. Based on those sorts of conversations, MySpace created a public service video called *Don't Stop the Dialogue* to help parents talk to their kids about online safety.[59]

As a parent, I know how hard this is to address. Even though I have been writing and teaching about privacy and harassment for a long time, that difficulty was painfully obvious to me after I learned about the rape and subsequent harassment of a sixteen-year-old girl in Steubenville, Ohio. On August 12, 2012, the Steubenville teen woke up to find tweets and texts with photographs of her partially nude body being dragged around by football players from her school. The night before, she had attended a party where she had passed out after drinking alcohol.

While unconscious, she was sexually assaulted by a group of teenage boys. Someone videotaped the assault and posted it on YouTube. The video was viewed over a million times before it was taken down. In the video, football players shouted at the camera, "They raped her more than the Duke Lacrosse Team" and "She is as dead as Trayvon Martin." In the days following the rape and the posting of the video, countless posts and tweets, written by teenagers, said the girl "deserved to be peed on" and raped.[60]

It is hard to talk to teens about sexually degrading, demeaning, and threatening harassment, let alone sexual abuse that the victim was forced to reexperience in photos, video, and taunts from anonymous commenters. But, as the Steubenville case shows, young people may not fully appreciate how harmful it is to forward, text, or post pictures and videos of someone being sexually abused and humiliated. We need to talk to our kids about the despair experienced when individuals are harassed online. That includes but isn't limited to sharing humiliating nude photos and tweeting that someone deserves to be sexually abused.[61]

Parents need to opt into their kids' use of networked technologies and the difficult challenges in navigating a world in which everyone is connected all of the time. Opting out of kids' online lives denies parents the chance to be more involved with their kids. It is crucial to talk to teenagers about responsible online engagement. Just as parents talk to their kids about drunk driving and schoolyard fights, they should discuss cyber harassment and cyber bullying. These conversations should start when children are young, should be tailored to their age, and should increase in frequency during their teenage years, when they are more likely to experiment with risky online behavior. Educating our kids about the destruction they can cause with networked tools is essential to preventing online abuse.

It is also important to talk to our kids about the damage that they can do to themselves. Young people often think that with all of the activity on social networks, no one cares about what they are saying besides their close friends. Unfortunately that is not the case. Once information is posted online, it can spread far beyond its intended audience. What teens write on Facebook often ends up reaching people they do not want seeing it. Even though people try hard to get their privacy settings right, they get them wrong most of the time. In a study of Columbia University students, over 90 percent of participants shared information on Facebook with people with whom they did not want to, even though they were mindful of their privacy settings. Much to their dismay, the study participants let the public and "friends of friends" see sensitive personal information.[62] Colleges and employers can use that information against them without their ever knowing.[63] Harassers and bullies can too. Young people need to keep these concerns in mind as they post, send e-mails, text, and chat online.

When I talk to parents of teenagers about cyber bullying and cyber harassment, they often wonder if their kids should be online at all. Banning kids from online life is neither realistic nor productive. Teens are notorious for working around their parents' prohibitions about Internet use. Study after study shows that when parents prohibit their teens from using social network sites, their kids maintain secret accounts. That seems like the worst result: kids interacting online without the benefit of parental guidance.[64]

Lots of good can come from social media use. In our digital age, social networks are indispensable for socializing and developing interests. Extracurricular clubs meet in social network groups and in person. Young adults experiment with different sides of their personalities in social networks, live gaming, and virtual worlds.[65] Of course, age is a crucial factor. Most social media providers do not allow kids under thirteen to join their sites. This has a lot to do with the federal Children's Online Privacy Protection Act, which requires sites to obtain parental consent if they collect personal information from kids who are twelve and younger. Whatever the reason, the age restriction is wise. Children who are not yet thirteen probably are not developmentally ready to interact on social network sites. Even if they are, their parents should not let them evade companies' age restrictions, as many do.[66]

Aside from talking to kids about online safety, what about monitoring their Internet use? When the school psychologist Susan Swearer's daughter got a Facebook account, she insisted that her daughter share her password. This allows Swearer to log in as her daughter and read her daughter's texts from time to time.[67] Dr. Elizabeth Englander, a cyber bullying researcher and psychologist, installed keystroke logger software on her family's computer. She affixed a note to the computer that says, "Don't Forget That Mom Sees Everything You Do Online." Englander hopes that the note and the monitoring software help remind her sons to think before they post, comment, or e-mail.[68] Although she does not often check her sons' online activities, she sees the software as a nudge in the right direction.

Monitoring strategies are not for everyone. Some parents have told me that they worry that asking for their kids' passwords sends the message that they do not trust them. Others just are uncomfortable. They want their kids to feel that Facebook and other social networks are their own private spaces. That is fine so long as parents stay engaged and do not plug out. Even if monitoring is more theater than fact, as Englander recognizes in her behavior, it helps remind kids that online activities have consequences. It can help push back against the feeling of anonymity that can unleash destructive behavior. It can slow down the tendency to lose oneself in a "game" of one-upmanship. Monitoring strategies could help bring out kids' better selves when they are most needed.

Without doubt, parents should take action if their kids behave irresponsibly or hurt others online.[69] That might mean taking away online privileges for a period of time. Bazelon reminds parents that no tool is more powerful in changing teens' behavior than the possibility that they might lose their Facebook accounts, cell phones, or computers.[70] Parents might need to use more serious punishments as well, but doing nothing or making excuses is the worst possible response.

With all of that said, sometimes parents do everything they can to be engaged in their kids' online lives, but still their kids get themselves into trouble by sharing nude photos of themselves with untrustworthy friends or by attacking others without thinking. Sometimes young people do everything they can to be mindful of others and protect their own and others' privacy, but still they face online abuse.

Last semester, a first-year law student came to my office and told me that her best friend from college had received several anonymous e-mails warning that the sender had her nude photo, which was attached, and was prepared to send it to her father unless she sent more. My student's friend had taken a nude self-shot but had never sent it to anyone. Her computer had clearly been hacked, and she felt helpless in the face of the threat. With my advice, the woman went to the police and told her father about what was happening. All her father can do now is help her work through whatever comes next. Her family's support will be indispensable.

By all public accounts, the teenage actor who was attacked on his fan site did nothing to provoke his classmates who overwhelmed the comment section with homophobic, frightening threats. His parents helped him cope with his emotional distress by enlisting a therapist. Ultimately his parents decided to move so that their son would not have to attend school with the individuals who targeted him. No matter if the bullying or harassment is on- or offline, the best parents can do is to help their kids cope with it.

The award-winning journalist Julia Angwin talked to me about her plans for active engagement in her kids' online lives. Her kids are still small, but she is already giving serious thought to what happens when they have networked devices of their own. Although Angwin wants her kids to enjoy online culture, she worries that the "Internet is like an unsafe playground." She does not want to censor them or chill their self-expression, but she wants to keep them safe.[71] When her kids get into the tween years, she plans to talk to them about protecting their privacy and treating others with respect online. She wants to be their go-to person for all things Internet. All parents should follow Angwin's lead. I am constantly trying to improve the lines of communication with my teenagers. I do not have all of the answers, but the effort is worth it.

Schools

Schools are increasingly involved in helping parents and students learn about online safety. Some school districts have adopted cyber bullying curricula to obtain federal funds earmarked for technology[72] or to comply with state laws requiring "character education" in public schools.[73] Their impetus has ethical roots as well. As the Supreme Court has underscored, schools nurture the "habits and manners of civility as values in themselves conducive to happiness and as indispensable to the practice of self-government."[74] At the turn of the twentieth century, the philosopher John Dewey observed that schools are uniquely situated to teach children and adults about the social meaning of citizenship because they bring diverse people together and thus "introduce deeper sympathy and wider understanding."[75] That is as true today as it was then.

Schools' "digital citizenship" initiatives are built around the values, ethics, and social norms that allow virtual communities, including social networks, to "facilitate constructive interaction and promote trust." Across the country, school districts have adopted antibullying and antiharassment policies. In-school and afterschool programs focus on treating others with respect off- and online.[76] Students learn to recognize cyber bullying, and educators talk to them about strategies for dealing with it. Teachers receive training to ensure they will take cyber bullying seriously rather than dismiss it as "boys being boys."[77] Parents are involved in the learning as well. A school official in Texas described his district's afterschool programs for parents as being centered on "digital responsibility—'Here's what we expect from your kids from a behavior standpoint when they're using technology and here are things that we do not allow.'"[78]

However schools design their digital citizenship curriculum, they should update it to accommodate changing technologies and return to its lessons often.[79] One-shot training about online safety, civility, and norms of respect does little to instill values. Beginning digital citizenship lessons in grade school makes it more likely that they will become ingrained. Then, too, schools should tie their cyber bullying lessons to lessons about bigotry and intolerance. Cyber bullying is the toughest on kids who belong to historically subordinated groups.[80] In discussing cyber bullying, schools should make clear that it is unacceptable to target students because they belong to a particular group. Staff should be trained to respond to bigoted taunting online. As Bazelon writes, schools should teach "there is nothing *wrong* with the sexuality of gay students or with the lives they will lead." The same should be said, again and again, about other groups targeted by bigoted bullying.

Schools' budgetary pressures can make it difficult to expand cyber literacy and digital citizenship lessons. Advocacy groups like the Anti-Defamation League have engaged in a multitude of efforts to help schools teach youth about cyber bullying and bigotry on- and offline. Interested Internet companies could support those efforts along the lines of MTV's A Thin Line project. The project's website is devoted to educating young people about digital abuse. Once users join the site, they can read about cyber bullying and strategies for coping with it. They can learn about how to "take a stand" against digital abuse and share their own stories.[81] Combining the efforts of advocacy groups, companies, parents, and schools will go a long way to helping young people internalize norms of respect and equality.

It is encouraging that Internet intermediaries are increasingly working to combat cyber harassment, stalking, bullying, and other forms of online abuse. They are leveraging their resources to defeat online abuse in steps small and large. Their efforts, reinforced by parents and schools, will have a powerful impact on the kind of Internet that is possible, one where norms of equality are nurtured and online users recognize their role as digital citizens to encompass treating others with respect.

Conclusion

In the spring of 2013, the revenge porn victim started speaking publicly about her cyber harassment experience. The support of law enforcement and her attorney gave her the strength that she needed to speak out against the abuse. She no longer felt unprotected and alone.

After talking to the media, she received hundreds of e-mails and comments on her anti-revenge porn site. Many accused her of being responsible for her predicament; they said she got what she deserved because she was stupid enough to share her nude photos with her ex. Didn't she know any better?

Recently she and other revenge porn victims have talked to many major media outlets about their experiences. Of late, the tone of the messages she has been receiving has shifted. For every two messages that blame her, twenty messages praise her for the work she is doing. Cyber harassment victims from all over the world have reached out to her. She has joined forces with them, including a woman who launched a "Stop Revenge Porn" campaign in Scotland.[1]

The revenge porn victim recently founded the antiharassment group called the Cyber Civil Rights Initiative (CCRI). I am on the board of directors, along with Professor Mary Anne Franks and Charlotte Laws, the mother of a revenge porn victim and an activist who is often called the Erin Brockovich of revenge porn. CCRI has been closely involved with efforts to criminalize revenge porn, helping lawmakers draft statutes and talking to the press about cyber harassment and its harms.

After getting her doctorate in industrial psychology, the revenge porn victim looked for jobs using two résumés; one included her anti–revenge porn work, which she sent to advocacy groups that she is interested in working for, and one did not mention it. During her search, she remained concerned about how her cyber harassment experience would be received in corporate settings. She hoped that when employers searched her name, they would see that she had the inner strength not only to fight back against her abuser but also to help other victims. Her personal strength paid off: she recently started a job with a well-known media company. The woman who hired her found her antiharassment work brave and impressive. On the job front, all is well.

Six years after being attacked online, the tech blogger is considering restarting her blog. She feels safer now than in the past because the individual behind the second wave of abuse ("weev," whose real name is Andrew Auernheimer) was recently sentenced to forty-one months in prison for hacking AT&T's customer information service. She wrote to me, "The morning after he went to prison, I woke up and realized I had not actually EXHALED in many years. And I felt lighter and happier than I had in years. I finished the book I had put on hold since the whole thing happened—I mean I wrote more in the first 6 weeks he was in prison than in the previous 6 years! And I decided at that moment that I would come back. That I would blog again."[2]

The law student works at the Department of Justice and loves it but is still dogged by the online abuse and wishes she could just forget about it. Married to a wonderful colleague of hers from law school, she says her life is full of joy. But the abuse cost her dearly, as it did the tech blogger and the revenge porn victim. She cannot undo that suffering.

Despite the vicious cyber mob attack that continues to this day, the media critic Anita Sarkeesian has not stopped working on her project about sexism in video games. Her Kickstarter campaign has far exceeded her goal of raising $6,000. As of January 2014, she had raised over $158,922. She explained, "I am certainly not the first woman to suffer this kind of harassment and sadly, I won't be the last. But I'd just like to reiterate that this is not a trivial issue. It can not and should not be brushed off by saying, 'oh well that's YouTube for you,' 'trolls will be trolls' or 'it's to be expected on the internet.' These are serious threats of violence, harassment and slander across many online platforms meant to intimidate and silence. And its not okay. Again, don't worry, this harassment will never stop me from making my videos! Thank you for all your support!"[3]

Since the earliest days of the Internet, scholars, activists, and early adopters have supported a cyber civil liberties agenda. The mantra "All information should be free" is a firmly entrenched norm in online communities. Although free speech concerns still require constant vigilance, civil libertarians have accomplished much in the past twenty years.

The Internet's impact on civil rights, however, has largely been neglected. The Internet and its potential as an engine of equality has all too often reflected and reinforced the power imbalances of our offline experiences. Eradicating bigoted cyber harassment is going to be a difficult task.

We have been here before and we have been successful. Only forty years ago, sexual harassment in the workplace and domestic violence in the home were viewed as normal practices that private individuals had to handle on their own. Women faced pervasive abuse at home and in the workplace with little means of recourse. In the 1970s and early

1980s, civil rights activists fought hard to get society to recognize those practices as harmful social problems.

Since law's recognition of women's suffering in the last quarter of the twentieth century, the home and workplace have become safer spaces for women. Change has been slow, however, because social attitudes were firmly entrenched. The notion that sexual harassment and domestic violence were trivialities had a strong hold on the public. In 1983 the New Jersey Supreme Court Task Force on Women in the Courts found that stereotyped myths, beliefs, and biases continued to affect attorneys' and court personnel's decision making in domestic violence and other areas. Despite clear changes in the law, some judges continued to marginalize domestic violence victims because they could just "get up and leave" to avoid the abuse.[4] Social norms might have changed more rapidly had the marginalization of sexual harassment and domestic violence not been so deeply ingrained.

Today we see the same pattern of subordination and exclusion in cyberspace. The notion that cyber harassment is trivial is widespread. A cyber civil rights legal agenda is essential to shift our cultural attitudes. Because legal reform won't come to fruition immediately and because law is a blunt instrument, changing social norms requires the help of online users, Internet companies, parents, and schools.

Some online communities are expressing their disapproval of cyber harassment rather than letting it continue without rebuke. Through software design and user policies, Internet companies are engaging in efforts to inculcate norms of respect. Parents and educators are teaching the young about cyber harassment's harms. This is a particularly opportune moment to educate the public about cyber harassment. If we act now, we could change social attitudes that trivialize cyber harassment and prevent them from becoming entrenched. Then future generations might view cyber harassment as a disgraceful remnant of the Internet's early history.

We are already seeing some change. After being told that cyber harassment was an uneventful part of online life that was partially their own fault and urged to leave online spaces if the Internet got too hot for them, the tech blogger, the law student, and the revenge porn victim defied that advice and refused to back down. The tech blogger spoke out publicly against the abuse and tried to enlist law enforcement's help. The law student brought a civil suit against her pseudonymous attackers. The revenge porn victim's ex-boyfriend is facing her civil suit, though the criminal case against him has been dropped.

These three women have contributed to a shift in our cultural attitudes. Through their efforts and the efforts of antiharassment advocacy groups, we are on the path to protect cyber civil rights and eradicate online harassment. As digital citizens, we must finish this work together.

Notes

Introduction

1. "Fatass Denial Bloggers," *Encyclopedia Dramatica,* https://encyclope diadramatica.es/Fatass_Denial_Bloggers.
2. Telephone interview with "Anna Mayer," October 21, 2011 (notes on file with author); see Marjorie Korn, "Cyberstalking," *Self Magazine,* January 2013, 107 (interviewing "Anna Mayer").
3. Proclamation No. 8769, 77 Fed. Reg. 211 (December 28, 2011) (announcing National Stalking Awareness Month).
4. Katrina Baum, Shannan Catalano, Michael Rand, and Kristina Rose, *Stalking Victimization in the United States,* Bureau of Justice Statistics, Special Report No. NCJ 224527 (January 2009), 8.
5. Hearing on Reauthorization of the Violence Against Women Act, before the S. Comm. on the Judiciary, 109th Cong., 27–28 (2005) (remarks of Mary Lou Leary, executive director, National Center for Victims of Crime).
6. Paul Bocij, *Cyberstalking: Harassment in the Internet Age and How to Protect Your Family* (Westport, CT: Praeger, 2004), 67. According to a recent Bureau of Justice Statistics report, a third of stalking incidents

involved more than one offender. Baum et al., *Stalking Victimization in the United States*, 12 (appendix table 3).

7. Martha C. Nussbaum, "Objectification and Internet Misogyny," in *The Offensive Internet: Speech, Privacy, and Reputation*, ed. Martha Nussbaum and Saul Levmore (Cambridge, MA: Harvard University Press, 2010), 73.

8. Callie Millner, "Public Humiliation over Private Photos," SFGate.com, February 10, 2013, http://www.sfgate.com/opinion/article/Public-humiliation-over-private-photos-4264155.php.

9. Nina Bahadur, "Victims of 'Revenge Porn' Open Up on Reddit about How It Impacted Their Lives," *Huffington Post* (blog), January 10, 2014, http://www.huffingtonpost.com/2014/01/09/revenge-porn-stories-real-impact_n_4568623.html.

10. Brian, "Craigslist Rapists Get 60 to Life: Ad Seeking Someone with 'No Regard' for Women Led to Rape," Victimized over the AOC (blog), July 3, 2010, http://victimsover18.blogspot.com/2010/07/craigslist-rapists-get-60-to-life-ad.html.

11. William Browning, "Wyo. Craigslist Rape Victim Speaks for the First Time," *AP Alert*, September 24, 2010.

12. William Browning, "Details Emerge in Web Rape Case," *Star-Tribune* (WY), February 5, 2010, http://trib.com/news/local/article_edb73077-0bbc-5bc2-b9ea-b3fe5c9aedce.html; Pete Kotz, "Jebidiah Stipe Used Craigslist Rape Fantasy Ad to Get Revenge on Ex Girlfriend," True Crime Report (blog), February 9, 2010 (11:13 A.M.), http://www.truecrimereport.com/2010/02/jebidiah_stipe_used_craigslist.php.

13. DeeDee Correll, "Craigslist Implicated in Rape Case: A Wyoming Man Is Accused of Using the Website to Engineer an Ex-Girlfriend's Assault," *Los Angeles Times*, January 11, 2010, A9.

14. Justin Jouvenal, "Stalkers Use Online Sex Ads as Weapons," *Washington Post*, July 14, 2013, http://www.washingtonpost.com/local/i-live-in-fear-of-anyone-coming-to-my-door/2013/07/14/26c11442-e359-11e2-aef3-339619eab080_print.html.

15. "Misogyny: The Sites," *Southern Poverty Law Center Intelligence Report*, Spring 2012, http://www.splcenter.org/get-informed/intelligence-report/browse-all-issues/2012/spring/misogyny-the-sites.

16. Telephone interview with Jessica Valenti, April 12, 2012 (notes on file with author).
17. D.C. v. R.R., 106 Cal. Rptr. 3d 399, 408 (Ct. App. 2010).
18. Leser v. Penido, 879 N.Y.S.2d 107 (Sup. Ct. 2009); Second Amended Complaint, Lester v. Mineta, No. C 04-03074 SI (N.D. Cal. Mar. 3, 2006).
19. Telephone interview with "Jennifer Ivanov," March 26, 2012 (notes on file with author).
20. Ibid.; e-mail from Jennifer Ivanov to author, March 25, 2012 (on file with author); e-mail from Jennifer Ivanov to author, July 10, 2012 (on file with author).
21. "Sacramento Woman Describes Pain of 'Revenge Porn,'" *News 10 ABC*, November 5, 2013, http://www.news10.net/story/local/2013/11/05/4766349/.
22. "Revenge Porn Websites Growing in Popularity," *ABC 22*, December 5, 2013, http://www.abc22now.com/shared/news/top-stories/stories/wkef_vid_17474.shtml (discussing teacher who was placed on administrative leave after her employer, a private school, discovered her naked image appeared on gossip site The Dirty.com).
23. Second Amended Complaint, Lester v. Mineta, No. 3:04-03074 SI (N.D. Cal. Mar. 3, 2006).
24. Alexis Shaw, "Virginia Woman Sues Ex-Boyfriend for Cyber Harassment," *ABC News*, February 7, 2013.
25. Matt Ivester, *lol . . . OMG! What Every Student Needs to Know about Online Reputation Management, Digital Citizenship and Cyberbullying* (Reno, NV: Serra Knight, 2011), 95.
26. Korn, "Cyberstalking," 107.
27. Comes v. Molalla Transport System, Inc., 831 P. 2d 1316, 1321 (Colo. 1992).
28. Penelope Trunk's Brazen Careerist, "Blog under Your Real Name, and Ignore the Harassment," Penelope Trunk (blog), July 19, 2007, http://blog.penelopetrunk.com/2007/07/19/blog-under-your-real-name-and-ignore-the-harassment/ (explaining that women who write under pseudonyms miss opportunities associated with blogging under their real names, such as networking opportunities and expertise associated with the author's name).

29. Ellen Nakashima, "Sexual Threats Stifle Some Female Bloggers," *Washington Post,* April 30, 2007, A1.

30. Seth Stevenson, "Popularity Counts," *Wired Magazine,* May 2012, 120.

31. Ibid.

32. Matt Ritchel, "I Was Discovered by an Algorithm," *New York Times,* April 28, 2013, Business 1.

33. Matt Nobles, Bradford Reyns, Bonnie Fisher, and Kathleen Fox, "Protection against Pursuit: A Conceptual and Empirical Comparison of Cyberstalking and Stalking Victimization among a National Sample," *Justice Quarterly* (2013), doi:10.1080/07418825.2012.723030.

34. Ibid.; "New Study Examines Victims and Cyberstalking," *Science Daily,* February 12, 2013, http://www.sciencedaily.com/releases/2013/02/130212075454.htm.

35. Posting of "M.L.," http://wrlds.com/case/transNoah/press12-17-10.htm (password protected) (on file with author).

36. Korn, "Cyberstalking."

37. Kenneth L. Karst, "Threats and Meanings: How the Facts Govern First Amendment Doctrine," *Stanford Law Review* 58 (2006): 1337–1412, 1342.

38. B. J. Lee, "Suicide Spurs Bid to Regulate the Net in South Korea," *Newsweek.com,* October 15, 2008, http://www.thedailybeast.com/newsweek/2008/10/14/when-words-kill.html.

39. Nobles et al., "Protection against Pursuit."

40. Nussbaum, supra note 8, at 75.

41. Annmarie Chiarini, "I Was a Victim of Revenge Porn: I Don't Want Anyone Else to Face This," *Guardian* (blog), November 19, 2013, http://www.theguardian.com/commentisfree/2013/nov/19/revenge-porn-victim-maryland-law-change.

42. Michele L. Ybarra, Marie Diener-West, Dana Markow, Philip J. Leaf, Merle Hamburger, and Paul Boxer, "Linkages between Internet and Other Media Violence with Seriously Violent Behavior by Youth," *Pediatrics* 122 (2008): 929–937, 933.

43. Robyn M. Cooper and Warren J. Blumenfeld, "Responses to Cyberbullying: A Descriptive Analysis of the Frequency of and Impact on LGBT and Allied Youth," *Journal of LGBT Youth* 9 (2012): 153–177.

44. Nina Burleigh, "Sexting, Shame & Suicide," *Rolling Stone,* September 26, 2013, 52.

45. Dean Praetorius, "Jamie Rodemeyer, 14 Year Old Boy, Commits Suicide after Gay Bullying, Parents Carry On," *Huffington Post*, September 20, 2011, http://www.huffingtonpost.com/2011/09/20/jamey-rodemeyer -suicide-gay-bullying_n_972023.html.

46. Gillian Shaw and Lori Culbert, "Port Coquitlam Teen Driven to Death by Cyberbullying," *Vancouver Sun*, October 12, 2012, http://www.van couversun.com/technology/Port+Coquitlam+teen+driven+death+cybe rbullying+with+video/7375941/story.html.

47. Scott H. Greenfield, "Credit Where Due," Simple Justice (blog), March 11, 2012 (6:32 A.M.), http://blog.simplejustice.us/2012/03/11 /credit-where-due/.

48. National Cybersecurity Alliance, "Cyberstalking Is a Real Crime: One in Five Americans Affected by Unwanted Contact," news release, January 15, 2013, http://www.prnewswire.com/news-releases/cyberstalking -is-a-real-crime-one-in-five americans-affected-by-unwanted-contact -186985781.html.

49. Molly M. Ginty, "Cyberstalking Turns Web Technologies into Weapons," *Ottawa Citizen*, April 7, 2012, J1.

50. Baum et al., *Stalking Victimization in the United States*, 5.

51. Bradford W. Reyns, "Being Pursued Online: Extent and Nature of Cyberstalking Victimization from a Lifestyle/Routine Activities Perspective," PhD diss., University of Cincinnati, 2010, 25–26 (reviewing literature on estimates of the extent of cyberstalking); see also Bonnie S. Fisher, "Being Pursued and Pursuing During the College Years," in *Stalking Crimes and Victim Protection*, ed. Joseph A. Davis (Boca Raton, FL: CRC Press, 2001), 207–238; L. P. Sheridan and T. Grant, "Is Cyberstalking Different?," *Psychology, Crime & Law* 13 (2007): 627–640.

52. M. Alexis Kennedy and Melanie A. Taylor, "Online Harassment and Victimization of College Students," *Justice Policy Journal* 7, no. 1 (2010), http://www.cjcj.org/uploads/cjcj/documents/online_harassment.pdf.

53. Reyns, "Being Pursued Online," 29–33, 98, 102.

54. "Stalking," National Institute of Justice, October 25, 2007, http://www .nij.gov/topics/crime/stalking/Pages/welcome.aspx.

55. Ginty, "Cyberstalking," J1.

56. Working to Halt Online Abuse, "Comparison Statistics 2000–2011," http://www.haltabuse.org/resources/stats/Cumulative2000-2011

.pdf. WHOA's statistics are gleaned from individuals who contact their organization through their website. The organization's statistics are not as comprehensive as those of the Bureau of Justice Statistics, which sponsored a national survey of individuals who experienced offline and online stalking. According to the Bureau of Justice Statistics, an estimated 3.4 million people experienced real-space stalking alone, while an estimated 850,000 experienced stalking with both online and offline features. Baum et al., *Stalking Victimization in the United States*, 4.

57. Baum et al., *Stalking Victimization in the United States*, 3.

58. Robert D'Ovidio and James Doyle, "A Study on Cyberstalking: Understanding Investigative Hurdles," *FBI Law Enforcement Bulletin*, March 2003, 10–17.

59. Robert Meyer and Michael Cukier, "Assessing the Attack Threat Due to IRC Channels," *Proceedings of the 2006 International Conference on Dependable Systems and Networks (DSN)* (Los Alamitos, CA: IEEE Computer Society, 2006), 467–472. The authors used simulated users with female names Cathy, Elyse, Irene, Melissa, and Stephanie, and simulated users with male names Andy, Brad, Gregg, and Kevin (460–470).

60. Reyns, "Being Pursued Online," 97.

61. Lisa Stone of BlogHer has observed that female bloggers who are famous, lesbian, and nonwhite receive the most vicious cyber harassment. Lisa Stone, "Hating Hate Speech: For Kathy Sierra and All Women Bloggers Online," BlogHer (blog), March 27, 2007 (12:47 A.M.), http://www.blogher.com/hating-hate-speech-safety-kathy-sierra -and-all-women-online. One blogger observed, "The fact is, to be a woman online is to eventually be threatened with rape and death." Yuki Onna, "Let Me Tell You about the Birds and the Bees: Gender and the Fallout over Christopher Priest," Rules for Anchorites: Letters from Proxima Thule (blog), April 6, 2012 (9:45 A.M.), http://yuki -onna.livejournal.com/675153.html.

62. John Scalzi, "The Sort of Crap I Don't Get," Whatever (blog), August 31, 2011, http://whatever.scalzi.com/2011/08/31/the-sort-of -crap-i-dont-get/.

63. Joan Walsh, "Men Who Hate Women on the Web," *Salon*, March 31, 2007, http://www.salon.com/2007/03/31/sierra/.

64. Avitable, "Where's My Reply, @OkCupid?," Avitable (blog), September 5, 2011, http://www.avitable.com/2011/09/05/wheres-my-reply-okcupid-prelude-to-a-lawsuit/.

65. PZ Myers, "Being a Woman on the Internet," Pharyngula (blog), November 7, 2011 (1:18 P.M.), http://freethoughtblogs.com/pharyngula/2011/11/07/being-a-woman-on-the-internet.

66. Michael Ezra, "Misogyny in the Blogosphere," Harry's Place (blog), November 11, 2011 (6:42 P.M.), http://hurryupharry.org/2011/11/11/misogyny-in-the-blogosphere/.

67. James Lasdun, *Give Me Everything You Have: On Being Stalked* (New York: Farrar, Straus and Giroux, 2013), 53, 110–115, 134.

68. Jerry Finn, "A Survey of Online Harassment at a University Campus," *Journal of Interpersonal Violence* 19 (2004): 468–483, 477.

69. Catharine Hill and Holly Kearl, *Crossing the Line: Sexual Harassment at School* (Washington, DC: American Association of University Women, 2011), 13–15.

70. Deborah Hellman, *When Is Discrimination Wrong?* (Cambridge, MA: Harvard University Press, 2008), 29.

71. Erving Goffman, *Stigma: Notes on the Management of Spoiled Identity* (New York: Simon & Schuster, 1963).

72. Anne Locksley, Eugene Borgida, Nancy Brekke, and Christine Hepburn, "Sex Stereotypes and Social Judgment," *Journal of Personality and Social Psychology* 39 (1980): 821–831; Anne Locksley, Christine Hepburn, and Vilma Ortiz, "Social Stereotypes and Judgments of Individuals: An Instance of the Base-Rate Fallacy," *Journal of Experimental Social Psychology* 18 (1982): 23–42.

73. Fiona Roberts, "'Rape of Emotions': Man 'Hacked into Women's E-mails and Stole Naked Photos,'" *Daily Mail* (U.K.), July 21, 2011, http://www.dailymail.co.uk/news/article-2017272/Joseph-Campbell-hacked-womens-e-mails-posted-naked-photos-Facebook.html.

74. Helen Lewis, "This Is What Online Harassment Looks Like," *New Statesman* (blog), July 6, 2012 (9:30 A.M.), http://www.newstatesman.com/blogs/internet/2012/07/what-online-harassment-looks.

75. Sady Doyle, "But How Do You Know It's Sexist?," Tiger Beatdown (blog), November 10, 2011 (6:33 P.M.), http://tigerbeatdown.com/2011/11/10/but-how-do-you-know-its-sexist-the-mencallmethings-round-up/.

76. Robin West, *Caring for Justice* (New York: New York University Press, 1997), 102–103 (discussing real-space rape).

77. Lenora M. Lapidus, Emily J. Martin, and Namita Luthra, *The Rights of Women: The Authoritative ACLU Guide to Women's Rights,* 4th ed. (New York: New York University Press, 2009).

78. Jill Filipovic, "'Revenge Porn' Is about Degrading Women Sexually and Professionally," *Guardian* (U.K.), January 28, 2013, http://www .theguardian.com/commentisfree/2013/jan/28/revenge-porn-degrades -women.

79. Cyber Civil Rights Statistics on Revenge Porn, October 11, 2013 (on file with author).

80. Charles R. Lawrence III, "If He Hollers Let Him Go: Regulating Racist Speech on Campus," *Duke Law Journal* (1990): 431–483, 461.

81. Tracey L. M. Kennedy, "An Exploratory Study of Feminist Experiences in Cyberspace," *Cyberpsychology and Behavior* 3 (2000): 707–719, 717.

82. Lena Chen, "I Was the Harvard Harlot," *Salon*, May 23, 2011, http:// www.salon.com/2011/05/24/harvard_harlot_sexual_shame/.

83. Lasdun, *Give Me Everything,* 135.

84. Blogger Elaine Vigneault assumes male pseudonyms to comment on male-dominated blogs. Elaine Vigneault, "Read My Mind, to Ignore Violence Is to Condone It," Elaine Vigneault (blog), April 13, 2007 (2:02 P.M.), http://elainevigneault.com/to-ignore-violence-is-to-condone-it .html (link unavailable; post on file with author).

85. Kenji Yoshino, *Covering: The Hidden Assault on Our Civil Rights* (New York: Random House, 2006), 22, 144.

86. Debra Winter and Chuck Huff, "Adapting the Internet: Comments from a Women-Only Electronic Forum," *American Sociologist* 27 (1996): 30–54, 50.

87. Dmitri Williams, Nicole Martins, Mia Consalvo, and James D. Ivory, "The Virtual Census: Representations of Gender, Race and Age in Video Games," *New Media and Society* 11 (2009): 815–834; Nick Yee, "Maps of Digital Desires: Exploring the Topography of Gender and Play in Online Games," in *Beyond Barbie and Mortal Kombat: New Perspectives on Gender and Gaming,* ed. Yasmin Kafai, Carrie Heeter, Jill Denner, and Jennifer Y. Sun (Boston: MIT Press, 2008), 83–96.

88. Yee, "Maps of Digital Desires," 94.

89. E-mail from "Marisa Layton" to author, March 13, 2009 (on file with author).

90. Martha C. Nussbaum, *Hiding from Humanity: Disgust, Shame, and the Law* (Princeton, NJ: Princeton University Press, 2004), 293.

91. Kenji Yoshino, "Assimilationist Bias in Equal Protection: The Visibility Presumption and the Case of 'Don't Ask, Don't Tell,'" *Yale Law Journal* 108 (1998): 485–572, 528.

92. E-mail from "Marisa Layton" to author, March 13, 2009 (on file with author).

93. Yoshino, *Covering*, 154–162. Legal scholar Kenji Yoshino has used the term *covering* to describe the tendency to disguise or suppress disfavored identity characteristics, including sex, often at tremendous personal cost and in a society in which laws do not adequately account for this phenomenon.

94. Korn, "Cyberstalking," 108.

95. Brendan O'Neill, "The Campaign to 'Stamp Out Misogyny Online' Echoes Victorian Efforts to Protect Women from Coarse Language," *Telegraph* (U.K.) (blog), November 7, 2011, http://blogs.telegraph.co .uk/news/brendanoneill2/100115868/the-campaign-to-stamp-out -misogyny-online-echoes-victorian-efforts-to-protect-women-from coarse-language/.

96. Comment of Fistandantalus to Posting to Rev. Bill Bob Gisher to Less People Less Idiots, Silence of the hams, http://lessidiots.blogspot .com/2007/04/silence-of-hams.html.

97. Nathan Jurgenson, "The IRL Fetish," New Inquiry Blog, June 28, 2012, http://thenewinquiry.com/essays/the-irl-fetish/.

98. Julie E. Cohen, *Configuring the Networked Self: Law, Code, and the Play of Everyday Practice* (New Haven, CT: Yale University Press, 2012).

99. Korn, "Cyberstalking," 107.

100. Laura Smith-Spark, "Calls for Action as Female Journalists Get Bomb Threats on Twitter," CNN, August 2, 2013, http://www.cnn .com/2013/08/01/world/europe/uk-twitter-threats/.

101. Simon Hattenstone, "Caroline Criado-Perez: 'Twitter Has Enabled People to Behave in a Way They Wouldn't Face-to-Face,'" *Guardian* (U.K.), August 4, 2013, http://www.theguardian.com/lifeandstyle /2013/aug/04/caroline-criado-perez-twitter-rape-threats.

102. Emma Margolin, "Twitter Rolls Out New Rules as Threats to Women Continue," MSNBC.com, August 5, 2013, http://www.msnbc.com /news-nation/twitter-rolls-out-new-rules-threats.

103. Alexandra Topping, "Caroline Criado-Perez Says Culture Must Change as Malicious Threats Continue," *Guardian* (U.K.), September 3, 2013, http://www.theguardian.com/uk-news/2013/sep/03/caroline -criado-perez-rape-threats-continue.

104. Stefan Fafinski, *U.K. Cybercrime Report* (Garlik, 2006), App. D.

105. "500,000 Brits Are Victims of Cyberstalking," *Mail Online* (U.K.), December 13, 2006, http://www.dailymail.co.uk/news/article-422200 /500-000-Brits-victims-cyberstalking.html.

106. Karen McVeigh, "Cyberstalking 'Now More Common' than Face-to-Face Stalking," *Guardian* (U.K.), April 8, 2011, http://www.guardian .co.uk/uk/2011/apr/08/cyberstalking-study-victims-men.

107. National Centre for Cyberstalking Research, "Cyberstalking in the United Kingdom: An Analysis of the ECHO Pilot Survey" (2011), 32, http://www.beds.ac.uk/__data/assets/pdf_file/0003/83109/ECHO _Pilot_Final.pdf.

108. Miriam Berger, "Brazilian 17-Year-Old Commits Suicide after Revenge Porn Posted Online," *Buzzfeed*, November 20, 2013, http:// www.buzzfeed.com/miriamberger/brazilian-17-year-old-commits -suicide-after-revenge-porn-pos.

109. Martha J. Langelan, *Back Off! How to Confront and Stop Sexual Harassment and Harassers* (New York: Simon & Schuster, 1993), 90.

110. Because computer forensic experts are expensive and because law enforcement budgets are limited, a criminal law agenda naturally has to wrestle with the reality of scarce resources. We also ought to recognize the costs of such abuse and the value of spending resources on combating it.

111. Robin West, "Toward a Jurisprudence of the Civil Rights Acts" (on file with author).

112. Jane Martinson, "Attempts to Shut Women Up Should Fail," *Guardian* (U.K.), November 8, 2011, http://www.guardian.co.uk/lifeand style/the-womens-blog-with-jane-martinson/2011/nov/08/women -sexist-abuse-online.

113. New York Times v. Sullivan, 376 U.S. 254 (1964).

114. Dan Fost, "The Attack on Kathy Sierra," Tech Chronicles (blog), March 27, 2007, http://blog.sfgate.com/techchron/2007/03/27/the -attack-on-kathy-sierra/.

1. Digital Hate

1. Scott Rosenberg, *Say Everything: How Blogging Began, What It's Becoming, and Why It Matters* (New York: Three Rivers Press, 2009), 251.
2. Jim Turner, "The Sierra Saga Part 1: Dissecting the Creation of the Kathy Sierra Blog Storm," One by One Media (blog), March 28, 2007, http://www.onebyonemedia.com/the-sierra-saga-part-1-dissecting-the -creation-of-the-kathy-sierra-blog-storm-4/.
3. Jim Turner, "My Epilogue and Editorial of the Kathy Sierra Saga," One by One Media (blog), April 9, 2007, http://www.onebyonemedia.com /my-epilogue-and-editorial-of-the-kathy-sierra-saga/.
4. Theresa Cook, "Female Bloggers Face Threats: What Can be Done?," *ABC News,* May 1, 2007, http://abcnews.go.com/TheLaw/story?id=3107139.
5. "Blog Death Threats Spark Debate," *BBC News,* March 27, 2007, http://news.bbc.co.uk/2/hi/6499095.stm.
6. Memphis Two [Weev], "[Full-disclosure] Kathy Sierra," Virus.org (mailing list archive), March 28, 2007 (7:54 P.M.) (on file with author).
7. Mattathias Schwartz, "The Trolls among Us," *New York Times Magazine,* August 3, 2008, http://www.nytimes.com/2008/08/03/magazine /03trolls-t.html?pagewanted=all.
8. "Kathy Sierra," Wikipedia, June 2, 2010 (8:49), http://en.wikipedia.org /wiki/Kathy_Sierra; "User Talk: Vandalism Warnings (Kathy Sierra)," Wikipedia, June 3, 2010 (14:49), http://en.wikipedia.org/wiki /User_talk:118.208.78.197.
9. Telephone interview with Kathy Sierra, November 8, 2011 (notes on file with author).
10. Kathy Sierra, November 7, 2011, comment on Danielle Citron, "Bigoted Harassment: Alive and Well Online," Concurring Opinions (blog), November 7, 2011 (10:56 A.M.), http://www.concurringopinions .com/archives/2011/11/bigoted-harassment-alive-and-well-online .html/comment-page-1#comment-77652.

11. Kathy Sierra, April 18, 2009, comment on Kamipono D. Wenger, "CCR Symposium: A Behavioral Argument for Stronger Protections," Concurring Opinions (blog), April 14, 2009 (6:04 P.M.), http://www.concurringopinions.com/archives/2009/04/ccr_symposium_a_1.html#comments.

12. Second Amended Complaint at paragraphs 22–24, Doe I and Doe II v. Mathew C. Ryan et al., No. 3:07-cv-00909-CFD (D. Conn. Aug. 5, 2008).

13. David Margolick, "Slimed Online: Two Lawyers Fight Cyberbullying," *Portfolio Magazine*, February 11, 2009.

14. Ibid.

15. "AutoAdmit," Wikipedia, http://en.wikipedia.org/wiki/AutoAdmit.

16. [Author redacted], "DoJ Attorneys: Beware of Lying Bitch Coworker [Nancy Andrews]," AutoAdmit, June 8, 2011 (5:53 P.M.), http://www.xoxohth.com/thread.php?thread_id=1669162&mc=11&forum_id=2.

17. Telephone interview with "Nancy Andrews," November 15, 2011 (notes on file with author).

18. Telephone interview with Holly Jacobs, November 5, 2012 (notes on file with author).

19. Ibid.

20. 17 U.S.C. § 101 (2012).

21. 17 U.S.C. § 106 (2012).

22. 17 U.S.C. § 512(c) (2012).

23. "Fighting Revenge Porn at the Dawn of Cyber Civil Rights," *Q with Jian Gomeshi*, Canadian Broadcast Company, June 13, 2013, http://www.cbc.ca/q/blog/2013/06/13/end-revenge-porn/. Jacobs and I appeared on the interview together to talk about advocacy work against revenge porn.

24. Ibid.

25. Danielle Citron, "How to Make Revenge Porn a Crime without Trampling Free Speech," *Slate*, November 7, 2013, http://www.slate.com/articles/news_and_politics/jurisprudence/2013/11/making_revenge_porn_a_crime_without_trampling_free_speech.html.

26. Pseudonymous interviews with Holly Jacobs can be found at Jessica Roy, "The Battle over Revenge Porn: Can Hunter Moore, the Web's

Vilest Entrepreneur, Be Stopped?," *New York Observer,* December 4, 2012, A1; Richard Lardner, "FBI Detoured from Usual Path in Petraeus Case," Associated Press, November 18, 2012.

27. Jessica Roy, "A Victim Speaks: Standing Up to a Revenge Porn Tormentor," *New York Observer,* May 1, 2013, http://betabeat.com/2013/05 /revenge-porn-holli-thometz-criminal-case/.

28. Katrina Baum, Shannan Catalano, Michael Rand, and Kristina Rose, *Stalking Victimization in the United States,* Bureau of Justice Statistics, Special Report No. NCJ 224527 (January 2009), 4.

29. Robert D'Ovidio and James Doyle, "A Study on Cyberstalking: Understanding Investigative Hurdles," *FBI Law Enforcement Bulletin,* March 2003, 10–17, 12.

30. Paul Bocij, *Cyberstalking: Harassment in the Internet Age and How to Protect Your Family* (Westport, CT: Praeger, 2004), 67. By contrast, most real-space stalking victims know their attackers' real names. When cyber stalkers targeting women are individuals with whom they have some personal connection, they tend to be victims' friends (15.5 percent), former intimates (8.8 percent), or work colleagues (1.8 percent), whereas real-space stalkers of women are predominately former intimates (59 percent) (68).

31. Baum et al., *Stalking Victimization in the United States,* 11 (appendix table 3).

32. Brian Leiter, "Cleaning Cyber-Cesspools: Google and Free Speech," in *The Offensive Internet: Speech, Privacy, and Reputation,* ed. Martha Nussbaum and Saul Levmore (Cambridge, MA: Harvard University Press, 2010), 155.

33. Matt Ivester, *lol . . . OMG! What Every Student Needs to Know about Online Reputation Management, Digital Citizenship and Cyberbullying* (Reno, NV: Serra Knight, 2011), 95.

34. People's Dirt centered on high school students; Revenge on Your Ex focuses on ex-partners; and Dumpster Sluts seeks gossip on promiscuous women.

35. Joe Mullin, "New Lawsuit against 'Revenge Porn' Site Also Targets GoDaddy," *Ars Technica,* January 22, 2013, http://arstechnica.com/tech -policy/2013/01/new-lawsuit-against-revenge-porn-site-also-targets -godaddy/.

36. "Revenge Porn Website Has Colorado Women Outraged," CBS4 (Denver), February 3, 2013, http://denver.cbslocal.com/2013/02/03/re venge-porn-website-has-colorado-woman-outraged/.

37. Complaint, Hollie Toups et al. v. GoDaddy.com, Texxxan.com, et al., No. D130018-C (Dist. Ct., Orange County Texas, filed January 18, 2013).

38. Camille Dodero, "Hunter Moore Makes a Living Screwing You," *Village Voice*, April 4, 2012, http://www.villagevoice.com/2012-04-04/news /revenge-porn-hunter-moore-is-anyone-up/5/.

39. Gabriella Coleman, "Anonymous in Context: The Politics and Power behind the Mask," Draft report for Center for International Governance Innovation (on file with author).

40. Claire Hardaker, "Trolling in Asynchronous Computer-Mediated Communication: From User Discussions to Academic Definitions," *Journal of Politeness Research* 6 (2010): 215–242.

41. Whitney Phillips, "Lords of the Web," unpublished manuscript, 2011.

42. Gabriella Coleman, "Our Weirdness Is Free," *Triple Canopy*, January 13, 2012, http://canopycanopycanopy.com/15/our_weirdness_is_free.

43. Schwartz, "The Trolls among Us."

44. Coleman, "Our Weirdness Is Free."

45. David Auerbach, "Anonymity as Culture: Treatise," *Triple Canopy*, February 9, 2012, http://canopycanopycanopy.com/15/anonymity_as _culture__treatise.

46. E-mail from Professor Gabriella Coleman to author and Whitney Phillips (on file with author).

47. Auerbach, "Anonymity as Culture: Treatise."

48. Ibid.

49. Michael S. Bernstein, Andrés Monroy-Hernández, Drew Harry, Paul André, Katrina Panovich, and Greg Vargas, "4chan and /b/: An Analysis of Anonymity and Ephemerality in a Large Online Community," *Fifth International AAAI Conference on Weblogs and Social Media*, July 5, 2011, http://www.aaai.org/ocs/index.php/ICWSM/ICWSM11/paper /view/2873/4398.

50. Lee Knuttila, "User Unknown: 4chan, Anonymity and Contingency," *First Monday* 16, no. 10 (October 3, 2011), http://www.firstmonday.org /htbin/cgiwrap/bin/ojs/index.php/fm/article/view/3665/3055.

51. Coleman, "Our Weirdness Is Free."

52. Cole Stryker, *Epic Win for Anonymous: How 4chan's Army Conquered the Web* (New York: Overlook Press, 2011), 163.

53. National Council of Churches, "Queens Federation of Churches Warns of On-Line Vandalism of Religious Sites," news release, August 4, 2008, http://www.ncccusa.org/news/080804queenswarns.html.

54. Terrence O'Brien, "4chan Cyberbully Jailed over E mailing Lewd Photos to School," Switched (blog), http://www.switched.com/2011/01/19/4chan-matthew-riskin-bean-jailed-lewd-photos/; "Face behind the Name: Meet Matthew Riskin Bean, Convicted 4chan Cyberstalker," The Smoking Gun (blog), January 25, 2011, http://www.thesmokinggun.com/buster/4chan/face-behind-name-meet-matthew-riskin-bean-convicted-4chan-cyberstalker.

55. Phillips, "Lords of the Web"; see also Nidhi Subbaraman, "Meet Dr. Troll," *Fast Company*, May 30, 2012, http://www.fastcompany.com/1838743/whitney-phillips-troll-hunter.

56. "Kathy Sierra," *Encyclopedia Dramatica*, https://encyclopediadramatica.es/Kathy_Sierra.

57. E-mail from Gabriella Coleman to author, June 21, 2013 (on file with author).

58. Coleman, "Anonymous in Context."

59. Helen Walters, "Peeking behind the Curtain at Anonymous: Gabriella Coleman at TEDGlobal 2012," TED Blog (blog), June 27, 2012 (8:19 A.M.), http://blog.ted.com/2012/06/27/peeking-behind-the-curtain-at-anonymous-gabriella-coleman-at-tedglobal-2012/.

60. Roy, "The Battle over Revenge Porn."

61. Adrian Chen, "'Weaponize the Media': An Anonymous Rapper's War on Steubenville," Gawker (blog), June 12, 2013, http://gawker.com/weaponize-the-media-an-anonymous-rappers-war-on-ste-512747826.

2. How the Internet's Virtues Fuel Its Vices

1. Jeff Pearlman, "Tracking Down My Online Haters," CNN, January 21, 2011, http://articles.cnn.com/2011-01-21/opinion/pearlman.online.civility_1_online-haters-twitter-online-behavior?_s=PM:OPINION.

2. David Margolick, "Slimed Online: Two Lawyers Fight Cyberbullying," *Portfolio Magazine*, February 11, 2009 (on file with author).

3. Patricia Wallace, *The Psychology of the Internet* (New York: Cambridge University Press, 2001), 124–125.

4. Arnold P. Goldstein, *The Psychology of Group Aggression* (New York: John Wiley and Sons, 2002), 32; Ralph H. Turner and Lewis M. Killian, *Collective Behavior,* 2nd ed. (Englewood Cliffs, NJ: Prentice-Hall, 1972), 165, 408.

5. Brian Mullen, "Operationalizing the Effect of the Group on the Individual: A Self-Attention Perspective," *Experimental Social Psychology Journal* 19 (1983): 295–322.

6. Goldstein, *Psychology;* Turner and Killian, *Collective Behavior.*

7. Edward Diener, Scott C. Frasier, Arthur L. Beamon, and Roger T. Kelem, "Effects of Deindividuation Variables on Stealing among Halloween Trick-or-Treaters," *Journal of Personality and Social Psychology* 33 (1976): 178–183.

8. E. Ashby Plant and Patricia G. Devine, "Internal and External Motivation to Respond without Prejudice," *Journal of Personality and Social Psychology* 75 (1998): 811–832.

9. Philip Zimbardo, *The Lucifer Effect: Understanding How Good People Turn Evil* (New York: Random House, 2007).

10. Philip Zimbardo, "The Human Choice: Individuation, Reason, and Order versus Deindividuation, Impulse, and Chaos," *Nebraska Symposium on Motivation* 15 (1969): 300.

11. Adam N. Joinson, *Understanding the Psychology of Internet Behaviour: Virtual Worlds, Real Lives* (New York: Palgrave Macmillan, 2003), 23. Studies also show an enormous amount of racial abuse by American customers against Indian help-line workers, confirming the notion that people are more likely to be hostile on the phone than they would be in person. Winifred R. Poster, "Who's on the Line? Indian Call Center Agents Pose as Americans for U.S.-Outsourced Firms," *Industrial Relations* 46 (2007): 271–304.

12. Katelyn Y. A. McKenna and John A. Bargh, "Plan 9 from Cyberspace: The Implications of the Internet for Personality and Social Psychology," *Personality and Social Psychology Review* 4 (2000): 57–75, 60.

13. In a series of early experiments, Sara Kiesler and her colleagues compared the interactions of groups of people whose names were attached to online messages to those whose actual names were absent from online messages. After tallying the number of hostile remarks, they found that the anony-

mous groups made more than *six* times as many uninhibited remarks as the non-anonymous groups. Sara Kiesler, Jane Siegel, and Timothy W. McGuire, "Social Psychological Aspects of Computer-Mediated Communication," *American Psychologist* 39 (1984): 1123–1134.

14. Wallace, *Psychology of the Internet,* 126.

15. Megan Gibson, "#Mencallmethings: Twitter Trend Highlights Sexist Abuse Online," *Time,* November 8, 2011, http://newsfeed.time.com /2011/11/08/mencallmethings-twitter-trend-highlights-sexist-abuse -online/.

16. Suzanne Weisband and Leanne Atwater, "Evaluating Self and Others in Electronic and Face-to-Face Groups," *Journal of Applied Psychology* 84 (1999): 632–639, 633.

17. "Part I of @AC360 Exclusive Interview with Man behind 'Jailbait'— Ex-Reddit Troll Michael Brutsch," CNN Press Room (blog), October 18, 2012 (9:58 P.M.), http://cnnpressroom.blogs.cnn.com/2012/10/18 /part-1-of-ac360-exclusive-interview-w-man-behind-jailbait-ex-reddit -troll-michael-brutsch/.

18. Teresa Wilz, "Cyberspace Shields Hateful Bloggers," *Journal Gazette* (Fort Wayne, IN), November 17, 2007, 2D.

19. Poster, "Who's on the Line?" Anonymity does not affect just the posters. When victims do not know who is coming after them, they are more likely to assume the worst. A study of undergraduate students explored the impact of sexual harassment in classrooms and online. Students were asked about different types of behavior, including exposure to sexual pictures, derogatory comments about women, pressure for sexual favors, and sexist comments regarding dress. The study's participants rated derogatory comments, requests for sexual favors, and sexual jokes made online as *more* harassing than if they were made in person. Why? The act of writing something down implied thought and seriousness, and the absence of cues about attackers led participants to fear the worst. Jodi K. Biber, Dennis Doverspike, Daniel Baznik, Alana Cober, and Barbara A. Ritter, "Sexual Harassment in Online Communications: Effects of Gender and Discourse Medium," *CyberPsychology and Behavior* 5 (2002): 33–42.

20. Brian Coffey and Stephen Woolworth, "'Destroy the Scum, and Then Neuter Their Families:' The Web Forum as a Vehicle for Community Discourse?," *Social Science Journal* 41 (2004): 1–14, 8–9.

21. Tim Adams, "How the Internet Created an Age of Rage," *Guardian* (U.K.), July 23, 2011, http://www.guardian.co.uk/technology/2011 /jul/24/internet-anonymity-trolling-tim-adams. As I will later discuss, this approach could be automated, such as by thanking someone for their comment in a way that underscores their identifiability.

22. Shirley S. Ho and Douglas M. McLeod, "Social-Psychological Influences on Opinion Expression in Face-to-Face and Computer-Mediated Communication," *Communication Research* 35 (2008): 190–207; McKenna and Bargh, "Plan 9 from Cyberspace," 64.

23. I am grateful to Biella Coleman for pointing out the site Urban Mommy, which is an anonymous supportive community where the anonymity allows new parents to be frank about how challenging raising children can be.

24. Alyssa Royse, "Rape and Death Threats and Batman, OH MY!," BlogHer (blog), August 3, 2008 (11:42 A.M.), http://www.blogher.com /rape-and-death-and-batman-oh-my.

25. Simon Wiesenthal Center, *Facebook, Youtube + How Social Media Outlets Impact Digital Terrorism and Hate* (New York: Simon Wiesenthal Center, 2009) (providing screenshots of social media websites promoting hate).

26. Brian Levin, "Cyberhate: A Legal and Historical Analysis of Extremists' Use of Computer Networks in America," *American Behavioral Scientist* 45 (2002): 958–988; Katelyn Y. A. McKenna and John A. Bargh, "Coming Out in the Age of the Internet: Identity 'Demarginalization' through Virtual Group Participation," *Journal of Personality and Social Psychology* 75 (1998): 681–694.

27. D.C. v. R.R., 106 Cal. Rptr. 3d 399, 422 (Ct. App. 2010).

28. Cass R. Sunstein, *Republic.com 2.0* (Princeton, NJ: Princeton University Press, 2007), 60.

29. John C. Turner, *Rediscovering the Social Group: A Self-Categorization Theory* (New York: Blackwell, 1987).

30. Cass R. Sunstein, *Going to Extremes: How Like Minds Unite and Divide* (New York: Oxford University Press, 2009).

31. Choon-Ling Sia, Bernard C. Y. Tan, and Kwok-Kee Wei, "Group Polarization and Computer-Mediated Communication: Effects of Communication Clues, Social Presence, and Anonymity," *Information Systems Research* 13 (2002): 70–90.

32. Russell Spears, Martin Lea, and Stephen Lee, "De-individuation and Group Polarization in Computer-Mediated Communication," *British Journal of Social Psychology* 29 (1999): 121–134.

33. Karen M. Douglas and Craig McGarty, "Understanding Cyberhate: Social Competition and Social Creativity in Online White Supremacist Groups," *Social Science Computer Review* 32 (2005): 68–76, 74.

34. Magdalena Wojcieszak, "'Don't Talk to Me:' Effects of Ideologically Homogeneous Online Groups and Politically Dissimilar Offline Ties on Extremism," *New Media and Society* 12 (2010): 644.

35. Susan C. Herring, "The Rhetorical Dynamics of Gender Harassment On-Line," *Information Society* 15 (1999): 151–167, 155–157.

36. Kathy Sierra, August 1, 2011 (11:24 A.M.), comment on "Why It Matters: Google+ and Diversity, Part 2," Liminal States (blog), July 27, 2011 (10:25 P.M.), http://www.talesfromthe.net/jon/?p=2918#comment-179952.

37. Jim Turner, "The Sierra Saga, Part I," One by One Media Blog, March 28, 2007, http://onebyonemedia.com/the-sierra-saga-part-1-dissecting-the-creation-of-the-kathy-sierra-blog-storm-4/.

38. "Part I of @AC360 Exclusive Interview."

39. David Weinberger, *Too Big to Know: Rethinking Knowledge Now That the Facts Aren't the Facts, Experts Are Everywhere, and the Smartest Person in the Room Is the Room* (New York: Basic Books, 2011), 84.

40. Spears et al., "De-Individuation," 133.

41. David G. Myers and George D. Bishop, "Discussion Effects on Racial Attitudes," *Science* 169 (1970): 778–779.

42. Maureen O'Connor, "Is Jessi Slaughter More Popular than Jesus?," Gawker, September 10, 2010, http://uk.gawker.com/5634814/is-jessi-slaughter-more-popular-than-jesus; Max Read, "Now on Tumblr: Jessi Slaughter Suicide Hoax," Gawker, July 18, 2010, http://gawker.com/5590294/now-on-tumblr-jessi-slaughter-suicide-hoax; Adrian Chen, "The Art of Trolling: Inside a 4chan Smear Campaign," Gawker, July 17, 2010, http://gawker.com/5589721/the-art-of-trolling-inside-a-4chan-smear-campaign.

43. "Jessi Slaughter," *Encyclopedia Dramatica,* http://encyclopediadramatica.ch/Jessi_Slaughter (accessed November 1, 2011).

44. David Easley and Jon Kleinberg, *Networks, Crowds, and Markets: Reasoning about a Highly Connected World* (New York: Cambridge University Press, 2010).

45. James Grimmelmann, "Some Skepticism about Search Neutrality," in *The Next Digital Decade,* ed. Berin Szoka and Adam Marcus (Washington, DC: Tech Freedom, 2010), 435–460. Grimmelmann writes, "Google's algorithm depends on more than 200 different factors. . . . The PageRank of any webpage depends, in part, on every other page on the Internet" (455).

46. James G. Webster, "User Information Regimes: How Social Media Shape Patterns of Consumption," *Northwestern University Law Review* 104 (2010): 593–612.

47. A plaintiff in Japan obtained a judgment against Google's Autocomplete for breach of privacy. See "Google Ordered to Delete Terms from Autocomplete," *Japan Times,* March 26, 2012, http://www.japantimes.co.jp/news/2012/03/26/news/google-ordered-to-delete-terms-from-autocomplete/#.UVxHqZM4t8E. Breach of privacy and defamation litigation against Google for its Autocomplete feature is ongoing in other countries (e.g., France, the United Kingdom, and Italy). See Nina Mandell, "Google Faces Lawsuit over 'Suggest' Results," *New York Daily News,* May 1, 2012, http://www.nydailynews.com/news/world/google-faces-lawsuit-suggest-search-results-article-1.1070636 (France); Kate Solomon, "Google Loses Autocomplete Lawsuit," *TechRadar,* April 8, 2011, http://www.techradar.com/us/news/internet/google-loses-autocomplete-lawsuit-941498 (Italy).

48. Eli Pariser, *The Filter Bubble: What the Internet Is Hiding from You* (New York: Penguin Press, 2011), 13–14.

49. Howard Rheingold, *Smart Mobs: The Next Social Revolution* (New York: Basic Books, 2002).

50. Jennifer Preston, "Movement Began with Outrage and a Facebook Page That Gave It an Outlet," *New York Times,* February 5, 2011, A10; Chrystia Freeland, "Lessons from Central Europe for the Arab Spring," *New York Times,* June 16, 2011, http://www.nytimes.com/2011/06/17/world/europe/17iht-letter17.html?pagewanted=all.

51. Abraham H. Foxman and Christopher Wolf, *Viral Hate: Containing Its Spread on the Internet* (New York: Palgrave Macmillan, 2013), 100.

52. Nicholas Jackson, "Ten Notorious Google Bombs," *Atlantic,* February 25, 2011, http://www.theatlantic.com/technology/archive/2011/02/10-notorious-google-bombs/71731/#slide4.

53. John W. Dozier Jr. and Sue Scheff, *Google Bomb* (Deerfield Beach, FL: Health Communications, 2009).

54. tigtog, "Jill Filipovic, Internet Searches and the Success of Personal-Political Collective Action," Larvatus Prodeo (blog), March 27, 2007, http://larvatusprodeo.net/2007/03/27/jill-filipovic-internet-searches-and-the-success-of-personal-political-collective-action/.

55. danah boyd, "Streams of Content, Limited Attention: The Flow of Information through Social Media," Web 2.0 Expo, New York, November 17, 2009, transcript available at http://www.danah.org/papers/talks/Web2Expo.html.

3. The Problem of Social Attitudes

1. Helen Lewis, "'You Should Have Your Tongue Ripped Out': The Reality of Sexist Abuse Online," *New Statesman* (blog), November 3, 2011 (1:51 P.M.), http://www.newstatesman.com/blogs/helen-lewis-hasteley/2011/11/comments-rape-abuse-women; Vanessa Thorpe and Richard Rogers, "Women Bloggers Call for a Stop to 'Hateful' Trolling by Misogynist Men," *Guardian* (U.K.), November 6, 2011, http://www.guardian.co.uk/world/2011/nov/05/women-bloggers-hateful-trolling.

2. Helen Lewis, "What about the Men?," *New Statesman* (blog), November 10, 2011 (2:45 P.M.), http://www.newstatesman.com/blogs/helen-lewis-hasteley/2011/11/online-abuse-women-male.

3. Laurie Penny, "A Woman's Opinion Is the Mini-Skirt of the Internet," *Independent* (U.K.), November 4, 2011, http://www.independent.co.uk/opinion/commentators/laurie-penny-a-womans-opinion-is-the-mini-skirt-of-the-internet-6256946.html.

4. Thorpe and Rogers, "Women Bloggers Call for a Stop."

5. Brendan O'Neill, "The Campaign to 'Stamp Out Misogyny Online' Echoes Victorian Efforts to Protect Women from Coarse Language," *Telegraph* (U.K.) (blog), November 7, 2011, http://blogs.telegraph.co.uk/news/brendanoneill2/100115868/the-campaign-to-stamp-out-misogyny-online-echoes-victorian-efforts-to-protect-women-from-coarse-language/.

6. Lewis, "'You Should Have Your Tongue Ripped Out'"; Thorpe and Rogers, "Women Bloggers Call for a Stop."

7. WebWeaver, "Kathy Sierra, Misogyny on the Web, and the Blogger's Code of Conduct," WebWeaver's World (blog), April 14, 2007, http://webweaversworld.blogspot.com/2007/04/kathy-sierra-misogyny-on-web-and.html.

8. Heretic, Alex Grogan, and Mark, comments on "Cute Kitty—Rage Boy," One Good Move (blog), April 2, 2007, (9:08 A.M.), http://onegoodmove.org/1gm/1gmarchive/2007/04/cute_kitty_rage.html.

9. Scott Greenfield, "The New Discrimination: Invisible," Simple Justice (blog), November 8, 2011, (7:21 A.M.), http://blog.simplejustice.us/2011/11/08/the-new-discrimination-invisible/.

10. Steven D, "Why the Lack of Concern for Kathy Sierra (w/poll)?," Daily Kos (blog), April 13, 2007, http://www.dailykos.com/story/2007/04/13/323019/-Why-the-lack-of-concern-for-Kathy-Sierra-w-poll; Laurel Papworth, "Kathy Sierra: Death Threats Ballyhoo," Laurel Papworth (blog), March 27, 2007, http://laurelpapworth.com/kathy-sierra-death-threats-ballyhoo/.

11. Jennifer, March 28, 2007 (12:17 P.M.), comment on Lynn Harris, "Death Threats Dog Female Blogger," *Salon*, March 28, 2007, http://www.salon.com/2007/03/28/kathy_sierra/singleton/#comment-212133.

12. Dylan Tweney, "Kathy Sierra Case: Few Clues, Little Evidence, Much Controversy," Wired Blog, April 16, 2007, http://www.wired.com/techbiz/people/news/2007/04/kathysierra.

13. Scott Rosenberg, *Say Everything: How Blogging Began, What It's Becoming, and Why It Matters* (New York: Three Rivers Press, 2009), 255.

14. Jason Geiger, "Kathy Sierra," JayGeiger (blog), March 29, 2007, http://www.jaygeiger.com/index.php/2007/03/29/kathy-sierra/.

15. kos, "Death Threats and Blogging," Daily Kos (blog), April 7, 2007, http://www.dailykos.com/story/2007/04/12/322169/-Death-threats-and-blogging.

16. "Cyber Harassment and the Law," *On Point with Tom Ashbrook*, NPR, March 3, 2009, http://onpoint.wbur.org/2009/03/03/cyber-harassment (comments of David Margolick).

17. Marc J. Randazza, July 22, 2008 (6:42 P.M.), comment on boskboks, "Pseudonymous Speech and Message Board 'Acting' and the AutoAdmit Case," The Legal Satyricon (blog), July 22, 2008, http://randazza.wordpress.com/2008/07/22/pseudonymous-speech-and-message

-board-acting-and-the-autoadmit-case/; "Cyber Harassment and the Law" (comments of Marc Randazza).

18. Ann Althouse, "For Many People the Internet Has Become a Scarlet Letter, an Albatross," Althouse (blog), March 7, 2007 (9:37 A.M.), http://althouse.blogspot.com/2007/03/for-many-people-internet-has -become.html.

19. Glenn Reynolds, "Suing AutoAdmit," Instapundit Blog, June 12, 2007, http://instapundit.com/archives2/006203.php.

20. Joan, comment on Paterrico, "Volokh on the AutoAdmit Lawsuit," Patterico's Pontifications Blog, June 13, 2007 (8:19 A.M.), http://patterico .com/2007/06/13/volokh-on-the-autoadmit-lawsuit/.

21. D.C. v. R.R., 106 Cal. Rptr. 3d 399 (Ct. App. 2010).

22. deek, comment on Kim Zetter, "Court: Cyberbullying Threats Are Not Protected Speech," *Wired* (blog), March 18, 2010 (3:23 P.M.), http:// www.wired.com/threatlevel/2010/03/cyberbullying-not-protected /#comment-128062106.

23. Michael Sullivan, March 30, 2007 (6:39 P.M.), comment on Joan Walsh, "Men Who Hate Women on the Web," *Salon*, March 30, 2007 (9:02 A.M.), http://www.salon.com/2007/03/31/sierra/#postID=163 7767&page=0&comment=214397.

24. "I Never Told Kathy Sierra to Shut Her Gob (But I Wish I Would Have)," Violent Acres (blog), March 27, 2007, http://www.violentacres .com/archives/147/i-never-told-kathy-sierra-to-shut-her-gob-but-i.

25. Mark, comment on "Cute Kitty—Rage Boy."

26. Callie Millner, "Public Humiliation over Private Photos," *SFGate*, February 10, 2013, http://www.sfgate.com/opinion/article/Public-humilia tion-over-private-photos-4264155.php.

27. Susan Reimer, "Intimate Photos That Wound Intimately," *Baltimore Sun*, October 30, 2013, http://articles.baltimoresun.com/2013-10-30 /news/bs-ed-reimer-revenge-porn-20131030_1_nude_pictures-revenge -intimate-photos.

28. Cassie, "Harvard Asian Slut to Be Next Kaavya," AutoAdmit, January 24, 2007, http://www.autoadmit.com/thread.php?thread_id=569172 &mc=19&forum_id=2.

29. Maureen O'Connor, "Lena Chen and the Case of the Naughty Nudie Pics," IvyGate (blog), December 22, 2007 (1:43 A.M.), http://www.ivy

gateblog.com/2007/12/lena-chen-and-the-case-of-the-naughty -nudie-pics/.

30. Amanda Hess, "Lena Chen on Assault by Photograph," *Washington City Paper,* April 1, 2010, http://www.washingtoncitypaper.com/blogs /sexist/2010/04/01/lena-chen-on-assault-by-photograph/.

31. [Author redacted], "LOL, cuntsfall for 'Feminist Coming Out Day' SCAM," AutoAdmit, March 3, 2011 (10:18 A.M.), http://www.auto admit.com/thread.php?thread_id=1578569&mc=1&forum_id=2.

32. Lena Chen, "The Five Types of Haters Female Bloggers Encounter (And What to Do about Them)," the ch!cktionary (blog), August 2010, http://thechicktionary.com/post/409408816/the-five-types-of-haters -female-bloggers-encounter-and.

33. josie, comment on Maureen O'Connor, "Lena Chen and the Case of the Naughty Nudie Pics," Ivy Gate Blog, December 22, 2007, http:// www.ivygateblog.com/2007/12/lena-chen-and-the-case-of-the -naughty-nudie-pics/.

34. Lisa Nakamura, *Cybertypes: Race, Ethnicity, and Identity on the Internet* (New York: Routledge, 2002), 45.

35. U.S. Department of Justice, *Cyberstalking: A New Challenge for Law Enforcement and Industry,* report from the attorney general to the vice president (Washington, DC: GPO, 1999).

36. Mary Brandel, "Online Harassment: Five Tips to Defeat Blog Trolls and Cyberstalkers," *CIO.com,* April 27, 2007, http://www.cio.com /article/106500/Online_Harassment_Five_Tips_to_Defeat_Blog_ Trolls_and_Cyberstalkers?page=1&taxonomyId=3089 (quoting Richard Silverstein).

37. John Hawkins, "Blogging While Female Part 2," *Right Wing News,* March 18, 2008, http://www.rightwingnews.com/uncategorized/blog ging-while-female-part-2-five-women-bloggers-talk-about-gender -issues-and-the-blogosphere/.

38. John Hampshire, March 30, 2007 (3:59 P.M.), comment on Walsh, "Men Who Hate Women on the Web."

39. Harris, "Death Threats Dog Female Blogger."

40. Rich Kyanka, "Won't Somebody Think of the Bloggers?," Something Awful (blog), April 3, 2007, http://www.somethingawful.com/d/hogo sphere/internet-death-threat.php.

41. Liz Tay, "Blogger Spat Rages over Sierra 'Death Threats,'" *Computerworld*, March 28, 2007, http://www.computerworld.com.au/article /180214/blogger_spat_rages_over_sierra_death_threats_/.

42. Mitch Wagner, "Death Threats Force Designer to Cancel ETech Conference Appearance," *InformationWeek*, March 26, 2007, http://www .informationweek.com/blog/229216545.

43. Laura Lemay, "Kathy Sierra, or Imminent Death of the Net Predicted," Lauralemay (blog), March 28, 2007, http://blog.lauralemay.com/2007 /03/kathy-sierra-or-imminent-death-of-the-net-predicted.html#more -1616.

44. Fred Strebeigh, *Equal: Women Reshape American Law* (New York: Norton, 2009), 272.

45. Lin Farley, *Sexual Shakedown: The Sexual Harassment of Women on the Job* (New York: McGraw-Hill, 1978), 126–127.

46. Catharine A. MacKinnon, *Sexual Harassment of Working Women* (New Haven: Yale University Press, 1979), 60–61.

47. Corne v. Bausch & Lomb, 390 F. Supp. 161, 163–164 (D. Ariz. 1975).

48. Martha J. Langelan, *Back Off! How to Confront and Stop Sexual Harassment and Harassers* (New York: Simon & Schuster, 1993), 39; Deborah L. Rhode, "Sexual Harassment," *Southern California Law Review* 65 (1992): 1459–1466, 1465.

49. James Ptacek, *Battered Women in the Courtroom: The Power of Judicial Responses* (Boston: Northeastern University Press, 1999), 4–5 (describing the case of Pamela Dunn, who was shot, stabbed, and strangled by her husband five months after a judge chastised her for requesting a police escort to her apartment to gather her belongings).

50. Lynn Hecht Schafran, "Documenting Gender Bias in the Courts: The Task Force Approach," *Judicature* 70 (1987): 280–290, 283.

51. State v. Black, 60 N.C. (Win.) 262 (1864).

52. R. Emerson Dobash and Russell Dobash, *Violence against Wives: A Case against Patriarchy* (New York: Free Press, 1979), 213; International Association of Police Chiefs, Training Key No. 16, Handling Disturbance Calls (1968–69), 94–95, quoted in Sue E. Eisenberg and Patricia L. Micklow, "The Assaulted Wife: 'Catch 22' Revisited," *Women's Rights Law Reporter* 3 (1977): 138–161, 156.

53. Dobash and Dobash, *Violence*, 210.

54. J. C. Barden, "Wife Beaters: Few of Them Ever Appear before a Court of Law," *New York Times,* October 21, 1974.

55. Dobash and Dobash, *Violence,* 213.

56. Louise F. Fitzgerald, "Who Says? Legal and Psychological Constructions of Women's Resistance to Sexual Harassment," in *Directions in Sexual Harassment Law,* ed. Reva Siegel and Catharine MacKinnon (New Haven, CT: Yale University Press, 2004), 94–110.

57. Farley, *Sexual Shakedown,* 198.

58. B. Glenn George, "The Back Door: Legitimizing Sexual Harassment Claims," *Boston University Law Review* 73 (1993): 1–38, 18.

59. Sally Quinn, "The Myth of the Sexy Congressmen," *Redbook,* October 1976, 96.

60. Martha C. Nussbaum, *Sex and Social Justice* (New York: Oxford University Press, 1999), 144.

61. Martha R. Mahoney, "Exit: Power and the Idea of Leaving in Love, Work, and the Confirmation Hearings," *Southern California Law Review* 65 (1992): 1283.

62. Carrie N. Baker, *The Women's Movement against Sexual Harassment* (Cambridge, UK: Cambridge University Press, 2008), 11.

63. Reva Siegel, "The Rule of Love: Wife Beating as Prerogative and Privacy," *Yale Law Journal* 105 (1996): 2117–2208, 2170.

64. Elizabeth Pleck, *Domestic Tyranny: The Making of American Social Policy against Family Violence from Colonial Times to the Present* (Urbana: University of Illinois Press, 2004), 136, 140–141.

65. Peter G. Jaffe, Elaine Hastings, Deborah Reitzel, and Gary W. Austin, "The Impact of Police Laying Charges," in *Legal Responses to Wife Assault,* ed. N. Zoe Hilton (Newbury Park, CA: Sage, 1993), 62–95, 64.

66. Pleck, *Domestic Tyranny,* 159.

67. Catharine A. MacKinnon, *Women's Lives, Men's Laws* (Cambridge, MA: Belknap Press, 2005), 291.

68. Strebeigh, *Equal,* 386.

69. R. Langley and R. Levy, *Wife Beating: The Silent Crisis* (New York: Pocket Books, 1977).

70. Mahoney, "Exit: Power and the Idea of Leaving."

71. MacKinnon, *Women's Lives,* 291.

72. Elizabeth M. Schneider, "Battered Women, Feminist Lawmaking, Privacy, and Equality," in *Women and the United States Constitution:*

History, Interpretation, and Practice, ed. Sibyl A. Schwarzenbach and Patricia Smith (New York: Columbia University Press, 2003), 197–220, 201.

73. Siegel, "Rule of Love," 2169.

74. State v. Rhodes, 61 N.C. (Phil.) 453, 454–457 (1868).

75. Marcia Rockwood, "Courts and Cops: Enemies of Battered Wives," *Ms. Magazine* 5 (April 1977): 19.

76. Dobash and Dobash, *Violence*, 210.

77. Kirsten S. Rambo, *"Trivial Complaints": The Role of Privacy in Domestic Violence Law and Activism in the U.S.* (New York: Columbia University Press, 2009), 33.

78. Dobash and Dobash, *Violence*, 221.

79. U.S. Department of Justice, *Cyberstalking*.

80. Katrina Baum, Shannan Catalano, Michael Rand, and Kristina Rose, *Stalking Victimization in the United States*, Bureau of Justice Statistics, Special Report No. NCJ 224527 (January 2009).

81. Bonnie S. Fisher, Francis T. Cullen, and Michael G. Turner, "Being Pursued: Stalking Victimization in a National Study of College Women," *Criminology and Public Policy* 1 (2002): 257–308.

82. Devennie Wauncka, "The Dangers of Cyberstalking: Educating Law Enforcement and Communities," *Unified Solutions Tribal Community Development Group, Inc., Training and Technical Assistance Newsletter*, March–April 2009, 9, www.unified-solutions.org/Pubs/Newletters/2009_march_april.pdf.

83. Christa Miller, "Cyber Stalking and Bullying—What Law Enforcement Needs to Know," *Law Enforcement Technology* 33, no. 4 (2006): 18.

84. Karen L. Paullet, "An Exploratory Study of Cyberstalking: Students and Law Enforcement in Allegheny County, Pennsylvania," PhD diss., Robert Morris University, 2009.

85. Amanda Hess, "Why Women Aren't Welcome on the Internet. The Next Frontier of Civil Rights," *Pacific Standard Magazine*, January 2014, 45.

86. Marjorie Korn, "Cyberstalking," *Self Magazine*, January 2013, 107.

87. "Man Sentenced to Five Years," CBS (Philadelphia), http://philadelphia.cbslocal.com/2011/03/22/todd-hart-sentenced-to-five-years-for-cyberstalking/ (discussing federal cyber stalking case against Todd Hart who was convicted of stalking and threatening his ex-girlfriend

via email and sentenced to five years in jail); United States v. Cassidy, 814 F. Supp. 2d 574, 576 (D. Md. 2011), *appeal dismissed* (4th Cir. April 11, 2012, 12–4048) (dismissing indictment against defendant who criticized and threatened female Buddhist sect leader because the federal cyber stalking statute, as applied, violated the First Amendment); United States v. Juliano, 2011 WL 635273 (W.D. Pa. Feb. 11, 2011) (dismissing federal cyber stalking charge in exchange for plea to a lesser charge of lying to government in case where defendant sent harassing and threatening e-mail messages to his ex-wife); United States v. Walker, 665 F.3d 212 (1st Cir. 2011), *cert. denied,* 132 S. Ct. 2713 (2012) (defendant was convicted of cyber stalking, and he did not appeal); United States v. Grob, 625 F.3d 1209 (9th Cir. 2010) (defendant pled guilty to one count of cyber stalking for sending twenty-two threatening e-mails and harassing texts to his ex-girlfriend that included pictures of dead and dismembered women); United States v. Humphries, No. 12 Cr. 347 (RWS), 2013 WL 5797116 (S.D.N.Y. Oct. 28, 2013); United States v. Nagel, 2011 WL 4025715 (E.D.N.Y. September 9, 2011) (jury convicted defendant of cyber stalking and physically stalking a television actress); United States v. Petrovic, 701 F.3d 849 (8th Cir. 2012) (jury convicted defendant of cyber stalking based on evidence that he created a website that revealed sexually explicit photographs and videos of his ex-wife and tried to extort his wife of money in exchange for removing them); United States v. Sayer, 2012 WL 1714746 (D. Me. May 15, 2012) (defendant pled guilty to cyber stalking charge based on his creation of fake porn advertisements and social media profiles suggesting that his ex-girlfriend was interested in having sex with strangers); United States v. Shepard, 2012 WL 113027 (D. Ariz. January 13, 2012) (jury convicted defendant of cyber stalking for creating fake porn advertisements and posting ex-girlfriend's naked photos online).

88. Spencer Ackerman, "'Shirtless' FBI Agent Who Hunted Petraeus Also Helped Stop LA Bombing," *Wired Blog,* November 14, 2012, http:// www.wired.com/dangerroom/2012/11/fbi-allen/.

89. U.S. Department of Justice, Office of Violence Against Women, *Report to Congress on Stalking and Domestic Violence, 2005 through 2006* (Rockville, MD: National Criminal Justice Referral Service, 2007), https:// www.ncjrs.gov/pdffiles1/ovw/220827.pdf.

90. Baum et al., *Stalking Victimization in the United States.*

91. Korn, "Cyberstalking," 107.

92. Ibid., 108.

93. Madeleine Davies, "Man Convicted for Horrific Cyber-Stalking of Classmate," *Jezebel*, January 23, 2012, http://jezebel.com/5878418/man-will-serve-2-years-after-horrific-cyb.

94. Meghan Lindner, "UCF Alumna Still Worried After Cyber Stalker's Sentencing," *Central Florida Future*, January 27, 2012, http://www.centralfloridafuture.com/news/ucf-alumna-still-worried-after-cyber-stalker-s-sentencing-1.2690118.

95. D.C. v. R.R., 106 Cal. Rptr. 3d 399 (Ct. App. 2010).

96. Ibid., 413.

97. Mary, February 18, 2008, comment on Christina Chatalian, "Cyber Stalker Terrorizing Family: Former Syracuse Woman Becomes a Target of Cyber Harassment," *CNYcentral.com*, February 15, 2008 (7:10 P.M.), http://www.cnycentral.com/news/news_story.aspx?id=96646#.Tq_57aiwXyo.

98. Ellen Nakashima, "Sexual Threats Stifle Some Female Bloggers," *Washington Post*, April 30, 2007, A1.

99. Telephone interview with Kathy Sierra, November 8, 2011 (notes on file with author).

100. Eric Kurhi, "Police Lack Standards for Cyber Criminals," *Contra Costa Times* (California), February 19, 2007.

101. Laura Cummings, Office of Legislative Research, *Charges and Convictions Under Cyberstalking Laws*, OLR Research Report (February 26, 2009), http://www.cga.ct.gov/2009/rpt/2009-R-0121.htm.

102. National Institute of Justice, *Stalking Research Workshop Meeting Summary* (June 17, 2010), 11, http://nij.gov/topics/crime/stalking/Documents/stalking-research-workshop-summary-june-2010.pdf.

103. Ibid.

104. Ibid., 9.

105. Samantha Nelson, "Annoying Online Posts Could Be Illegal," *PC World*, January 13, 2006, http://www.pcworld.com/article/124373/annoying_online_posts_could_be_illegal.html.

106. National Center for Victims of Crime, "State Laws Falling Short of Current Stalking Realities," news release, January 12, 2007.

107. Trishula Patel, "Prince George's Man Who Used Social Media to Stalk Ex-Wife Sentenced to 85 Years," *Washington Post*, July 18, 2013,

http://www.washingtonpost.com/local/pr-georges-man-who-used
-social-media-to-stalk-ex-wife-is-to-be-sentenced/2013/07/17
/8e86d21c-ed75-11e2-9008-61e94a7ea20d_story.html.

4. Civil Rights Movements, Past and Present

1. Catharine A. MacKinnon, "Sexual Harassment: Its First Decade in Court," in *Feminism Unmodified: Discourses on Life and Law* (Cambridge, MA: Harvard University Press, 1987), 103.

2. Fred Strebeigh, *Equal: Women Reshape American Law* (New York: Norton, 2009), 219; Lin Farley, *Sexual Shakedown: The Sexual Harassment of Women on the Job* (New York: McGraw-Hill 1978), 171.

3. Strebeigh, *Equal,* 224, 219.

4. Clara Bingham and Laura Leedy Gansler, *Class Action* (New York: Anchor Books, 2002), 70.

5. Ibid., 72.

6. Abigail C. Saguy, *What Is Sexual Harassment? From Capitol Hill to the Sorbonne* (Berkeley: University of California Press, 2003), 29–30.

7. Carrie N. Baker, *The Women's Movement against Sexual Harassment* (Cambridge, UK: Cambridge University Press, 2008), 35, 40.

8. Ibid., 40.

9. Elizabeth Schneider, "Battered Women and Feminist Lawmaking," *Women's Rights Law Reporter* 23 (2002): 243–246.

10. Andrea Dworkin, "The Bruise That Doesn't Heal," *Mother Jones* (July 1978): 35.

11. Ibid.; Note, "Legal Responses to Domestic Violence," *Harvard Law Review* 106 (1993): 1498–1620.

12. Kathleen Tierney, "The Battered Women Movement and the Creation of the Wife Beating Problem," *Social Problems* 29 (1982): 207–220, 210.

13. Jack M. Balkin, *Constitutional Redemption* (Cambridge, MA: Harvard University Press, 2011).

14. Reva Siegel, "The Rule of Love: Wife Beating as Prerogative and Privacy," *Yale Law Journal* 105 (1996): 2117–2208, 2173.

15. See generally Leigh Goodmark, *A Troubled Marriage: Domestic Violence and the Legal System* (New York: New York University Press, 2011) (exploring how excessive focus on physical violence prevents the legal system from tackling serious harms inflicted by domestic abusers and cri-

tiquing mandatory arrest policies as insufficiently attentive to victims' autonomy).

16. A study conducted in 1986 found that while 63 percent of domestic violence victims agreed with the statement "The best way to deal with marital violence is to arrest the offender," only 4 percent of police officers shared that sentiment. More than five years after the battered women's movement had caught the public's attention, the police continued to attribute responsibility to victims in the view that victims brought the violence on themselves, could have avoided the violence by being quiet, or enjoyed being hit. Although police attitudes have evolved with the help of legal change, domestic violence remains a rampant problem. N. Zoe Hilton, "Police Intervention and Public Opinion," in *Legal Responses to Wife Assault*, ed. N. Zoe Hilton (Newbury Park, CA: Sage, 1993), 37–61, 40–41.

17. Martha R. Mahoney, "Exit: Power and the Idea of Leaving in Love, Work, and the Confirmation Hearings," *Southern California Law Review* 65 (1992): 1283–1320.

18. Patricia Sanchez Abril explains that online social networking sites generally refuse to take down material that is purportedly defamatory or embarrassing. Patricia Sanchez Abril, "A (My)Space of One's Own: On Privacy and Online Social Networks," *Northwestern Journal of Technology and Intellectual Property* 6 (2007): 73–89, 82.

19. "Washington Hears Range Women Advocates," *Hibbing (MN) Daily Tribune*, May 29, 2011, http://www.hibbingmn.com/community_voice /milestones/article_2c0ac669-5f2c-5313-bac3-b0db02aa0797.html (citing testimony of the National Network to End Domestic Violence and the Minnesota Coalition for Battered Women in roundtable discussion with Senator Al Franken).

20. Michael Ellsberg, "Tucker Max Gives Up the Game," *Forbes*, January 18, 2012, http://www.forbes.com/sites/michaelellsberg/2012/01/18/tucker -max-gives-up-the-game/; Tucker Max, http://www.tuckermax.com/.

21. Deborah L. Rhode, "Sexual Harassment," *Southern California Law Review* 65 (1992): 1459–1466, 1462.

22. Nathan Jurgenson, "The IRL Fetish," The New Inquiry Blog, June 28, 2012, http://thenewinquiry.com/essays/the-irl-fetish/.

23. Julie E. Cohen, *Configuring the Networked Self: Law, Code, and the Play of Everyday Practice* (New Haven, CT: Yale University Press, 2012).

24. Paul Bocij, *Cyberstalking: Harassment in the Internet Age and How to Protect Your Family* (Westport, CT: Praeger, 2004), 165–166.

25. La. Rev. Stat. Ann. § 14:40.2 (West 2012); Vt. Stat. Ann. tit. 13, § 1061 (West 2012).

26. National Center for Victims of Crime, *The Model Stalking Code Revisited: Responding to the New Realities of Stalking* (Washington, DC: National Center for Victims of Crime, 2007), 16, http://www.victimsof crime.org/docs/src/model-stalking-code.pdf?sfvrsn=0.

27. Hearing on H.R. 1869, the Stalking and Victim Protection Act of 1999, before the H. Comm. on the Judiciary, 106th Cong. (1999) (statement of Jayne Hitchcock).

28. Jayne Hitchcock, *Net Crimes and Misdemeanors: Outmaneuvering Web Spammers, Stalkers, and Con Artists* (Medford, MA: Information Today, 2006), 8–9.

29. Hearing on H.R. 1869, the Stalking and Victim Protection Act of 1999, before the H. Comm. on the Judiciary, 106th Cong. (1999) (statement of Jayne Hitchcock).

30. Michael Dresser, "New Md. Law Will Ban Harassment by Email," *Baltimore Sun,* May 21, 1998, http://articles.baltimoresun.com/1998 -05-21/news/1998141126_1_harassment-e-mail-message-hitchcock.

31. Hearing on H.R. 1869, the Stalking and Victim Protection Act of 1999, before the H. Comm. on the Judiciary, 106th Cong. (1999) (statement of Jayne Hitchcock).

32. Hearing on H.R. 1869, the Stalking and Victim Protection Act of 1999, before the H. Comm. on the Judiciary, 106th Cong. (1999) (statement of David Beatty, director of public policy, National Center for Victims of Crime).

33. Molly M. Ginty, "Cyberstalking Turns Web Technologies into Weapons," *Ottawa Citizen,* April 7, 2012, J1.

34. End Revenge Porn, http://www.endrevengeporn.org.

35. Rhoda Kelly (pseudonym), "My Ex Posted 'Revenge Porn' Photos of Me," *Nerve,* January 8, 2013, http://www.nerve.com/love-sex/true -stories/my-ex-posted-revenge-porn-photos-of-me.

36. Bekah Wells, "Revenge Porn: Whose Fault Is It Anyway?," Women against Revenge Porn (blog), no date, http://www.womenagainstre vengeporn.com/blog/.

37. Brad Stone, "A Call for Manners in the World of Nasty Blogs," *New York Times*, April 9, 2007, A1.

38. Cheryl Lindsey Seelhoff, "A Chilling Effect: The Oppression and Silencing of Women Journalists and Bloggers Worldwide," *Off Our Backs* 37, no. 1 (2007): 18–21, 20.

39. Robert Scoble, "Taking the Week Off," Scobleizer (blog), March 26, 2007, http://scobleizer.com/2007/03/26/taking-the-week-off/; comment of Robert Scoble to same post, March 26, 2007 (4:34 P.M.).

40. Tim Adams, "How the Internet Created an Age of Rage," *Observer* (U.K.), July 23, 2011, http://www.guardian.co.uk/technology/2011/jul/24/internet-anonymity-trolling-tim-adams.

41. "Cyber Harassment and the Law," *On Point with Tom Ashbrook*, NPR, March 3, 2009, http://onpoint.wbur.org/2009/03/03/cyber-harassment.

42. Alyssa Rosenberg, "Threat of the Day," Think Progress (blog), November 3, 2011 (1:34 P.M.), http://thinkprogress.org/alyssa/2011/11/04/361717/threat-of-the-day/.

43. Kathy Sierra, "What Happened," Head Rush (blog), May 30, 2007, http://headrush.typepad.com/whathappened.html.

44. David Fagundes, "CCR Symposium: In Defense of Self Defense," Concurring Opinions (blog), April 16, 2009, http://www.concurringopinions.com/archives/2009/04/ccr_symposium_i.html.

45. thewhatifgirl, October 11, 2011, comment on Mary, "Online Harassment as a Daily Hazard: When Trolls Feed Themselves," Geek Feminism (blog), October 11, 2011, http://geekfeminism.org/2011/10/11/online-harassment-as-a-daily-hazard-when-trolls-feed-themselves/.

46. Dale Spender, *Nattering on the Net: Women, Power and Cyberspace* (North Melbourne, Australia: Spinifex Press, 1995), 210.

47. National Centre for Cyberstalking Research, *Cyberstalking in the United Kingdom*, 28, http://www.bedo.ac.uk/__data/assets/pdf_file/0003/83109/ECHO_Pilot_Final.pdf.

48. Interview with Dissent Doe, Washington, DC, June 4, 2012 (notes on file with author).

49. Jill Filipovic, "AutoAdmit's Anthony Ciolli Loses Job Offer," Feministe (blog), May 3, 2007, http://www.feministe.us/blog/archives/2007/05/03/autoadmits-antho.

50. "Official Jill Filipovic RAPE Thread," AutoAdmit, April 27, 2007 (8:33 A.M.), http://www.xoxohth.com/thread.php?thread_id=621704 &forum_id=2; "Jill Filipovic Has a Sister," AutoAdmit, June 3, 2007 (10:42 P.M.), http://www.autoadmit.com/thread.php?thread_id=639 509&mc=3&forum_id=2.

51. Jill Filipovic, "'Revenge Porn' Is about Degrading Women Sexually and Professionally," *Guardian* (U.K.), January 28, 2013, http://www. theguardian.com/commentisfree/2013/jan/28/revenge-porn-degrades -women.

52. Valerie Aurora, "Adria Richards' Story Shows How Sexual Harassment Endures in Tech Community," *Slate,* March 25, 2013, http:// www.slate.com/blogs/future_tense/2013/03/25/adria_richards_her _firing_online_harassment_show_how_sexual_harassment_endures .html.

53. Kris Holt, "As Adria Richards Backlash Grows Violent, SendGrid Publicly Fires Her," The Daily Dot (blog), March 21, 2013, http:// www.dailydot.com/news/adria-richards-fired-sendgrid-violent-back lash/.

54. Kashmir Hill, "'Sexism' Public Shaming via Twitter Leads to Two People Getting Fired (Including the Shamer)," *Forbes.com,* March 21, 2013, http://www.forbes.com/sites/kashmirhill/2013/03/21/sexism -public-shaming-via-twitter-leads-to-two-people-getting-fired-includ ing-the-shamer/.

55. Vindu Goel, "Fight Back against the Cyberbullies and Trolls," Vindu's Views from the Valley (blog), *San Jose Mercury-News,* April 1, 2007 (11:00 P.M.) (on file with author).

56. Steven D, "Kathy Sierra and Online Hate Crimes," Booman Tribune, April 2, 2007, http://www.boomantribune.com/story/2007/4/2/203416 /5935.

57. Anony Mouse, April 11, 2007 (1:39 P.M.), comment on Tim O'Reilly, "Code of Conduct: Lessons So Far," O'Reilly Radar (blog), April 11, 2007, http://radar.oreilly.com/2007/04/code-of-conduct-lessons -learne.html (comments no longer available online).

58. Laura Lemay, "Kathy Sierra, or Imminent Death of the Net Predicted," Lauralemay (blog), March 28, 2007, http://blog.lauralemay.com/2007 /03/kathy-sierra-or-imminent-death-of-the-net-predicted.html#more -1616.

59. Erik Ortiz, "Steubenville High School Students Joke about Alleged Rape in Highly-Charged Case against Big Red Football Players," *New York Daily News*, January 3, 2013, http://www.nydailynews.com/news /crime/steubenville-students-laugh-alleged-rape-article-1.1232113.

60. Adrian Chen, "The FBI Raided the Steubenville Anonymous Guy's House. Here He Is," *Gawker*, June 6, 2013, http://gawker.com/the-fbi -raided-steubenville-anonymous-guys-house-heie-511634071.

61. [Author redacted], "Better Titty Fuck: [woman's name] or [woman's name]?," AutoAdmit, June 7, 2011 (2:14 P.M.), http://www.xoxohth .com/thread.php?thread_id=1667847&mc=1&forum_id=2.

62. [Author redacted], "Anyone at Northwestern know this [woman's name] whore?," AutoAdmit, February 24, 2011 (5:53 P.M.), http://auto admit.com/thread.php?thread_id=1572160&mc=17&forum_id=2.

63. Lori Andrews, *I Know Who You Are and I Saw What You Did: Social Networks and the Death of Privacy* (New York: Free Press, 2011), 135.

64. Patrickhammscandal, "Scandal Hits Harvard," *Newsvine*, June 7, 2008, http://patrickhammscandal.newsvine.com/_news/2008/06/07 /1551800-scandal-hits-harvard.

65. Lena Chen, "Slut-Shaming in Action: A Warning to Readers," The Chicktionary (blog), January 24, 2011, http://thechicktionary.com/post /2915627917/slut-shaming in action-a-warning-to-readers.

66. "Is this Gina Chen the Slut Sister of Porn Star Lena Chen?," Meme Generator, http://memegenerator.net/instance/2981217 (no longer available online).

67. [Author redacted], "Lena Chen Interview on Lena Chen Nude Pix Scandal," AutoAdmit, January 9, 2010 (4:05 P.M.), http://www.xoxohth .com/thread.php?thread_id=1185708&forum_id=2.

68. Lena Chen, "What Slut Shaming Looks Like," The Chicktionary (blog), May 25, 2011, http://thechicktionary.com/post/5838755243/this -is-what-slut-shaming-looks-like.

69. Yeah O, "Oops! Herpesblog Surfers Revealed," Who's Enabling Lena Chen's Bipolar Nymphomania? (blog), March 12, 2011, http://lenachen -enablers.blogspot.com/2011/03/oops-herpesblog-surfers-revealed .html (on file with author).

70. [Author redacted], "LOL . . . Lena Chen Bitches about People Mocking Her AGAIN," AutoAdmit, January 24, 2011 (7:16 P.M.), http://www .xoxohth.com/thread.php?forum_id=2&thread_id=1544376.

71. Obama's Teleprompter, "Whatever Happened to Lena Chen (Harvard Slut)?," AutoAdmit, March 20, 2009 (2:21 A.M.), http://www.xoxohth .com/thread.php?thread_id=956025&mc=16$forum_id=2.

72. Telephone interview with Lena Chen, October 12, 2011 (notes on file with author).

73. Yeah O, "Oops! Herpesblog Surfers Revealed."

74. Chen, "Slut Shaming in Action."

75. Stephanie Brail, "The Price of Admission: Harassment and Free Speech in the Wild, Wild West," in *Wired Women: Gender and New Realities in Cyberspace,* ed. Lynn Cherny and Elizabeth Reba Weise (Seattle: Seal Press, 1996), 141–157, 147.

5. What Law Can and Should Do Now

1. Restatement (Second) of Torts 559 (1969).

2. Benjamin Zipursky, "Snyder v. Phelps, Outrageousness and the Open Texture of Tort Law," *DePaul Law Review* 60 (2011): 473–520.

3. Restatement (Second) of Torts § 559 (1969); William L. Prosser, *Handbook of the Law of Torts,* 4th ed. (St. Paul, MN: West, 1971), § 117, at 816. Hacking someone's password-protected account implicates the intrusion-upon-seclusion tort, which covers the disruption of someone's private affairs in a manner that would be highly offensive to a reasonable person. Steinbach v. Village of Forest Park, No. 06-4215, 2009 WL 2605283 (N.D. Ill. Aug. 25, 2009) (finding that the unauthorized forwarding of e-mail messages amounted to intrusion upon seclusion).

4. Daniel J. Solove and Paul M. Schwartz, *Privacy Law Fundamentals 2013* (Portsmouth, NH: International Association of Privacy Professionals, 2013), 42.

5. Derek Bambauer, "Exposed," *Minnesota Law Review* 98 (forthcoming 2014); Derek Bambauer, "Beating Revenge Porn with Copyright," January 25, 2013, https://blogs.law.harvard.edu/infolaw/2013/01/25 /beating-revenge-porn-with-copyright/.

6. Meg Garvin, Alison Wilkinson, and Sarah LeClair, "Protecting Victims' Privacy Rights: The Use of Pseudonyms in Civil Suits," *Violence against Women Bulletin,* July 2011, http://law.lclark.edu/live/files /11778-protecting-victims-privacy-rights-the-use-of.

7. Those collateral consequences can be harsh and particularly troubling for racial minorities, as we have seen when it comes to drug crimes. My colleague Michael Pinard has done important work on the collateral consequences of convictions. See Michael Pinard, "Collateral Consequences of Criminal Convictions: Confronting Issues of Race and Dignity," *New York University Law Review* 85 (2010); Michael Pinard, "An Integrated Perspective of the Collateral Consequences of Criminal Convictions and the Reentry of Formerly Incarcerated Individuals," *Boston University Law Review* 85 (2006). As I explore in Chapter 7, cyber harassment laws are seriously underenforced, muting some of the concerns surrounding a legal agenda including overcriminalization and its disparate impact on race.

8. United States v. Kammersell, 196 F.3d 1137 (10th Cir. 1999) (affirming a conviction under 18 U.S.C. § 875 after the defendant sent a bomb threat over instant messenger to his girlfriend's computer in the same state in the hope that the threat would allow the defendant's girlfriend to leave work early); Holcomb v. Commonwealth, 709 S.E.2d 711 (Va. Ct. App. 2011) (upholding a conviction under Virginia's threat statute Section 18.2-60(A)(1) for threats made on a defendant's MySpace profile because threats need not be sent to a victim directly and can be publicly posted online, where the defendant proclaimed that he "just had to stab" the victim and "slit [her] neck into a fountain drink" and stated, "Never lettin' go ya throat becomes my obsession" and "Murder makes me so happy").

9. Cal. Rev. Code Ann. § 422 (West 2012). A California security guard pled guilty to cyber stalking for impersonating a woman in chat rooms, revealing her home address, and stating that she had rape fantasies, which led to six men coming to her home at night and saying that they wanted to rape her. *Cyberstalking: A New Challenge for Law Enforcement and Industry*, Report from the attorney general to the vice president (Washington, DC: U.S. Department of Justice, 1999); Greg Miller and Davan Mahraj, "North Hollywood Man Charged in 1st Cyberstalking Case," *Los Angeles Times*, January 22, 1999, A1.

10. Susan Price, Office of Legislative Research, "OLR Backgrounder: Cyberstalking," August 7, 2012; Alison M. Smith, "Protection of Children Online: Federal and State Laws Addressing Cyberstalking, Cyberharassment, and Cyberbullying," Congressional Research Service,

RL 34651, October 19, 2009. See, for example, Cal. Penal Code § 646.9 (West 2012).

11. Naomi Harlin Goono, "Cyberstalking, a New Crime: Evaluating the Effectiveness of Current State and Federal Laws," *Missouri Law Review* 72 (2007): 125–198, 134–135.

12. Ala. Code § 13A-11-8 (West 2012); Ariz. Rev. Stat. Ann. § 13-2921 (West 2012); Cal. Penal Code § 653m (West 2012); Colo. Rev. Stat. § 18-9-111 (West 2012).

13. Price, "Cyberstalking" (describing variations in the thirty-four state cyber stalking laws surveyed by the National Conference of State Legislatures).

14. 18 U.S.C. § 2261A(2) (2012).

15. Hearing on Reauthorization of the Violence against Women Act, before the S. Comm. on the Judiciary, 109th Congress 28 (2005) (statement of Mary Lou Leary, executive director of the National Center for Victims of Crime).

16. 47 U.S.C. § 223(a)(1)(c) (2006).

17. For instance, in *United States v. Bowker*, 372 F.3d 365 (6th Cir. 2004), a defendant was convicted under VAWA for making more than a hundred anonymous phone calls to a television news reporter that were threatening and sexual in nature.

18. Ohio Rev. Code Ann. § 2903.211(A)(2) (West 2009).

19. Cal. Penal Code § 653.2 (West 2012).

20. Cal. Penal Code § 528.5 (West 2012).

21. Xiaomin Huang, Peter Radkwoski, and Peter Roman, "Computer Crimes," *American Criminal Law Review* 44 (2007): 285–336, 298.

22. United States v. Sutcliffe, 505 F.3d 944, 959 (9th Cir. 2007).

23. Catharine MacKinnon made this point in her transformative book *Sexual Harassment of Working Women*. As she explained, torts redress injuries to one's person rather than to public and shared social existence. Catharine A. MacKinnon, *Sexual Harassment of Working Women* (New Haven, CT: Yale University Press, 1979), 88. She argued that to the extent that tort theory "failed to capture the broadly social sexuality/employment nexus that comprises the injury of sexual harassment, by treating the incidents as if they are outrages particular to an individual woman rather than integral to her social status as a woman worker, the personal approach on the legal level fails to analyze the relevant dimensions of the problem" (88).

24. C.L., March 12, 2009 (10:37 P.M.), comment on Danielle Citron, "Cyber Harassment: Yes, It Is a Woman's Thing," Concurring Opinions (blog), March 10, 2009 (11:23 A.M.), http://www.concurringopinions .com/archives/2009/03/cyber_harassmen.html/comment-page-1#comment-44054.

25. Amanda Hess, "Why Women Aren't Welcome on the Internet: The Next Frontier of Civil Rights," *Pacific Standard Magazine,* January 2014, 45.

26. "Female Bloggers Face Harassment," *Women in Higher Education,* June 1, 2007, 5.

27. Frederick M. Lawrence, *Punishing Hate: Bias Crimes under American Law* (Cambridge, MA: Harvard University Press, 1999), 167–169.

28. Lisa Nakamura, *Digitizing Race: Visual Cultures of the Internet* (Minneapolis: University of Minnesota Press, 2008).

29. Martha Chamallas, *Introduction to Feminist Legal Theory,* 2nd ed. (New York: Aspen, 2003), 57–58.

30. 720 Ill. Comp. Stat. 5/12-7.1 (2012).

31. Mass. Gen. Laws ch. 265, § 37 (2012).

32. See, e.g., Fla. Stat. 760.51 (2012).

33. See, e.g., Ala. Code 13A-5-13 (2012); Cal. Penal Code 422.7 (2012).

34. Fred Strebeigh, *Equal: Women Reshape American Law* (New York: Norton, 2009).

35. Catharine A. MacKinnon, "The Logic of Experience: Reflections on the Development of Sexual Harassment Law," *Georgetown Law Journal* 90 (2002): 813–833, 826, 830.

36. Ibid., 831; U.S. Equal Employment Opportunity Commission, "Harassment Charges: FY 1992–FY 1996," accessed July 8, 2013, http:// www.eeoc.gov/eeoc/statistics/enforcement/harassment-a.cfm.

37. Martha Nussbaum, *Sex and Social Justice* (New York: Oxford University Press, 1999), 20.

38. Jack M. Balkin, *Cultural Software: A Theory of Ideology* (New Haven, CT: Cambridge University Press, 1998), 14.

39. United States v. Sutcliffe, 505 F.3d 944 (9th Cir. 2007).

40. Jerry DeMarco, "NJ 'Devilfish' Gets 5 Years in Federal Prison for Threatening Latino Civil Rights Groups," *Cliff View Pilot* (NJ), April 18, 2011.

41. Indictment, United States v. Vincent Johnson, No. 3:10-cr-0076-AET (D.N.J. Feb. 4, 2010).

42. Colo. Rev. Stat. Ann. § 18-3-602 (West 2012).
43. Robert D'Ovidio and James Doyle, "A Study on Cyberstalking: Understanding Investigative Hurdles," *FBI Law Enforcement Bulletin*, March 2003, 14.
44. See, e.g., Ala. Code § 13A-5-13 (2012); Cal. Penal Code § 422.7 (2012); Del. Code Ann. tit. 11, § 1304 (2012); Haw. Rev. Stat. § 706-662 (2012); Ky. Rev. Stat. Ann. § 532.031 (2012); Md. Code Ann., Crim. Law § 10-304 (West 2012); Mich. Comp. Laws § 750.147b (2012); Miss. Code Ann. § 99-19-305 (2012); Mo. Rev. Stat. § 557.035 (2012); Neb. Rev. Stat. § 28-11 (2012); Nev. Rev. Stat. § 193.1675 (2012); N.M. Stat. Ann. § 31-18B-3 (2012); N.Y. Penal Law § 485.05 (McKinney 2012); Ohio Rev. Code Ann. § 2927.12 (2012); 18 Pa. Const. Stat. Ann. § 2710 (2012); R.I.Gen. Laws § 12-19-38 (2012); Vt. Stat. Ann. tit. 13, § 1455 (2012); W. Va. Code § 61-6-21 (2012); Wis. Stat. § 939.645 (2012). Although the hate crimes statute in Missouri creates an additional offense when a perpetrator commits harassment motivated by hate, a portion of the harassment statute—Mo. Rev. Stat. § 565.090.1(5) (2012)—was recently ruled unconstitutional. State v. Vaughn, 366 S.W.3d 513, 519–20 (Mo. 2012) (holding that 565.090.1(5), which criminalizes conduct when a perpetrator "knowingly makes repeated unwanted communication to another person," is unconstitutionally overbroad but severable from the rest of the harassment statute).
45. My research assistants and I discovered these ten cases by researching electronic case system PACER, Westlaw, and online search engines.
46. "Man Sentenced to Five Years," CBS (Philadelphia), http://philadelphia.cbslocal.com/2011/03/22/todd-hart-sentenced-to-five-years-for-cyberstalking/ (discussing federal cyber stalking case against Todd Hart who was convicted of stalking and threatening his ex-girlfriend via email and sentenced to five years in jail); United States v. Juliano, No. 2:10CR00234 (W.D. Pa. May 3, 2011) (dismissing federal cyber stalking charge in exchange for plea to a lesser charge of lying to government in case where defendant sent harassing and threatening e-mail messages to his ex-wife); United States v. Walker, 665 F.3d 212 (1st Cir. 2011) (defendant was convicted of cyber stalking; he did not appeal his conviction); United States v. Grob, 625 F.3d 1209 (9th Cir. 2010) (defendant pled guilty to one count of cyber stalking for sending twenty-two threatening e-mails and harassing texts to his ex-girlfriend that

included pictures of dead and dismembered women); United States v. Nagel, 2011 WL 4025715 (E.D.N.Y. Sept. 9, 2011) (jury convicted defendant of cyber stalking and physically stalking a television actress); United States v. Petrovic, 701 F.3d 849 (8th Cir. 2012) (jury convicted defendant of cyber stalking based on evidence that he created a website that revealed sexually explicit photographs and videos of his ex-wife and tried to extort his wife of money in exchange for removing them); United States v. Sayer, No. 11-cr-00113-DBH, 2012 WL 6676889 (D. Me. Aug. 9, 2012) (defendant pled guilty to cyber stalking charge based on his creation of fake porn advertisements and social media profiles suggesting that his ex-girlfriend was interested in having sex with strangers); United States v. Shepard, 2012 WL 113027 (D. Ariz. Jan. 13, 2012) (jury convicted defendant of cyber stalking for creating fake porn advertisements and posting ex-girlfriend's nude photos online); United States v. Humphries, No. 12 Cr. 347 (RWS), 2013 WL 5797116 (S.D.N.Y. Oct. 28, 2013); United States v. Cassidy, 814 F. Supp. 2d 574 (D. Md. 2011) (vacating cyber stalking conviction in case involving tweets directed to a Buddhist monk because online abuse concerned protected speech about matter of public importance).

47. 18 U.S.C. 245(b)(5) (2012).

48. Colo. Rev. Stat. Ann. § 18-9-121 (West 2012).

49. Fed. R. Civ. P. 10(a) ("title of the complaint must name all the parties"); Fed. R. Civ. P. 17(a)(1) ("action must be prosecuted in the name of the real party in interest").

50. Gonsalves v. Conseco Insurance Co., No. Civ. S-06-0058, 2006 WL 3486962, at *6 (E.D. Cal. Dec. 1, 2006) (denying defendant's motion for summary judgment because a reasonable jury could find that posting plaintiff's name and social security number on a website amounted to extreme and outrageous conduct); Delfino v. Agilent Techs., Inc., 52 Cal. Rptr. 3d 376, 382 n.6, 392 (Ct. App. 2006) (concluding that e-mail messages and postings threatening, "You can look forward to all your fingers getting broken, several kicks to the ribs and mouth, break some teeth, and a cracked head," may constitute extreme and outrageous acts).

51. Doe I v. Individuals, 561 F. Supp. 2d 249, 256–57 (D. Conn. 2008).

52. In privacy suits, this backlash phenomenon is often referred to as the "Streisand effect." Barbra Streisand sued a photographer whose aerial

photograph of her mansion appeared in an online collection of pictures. Before Streisand filed the suit, the image had hardly been viewed. Once word of the suit got out, hundreds of thousands of people downloaded the image. In some respects, the Streisand effect does not capture what happened to the law student because posters seemingly sought to punish her for suing, a retaliation of sorts. The Streisand effect does not implicate the same sort of malice, at least in the way that it has been understood as the lesson that making a fuss over privacy can end up drawing attention to the information that the person wants to keep private. Criminal punishments generally have not provoked retaliatory online abuse, perhaps because a prosecutor's willingness to pursue criminal charges deters the defendant's supporters from risking their own criminal prosecution.

53. Conn. Gen Stat. § 46a-58 (2012).

54. Conn. Gen. Stat. § 53A-1811-L (2012).

55. Susan Price, "OLR Backgrounder: Cyberstalking," *OLR Research Report*, August 7, 2012, http://www.cga.ct.gov/2012/rpt/2012-R-0293.htm (explaining that until 2012 Connecticut's stalking law required that the defendant "lie in wait" for victim or appear in close physical proximity to the victim).

56. Conn. Gen. Stat. § 53A-182B (2012); Conn. Gen. Stat. 53A-183 (2012).

57. The privacy scholars Daniel Solove and Joel Reidenberg helpfully talked me through these and other problems related to prosecuting cyber mobs.

58. United States v. Bayer, 331 U.S. 532, 542 (1947).

59. 18 U.S.C. § 371 (2012).

60. The federal cyber stalking statute would not cover the abuser's actions because it applies only to defendants who live in different states from their victims.

61. United States v. Petrovic, No. S1-4:10CR415 HEA, 2011 WL 3880581 (E.D. Mo. Mar. 17, 2011), *report and recommendation adopted*, 2011 WL 3880504 (E.D. Mo. Sept. 2, 2011), *aff'd*, 701 F.3d 849 (8th Cir. 2012).

62. United States v. Sayer, No. 2:11-CR-113-DBH, 2012 WL 1714746 (D. Me. May 15, 2012); Susan Brenner, "Wi-Fi, Curtilage and Kyllo," Cyb3rcrim3 (blog), June 27, 2012, http://cyb3rcrim3.blogspot.com/2012/06/wi-fi-curtilage-and-kyllo.html; "Biddeford Man Indicted on Cy-

berstalking, Identity Theft," *Bangor (ME) Daily News,* July 14, 2011, http://bangordailynews.com/2011/07/14/news/portland/biddeford -man-indicted-in-cyberstalking-id-theft/. In another case, Shawn Memarian pleaded guilty to cyber stalking under Section 2261A(2)(B), admitting that he sent threatening e-mails to the victim and created fake personal advertisements in which he impersonated the victim, provided her home address, and claimed her interest in sex, after which over thirty men showed up at her house seeking sex. Plea Agreement, United States v. Shawn Memarian, Civil No. 10-0870-CV-W-NKL,Crim. No. 08-CR-00128-W-NKL (W.D. Mo. January 8, 2009).

63. Fla. Stat. Ann. § 784.048 (2012).

64. Daniel J. Solove, *The Future of Reputation: Gossip, Rumor, and Privacy on the Internet* (New Haven, CT: Yale University Press, 2007), 119.

65. Daniel J. Solove and Paul M. Schwartz, *Information Privacy Law,* 4th ed. (New York: Aspen, 2012).

66. See, e.g., Daily Times Democrat v. Graham, 162 So.2d 474 (Ala. 1964) (upholding public disclosure claim in case where newspaper published a photo in which the wind had blown a woman's skirt high enough to reveal her underwear).

67. Doe v. Hofstetter, No. 11-cv-02209-DME-MJW, 2012 WL 2319052, at *1, *8–9 (June 13, 2012). Not only did the court find that the plaintiff sufficiently stated a claim for intentional infliction of emotional distress, but it upheld the plaintiff's claim for negligent infliction of emotional distress despite the general requirement of physical injury because the unique circumstances of the case made clear that the plaintiff's distress was trustworthy and genuine. See also Doe v. Hofstetter, No. 11-cv-02209-DME-MJW, 2012 WL 2319052, at *7 (June 13, 2012) (awarding plaintiff damages for intentional infliction of emotional distress where defendant posted her intimate photographs online, e-mailed them to her husband, and created fake Twitter accounts displaying them).

6. Updating the Law: The Harassers

1. People v. Barber, 2014 N.Y. Slip. Op. 50193(U) (N.Y. Sup. Ct. Feb. 18, 2014); Erin Donaghue, "Judge Throws Out New York Revenge

Porn Case," CBS.com, February 25, 2014, http://www.cbsnews.com /news/judge-throws-out-new-york-revenge-porn-case/.

2. See, e.g., La. Rev. Stat. Ann. § 14:40.2 (West 2012); Vt. Stat. Ann. tit. 13, § 1061 (West 2012).

3. National Center for Victims of Crimes, *The Model Stalking Code Revisited: Responding to the New Realities of Stalking* (Washington, DC: National Center for Victims of Crime, 2007), 16, http://www.victim sofcrime.org/docs/src/model-stalking-code.pdf?sfvrsn=0.

4. 47 U.S.C.A. § 223(a)(1)(C) (West 2013).

5. Sonia E. Velazquez, Michelle Garcia, and Elizabeth Joyce, "Mobilizing a Community Response to Stalking: The Philadelphia Story," *Police Chief Magazine,* January 2009, http://www.policechiefmagazine .org/magazine/index.cfm?fuseaction=display_arch&article_id=1702 &issue_id=12009.

6. As I shall soon discuss, Jane had no leverage to press the site operator to take down the post, and the site operator refused to do so unless she paid for the site's takedown services. She was terrified for her life. I spoke to Jane just after the post appeared online, and she felt so afraid that she did not go into work for days. Telephone interview with "Jane," May 7, 2013 (notes on file with author).

7. Revenge porn is also sometimes referred to as "nonconsensual pornography" and "involuntary pornography."

8. Samuel Warren and Louis Brandeis, "The Right to Privacy," *Harvard Law Review* 4 (1890): 193–220, 219. Warren and Brandeis noted that possible criminal legislation could punish as a felony the publication of "any statement concerning the private life or affairs of another, after being requested in writing not to publish such statement," provided the statement does not concern someone's qualifications for public office or profession or involve a matter of public interest (219 n.3).

9. 5 U.S.C. § 552(i)(1).

10. 42 U.S.C.A. § 1320d-6.

11. Rebecca Rosenbaum, "Banker Filming Trysts," *New York Post,* December 16, 2014, http://nypost.com/2014/01/16/money-manager-says-sex -cams-were-for-his-dog/.

12. Professor Mary Anne Franks and I explore these issues in our forthcoming essay, "Criminalizing Revenge Porn," which will be published in the *Wake Forest Law Review.*

13. See Helen Nissenbaum, "Privacy as Contextual Integrity," *Washington Law Review* 79 (2004): 119–158.

14. *Protecting Consumer Privacy in an Era of Rapid Change: A Proposed Framework for Businesses and Policymakers,* preliminary FTC staff report (December 2010), http://www.ftc.gov/os/2010/12/101201privacy report.pdf.

15. 18 U.S.C. § 1801 (2012).

16. N.J. Stat. Ann. § 2C:14-9 (West 2012).

17. N.J. Stat. Ann. §§ 2C:43-1 through 43-3 (West 2012).

18. State v. Parsons, 2011 WL 6089210 (N.J. Super. Ct. App. Div. Dec. 8, 2011).

19. "State 'Revenge Porn' Legislation," National Council for State Legislatures, March 23, 2014, http://www.ncsl.org/research/telecommunica tions-and-information-technology/state-revenge-porn-legislation.aspx.

20. Thomas Peter, "'Tainted Love: US Lawmakers Move to Make Revenge Porn Illegal," *RT,* January 31, 2014, http://rt.com/usa/revenge-porn -illegal-states-482/.

21. Associated Press, "Revenge Porn Victims Press for New Laws," November 15, 2013, http://abclocal.go.com/ktrk/story?section=news/national _world&id=9326829.

22. See Danielle Keats Citron and Mary Anne Franks, "Criminalizing Revenge Porn," *Wake Forest Law Review* (forthcoming).

23. Mary Anne Franks, "Why We Need a Federal Criminal Law Response to Revenge Porn," Concurring Opinions (blog), February 15, 2013 (9:51 A.M.), http://www.concurringopinions.com/archives/2013/02/why -we-need-a-federal-criminal-law-response-to-revenge-porn.html.

24. I am grateful to Lee Rowland, who encouraged me to think about a takedown remedy in the federal context. Rowland wisely noted that in the copyright context, individuals issue takedown notices to site operators without court orders. Sites comply with them because they want to avoid liability. In the criminal context, a takedown order would issue only after the criminal matter was adjudicated with all of the protections of a criminal trial.

25. Helen Lewis, "Dear the Internet, This is Why You Can't Have Anything Nice," *New Statesman* (blog), June 12, 2012 (11:34 A.M.), http:// www.newstatesman.com/blogs/internet/2012/06/dear-internet-why -you-cant-have-anything-nice.

26. E-mail from Anita Sarkeesian to author, February 6, 2014.

27. Interview with Anita Sarkeesian, September 14, 2013 (notes on file with author).

28. Helen Lewis, "This Is What Online Harassment Looks Like," *New Statesman* (blog), July 6, 2012 (9:30 A.M.), http://www.newstatesman.com/blogs/internet/2012/07/what-online-harassment-looks.

29. Kevin Morris, "Anita Sarkeesian Haters Flood TED Talk with Misogynist Comments," The Daily Dot, December 6, 2012, http://www.daily dot.com/culture/anita-sarkeesian-ted-talk-misogynist-comments/.

30. Lewis, "This Is What Online Harassment Looks Like."

31. E-mail from Anita Sarkeesian to author, January 26, 2014 (on file with author); e-mail from Anita Sarkeesian to author, February 6, 2014 (on file with author).

32. Office of Attorney General of California, "California's Criminal and Civil Laws Related to Hate Crimes," http://oag.ca.gov/civil/htm/laws (updated February 25, 1999).

33. "Not Alone: Widespread Internet Hate," New Wave Radical (blog), August 8, 2007, http://newwaveradfem.wordpress.com/?s=attack.

34. E-mail from Anita Sarkeesian to author, January 26, 2014.

35. danah boyd, "Safe Havens for Hate Speech Are Irresponsible," Zephoria (blog), March 26, 2007, http://www.zephoria.org/thoughts/archives/2007/03/26/safe_havens_for.html.

36. 42 U.S.C. § 1981 (2006).

37. Vietnamese Fishermen's Ass'n v. Knights of the Ku Klux Klan, 518 F. Supp. 993, 1001–1004 (S.D. Tex. 1981) (upholding judgment in a Section 1981 case, where hooded Klan members threatened violence and burned crosses to prevent Vietnamese fishermen from fishing in Gulf waters).

38. 42 U.S.C. § 2000e-2 (2006).

39. Professor Mary Anne Franks creatively argues that we ought to recognize claims for hostile sexual environments under Title VII for harassing activity that occurs online but produces effects in the workplace, which is protected under the statute. In her proposal, Title VII would be amended to extend its mandates to site operators who have effective control over the setting of cyber harassment. Site operators could be held liable for sexual harassment by amending current federal sex discrimination law and by amending a federal statute that has been inter-

preted to immunize site operators from liability for the postings of others. Mary Anne Franks, "Sexual Harassment 2.0," *Maryland Law Review* 71 (2012): 655–704.

40. United States v. Original Knights of Ku Klux Klan, 250 F. Supp. 330, 349 (E.D. La. 1965); see also Heart of Atlanta Hotel, Inc. v. United States, 379 U.S. 241, 250 (1964).

41. Letter of Department of Education, Office for Civil Rights, "Harassment and Bullying," October 26, 2010.

42. 18 U.S.C. § 241–249 (2012).

43. Jerry Demarco, "NJ 'Devilfish' Gets 5 Years in Federal Prison for Threatening Latino Civil Rights Groups," *Cliff View Pilot* (NJ), April 18, 2011; Indictment, United States v. Vincent Johnson, No. 3:10-cr-0076-AET (D.N.J. Feb. 4, 2010). A jury convicted Richard Machado of violating the civil rights of sixty Asian American college students in e-mails, written under the alias "Asian Hater," that threatened, "If you don't [leave the university] I will hunt you down and kill your stupid asses." "Machado Case History," Computingcases.org, accessed December 17, 2013, http://www.computingcases.org/case_materials/machado/case_history/case_history.html.

44. Plea Agreement, United States v. Mohamad Fouad Abdallah, Cr. 08-20223, (E.D. Mich. filed June 26, 2008).

45. James E. Kaplan and Margaret P. Moss, Partners against Hate, "Investigating Hate Crimes on the Internet," Technical Assistance Brief (2003), 5, http://www.partnersagainsthate.org/publications/investigating_hc.pdf.

46. 42 U.S.C. § 1985(3) (2006).

47. 18 U.S.C. § 241 (2012).

48. L. P. Sheridan and T. Grant, "Is Cyberstalking Different?," *Psychology, Crime & Law* 13 (2007): 627–640, 637.

49. Ellen Nakashima, "Harsh Words Die Hard on the Net," *Washington Post*, March 7, 2007, A1 (explaining that women attacked online by anonymous posters suspend their blogging, turn to private forums, or use gender-neutral pseudonyms).

50. Alyssa Royse comment on Alyssaroyse, "Rape and Death and Batman Oh My," Alyssa Royse's Personal Blog on Blogher (blog), August 4, 2008 (5:38 P.M.), http://www.blogher.com/rape-and-death-and-batman-oh-my.

51. Penelope Trunk's Brazen Careerist, "Blog under Your Real Name, and Ignore the Harassment," Penelope Trunk (blog), July 19, 2007, http://blog.penelopetrunk.com/2007/07/19/blog-under-your-real-name-and-ignore-the-harassment/ (explaining that women who write under pseudonyms miss opportunities associated with blogging under their real names, such as networking opportunities and expertise associated with their name).

52. Ellen Nakashima, "Sexual Threats Stifle Some Female Bloggers," *Washington Post,* April 30, 2007, A1.

53. Seth Stevenson, "Popularity Counts," *Wired Magazine,* May 2012, 120.

54. United States v. Cruikshank, 92 U.S. 542, 554–55 (1875).

55. For instance, in *United States v. Bowker,* 372 F.3d 365 (6th Cir. 2004), a defendant was convicted under VAWA for making more than a hundred anonymous phone calls to a television news reporter that were threatening and sexual in nature. The statute was recently amended to apply to harassing online postings and not just direct communications, such as e-mail. 47 U.S.C.A. § 223(a)(1)(C) (West 2013).

56. See Danielle Keats Citron, "Cyber Civil Rights," *Boston University Law Review* 89 (2009): 61–126, 76–77; see also Jill, "What Do We Do about Online Harassment?," Feministe (blog), August 9, 2007 (22:36), http://www.feministe.us/blog/archives/2007/08/09/what-do-we-do-about-online-harassment/.

57. Emily Bazelon, "Trolls, the Bells Toll for Thee," *New York Times Magazine,* April 24, 2011, 10.

58. Telephone interview with Ms. Harvard, July 20, 2011 (notes on file with author).

59. Doe v. Smith, 429 F.3d 706 (7th Cir. 2005).

60. Fed. R. Civ. P. 11.

61. Daniel J. Solove, *The Future of Reputation: Gossip, Rumor, and Privacy on the Internet* (New Haven, CT: Yale University Press, 2007).

62. Thanks to the journalist Julia Angwin for suggesting this possibility.

63. I have conducted extensive interviews with "Ms. Harvard," and we worked together in support of proposed legislation, which passed into law in Hawaii. "Collected Written Testimony," The Judiciary, State of Hawaii, accessed July 12, 2013, http://www.capitol.hawaii.gov/session 2011/testimony/SB77_TESTIMONY_JDL_LATE.pdf.

64. Ernesto, "How Long Does Your ISP Store IP Address Logs?," Torrent Freak (blog), June 29, 2012, http://torrentfreak.com/how-long-does -your-isp-store-ip-address-logs-120629/.

65. Nate Anderson, "How a Fake Justin Bieber 'Sextorted' Hundreds of Girls through Facebook," Ars Technica, May 1, 2012 (2:45 P.M.), http:// arstechnica.com/tech-policy/2012/05/how-a-fake-justin-bieber -sextorted-hundreds-of-girls-through-facebook/ (explaining that police tracked a suspect in a sextortion scheme using his IP address, user information provided voluntarily by Facebook, and account information from an ISP); Leo Traynor, "The Day I Confronted My Troll," *Guardian* (U.K.), September 26, 2012 (4:31 A.M.), http://www.the guardian.com/commentisfree/2012/sep/26/day-confronted-troll (describing how the author used IP and ISP information to track and identify the troll who harassed him and his family).

66. Paul Bocij and Leroy McFarlane, "Cyberstalking: The Technology of Hate," *Police Journal* 76 (2003): 204–221.

67. David Robinson, "CCR Symposium: Screening Software," Concurring Opinions (blog), April 16, 2009 (12:45 P.M.), http://www.concurringo pinions.com/archives/2009/04/ccr_symposium_s_1.html.

68. Amir Efrati, "Subpoenas Allowed in AutoAdmit Suit," *Wall Street Journal Law Blog* (blog), January 30, 2008 (9:08 A.M.), http://blogs.wsj .com/law/2008/01/30/subpoena-allowed-in-autoadmit-suit/ (quoting Zittrain).

69. Robinson, "CCR Symposium: Screening Software."

70. Harlan Yu, "The Traceability of an Anonymous Online Comment," Freedom to Tinker (blog), February 10, 2010, http://www.freedom-to -tinker.com/blog/harlanyu/traceability-anonymous-online-comment.

71. Motion to Expedite, Doe v. Ciolli, 3:07-cv-909 (D. Conn. Jan. 24, 2008).

7. Legal Reform for Site Operators and Employers

1. Kashmir Hill, "Hunter Moore Will Post Your Nude Photos but Will Only Include Your Home Addresses If He Thinks You're a Horrible Person," *Forbes.com*, December 5, 2012 (5:16 P.M.), http://www.forbes .com/sites/kashmirhill/2012/12/05/hunter-moore-is-going-to-start

-posting-your-nude-photos-again-but-will-only-post-your-home-ad dress-if-he-thinks-youre-a-horrible-person/.

2. Statement of Hollie Toups (on file with author).
3. Cubby v. CompuServe, 776 F. Supp. 135 (S.D.N.Y. 1991).
4. Mike Godwin, *Cyber Rights: Defending Free Speech in the Digital Age* (Boston: MIT Press, 2003), 95.
5. A 2013 Martin Scorsese movie, *The Wolf of Wall Street*, recounts the fraud and eventual arrest of Stratton Oakmont's president. Ronald L. Rubin, "How the 'Wolf of Wall Street' Really Did It," *Wall Street Journal* (blog), January 3, 2014, http://online.wsj.com/news/articles/SB100 01424052702303453004579290450707920302 .
6. Stratton Oakmont, Inc. v. Prodigy Servs. Co., 1995 WL 323710, at *1 (N.Y. Sup. Ct. May 24, 1995), *superseded by statute,* Telecommunications Act of 1996, Pub L. No. 104-104, 110 Stat. 56, *as recognized in* Shiamili v. Real Estate Grp. of N.Y., Inc., 17 N.Y.S.2d 19, 24 (Sup. Ct. App. Div. 2011).
7. Representative Bob Goodlatte explained, "Currently . . . there is a tremendous disincentive for online service providers to create family friendly services by detecting and removing objectionable content. These providers face the risk of increased liability where they take reasonable steps to police their systems. A New York judge recently sent the online services the message to stop policing by ruling that Prodigy was subject to a $200 million libel suit simply because it did exercise some control over profanity and indecent material." 141 Cong. Rec. 22,047 (Aug. 4, 1995) (statement of Rep. Goodlatte).
8. S. 314, 104th Cong. (1995).
9. S. Rep. No. 104-23, at 59 (1995).
10. H.R. Rep. No. 104-223, Amendment No. 2-3 (1995) (proposed to be codified at 47 U.S.C. § 230).
11. H. Conf. Rep. No. 104-458, at 193 (1996).
12. H.R. Rep. No. 104-223, Amendment No. 2-3 (1995) (proposed to be codified at 47 U.S.C. § 230).
13. 47 U.S.C. § 230(b) (2006).
14. See, e.g., Chicago Lawyers' Committee for Civil Rights Under Law, Inc. v. Craigslist, Inc., 519 F.3d 666, 670 (7th Cir. 2008) (finding site host Craigslist immune from liability under federal housing antidiscrimination law for users' discriminatory housing advertisements).

15. Jessica Roy, "Revenge Porn King Indicted on Federal Charges," *Time*, January 24, 2014, http://newsfeed.time.com/2014/01/23/revenge-porn-king-hunter-moore-indicted-by-fbi/.
16. Hill, "Hunter Moore Will Post Your Nude Photos." The Senate Judiciary Committee recently approved a bill that makes it a crime to make an online app whose primary use is to facilitate cyber stalking. "Senate Judiciary Committee Approves Bill That Would Ban Creation of Cyberstalking Apps on Cellphones Often Used to Track Spouses," *New York Daily News*, December 13, 2012, http://www.ny dailynews.com/news/national/bill-strikes-cellphone-stalking-apps -article-1.1219887.
17. Site operators are not liable for infringement if they take down the allegedly infringing content. See 17 U.S.C. § 512(a) (2012).
18. Complaint, Hollie Toups v. GoDaddy.com, Texxxan.com., No. D130018-C (Tex. Dist. Ct. filed Jan. 18, 2013).
19. Revenge porn operators should take note because at least one court pierced the safe harbor for a cyber cesspool site operator. In 2011 a federal district court permitted a woman to sue the site operator of TheDirty.com for defamation on the grounds that Section 230 is forfeited if the site owner "invites the posting of illegal materials or makes actionable postings itself." Hollis B S v. Dirty World Entertainment Recordings LLC, 766 F. Supp. 2d 828, 836 (E.D. Ky. 2011).
20. M.A. v. Village Voice Media Holdings, 809 F. Supp. 2d 1041, 1041 (E.D. Mo. 2011); Goddard v. Google, Inc., 640 F. Supp. 2d 1193 (N.D. Cal. 2009).
21. Fair Hous. Council v. Roommates.com, 521 F.3d 1157, 1167–1168 (9th Cir. 2008).
22. William H. Freivogel, "Does the Communications Decency Act Foster Indecency?," *Communication, Law & Policy Journal* 16 (2011): 17–48, 30–31.
23. Fair Hous. Council v. Roommates.com, 666 F.3d 1216 (9th Cir. 2012).
24. "Revenge Porn Websites Growing in Popularity," *ABC22Now,* December 5, 2013, http://www.abc22now.com/shared/news/top-stories /stories/wkef_vid_17474.shtml
25. "'Revenge Porn' Website Has Colorado Women Outraged," CBS Denver, February 3, 2013, http://denver.cbslocal.com/2013/02/03/revenge -porn-website-has-colorado-woman-outraged/; Jessica Valenti, "How

the Web Became a Sexists' Paradise," *Guardian* (U.K.), April 6, 2007, http://www.guardian.co.uk/world/2007/apr/06/gender.blogging.

26. Jessica Roy, "Even as He Promises to Close 'Is Anybody Down,' Craig Brittain Covertly Plans a New Revenge Porn Site," *Observer.com*, April 5, 2013 (11:57 A.M.), http://betabeat.com/2013/04/craig-brittain-revenge -porn-is-anybody-down-obama-nudes/.

27. It's believed that the same person owns and operates WinByState and the takedown site. Adam Steinbaugh, "Casey Meyering's Revenge Porn Forum Rips Off 'Takedownhammer' Scam," Adam Steinbaugh's Blog about Law and Technology, June 7, 2013, http://adamsteinbaugh.com /tag/revenge-porn/.

28. MyEx, "Contact Us," http://myex.com/contact-us/.

29. Lee Munson, "Revenge Porn Operator Faces Charges on Conspiracy, Extortion, and Identity Theft," Naked Security, December 11, 2013, http://nakedsecurity.sophos.com/2013/12/11/revenge-porn-operator -facing-charges-of-conspiracy-extortion-and-identity-theft/.

30. Mary Anne Franks, "The Lawless Internet? Myths and Misconceptions about Section 230," *Huffington Post*, December 18, 2013, http://www .huffingtonpost.com/mary-anne-franks/section-230-the-lawless-inter net_b_4455090.html.

31. Sam Bayard, "New Jersey Prosecutors Set Sights on Juicy Campus," Digital Media Law Project (blog), March 21, 2008, http://www.dmlp .org/blog/2008/new-jersey-prosecutors-set-sights-juicycampus.

32. Mike Masnick, "More Details Emerge as States' Attorneys General Seek to Hold Back Innovation on the Internet," Techdirt (blog), June 19, 2013 (4:16 P.M.), http://www.techdirt.com/blog/innovation/articles /20130619/01031623524/more-details-emerge-as-states-attorneys -general-seek-to-hold-back-innovation-internet.shtml.

33. In a case involving a violation of fair housing laws, Judge Easterbrook noted that the expansive interpretation of Section 230 does not har- monize with the "decency" name of the statute because broad protec- tion induces online computer services to "do nothing about the dis- tribution of indecent and offensive materials." Chicago Lawyers Comm. for Civil Rights v. Craigslist, 519 F.3d 666, 670 (7th Cir. 2008).

34. Danielle Keats Citron, letter to the editor, "Sunday Dialogue: Ano- nymity and Incivility on the Internet," *New York Times*, November 27, 2011, SR2.

35. I thank Emily Bazelon for talking through the merits of this proposal with me and providing guidance.

36. Comment of Jimmy, to Jack Balkin, "The Autoadmit Controversy: Some Notes about Social Software, Code, and Norms," Balkinization (blog), March 9, 2007, http://balkin.blogspot.com/2007/03/auto admit-controversy-some-notes-about.html.

37. Felix Wu, "Collateral Censorship and the Limits of Intermediary Im munity," *Notre Dame Law Review* 87 (2011): 293–349.

38. Emily Bazelon, "Fighting Back against Revenge Porn," *Slate,* January 23, 2013 (4:25 P.M.), http://www.slate.com/blogs/xx_factor/2013/01 /23/women_sue_to_fight_back_against_revenge_porn.html.

39. Robert L. Rabin, "Enabling Torts," *DePaul Law Review* 49 (1999): 435–454, 437 n.14.

40. Remsburg v. Docusearch, 816 A.2d 1001, 1007–08 (N.H. 2003).

41. Frank Pasquale, "Reputation Regulation: Disclosure and the Chal-lenge of Clandestinely Commensurating Computing," in *The Offen-sive Internet: Speech, Privacy, and Reputation,* ed. Martha Nussbaum and Saul Levmore (Cambridge, MA: Harvard University Press, 2010), 110.

42. Act on the Protection of Privacy in Working Life, No. 759 of 2004.

43. William McGeveran, "Finnish Employers Cannot Google Applicants," Info/Law (blog), November 15, 2006, https://blogs.law.harvard.edu/in folaw/2006/11/15/finnish-employers-cannot-google-applicants/.

44. Md. Code Ann., Lab. & Empl. § 3-712 (West 2013). According to the National Conference of State Legislatures, twelve other states have in-troduced legislation that would restrict employers from requesting ac-cess to individuals' social network user names and passwords.

45. I thank privacy law expert Professor Chris Hoofnagle for suggesting this strategy to me.

46. Johnson v. Ry. Express Agency, Inc., 421 U.S. 454 (1975), *superseded by statute on other grounds,* Civil Rights Act of 1991, Pub. L. No. 102-166, 105 Stat. 1071, *as recognized in* Sims v. Viacom, Inc., No. 12-166, 2012 WL 6962225 (W.D. Pa. Nov. 26, 2012).

47. 42 U.S.C. 2000e-2(k)(1) (2006).

48. EEOC, Policy Guidance on the Consideration of Arrest Records, 915.061, September 7, 1990, http://www.eeoc.gov/policy/docs/arrest _records.html. Arrest records can be the basis for an employment

decision only if it appears that the applicant engaged in the illegal conduct and the conduct is recent and job-related.

49. Amos Tversky and Daniel Kahneman, "Availability: A Heuristic for Judging Frequency and Probability," *Cognitive Psychology* 5 (1973): 207–232.

50. Clive Thompson, "Why Johnny Can't Search," *Wired Magazine*, November 2011, 62. A group of researchers asked college students to look up the answers to a handful of questions. The students generally relied on the web pages at the top of Google's results list. Researchers changed the order of the results for some students, who more often than not used the falsely top-ranked pages. The researchers concluded that the students were not assessing information sources on their own merit.

51. Laura Brandimarte, Alessandro Acquisti, and Joachim Vosgerau, "Discounting the Past: Bad Weighs Heavier than Good," presentation, November 2010, http://www.truststc.org/pubs/775.html.

52. Linda J. Skitka et al., "Automation Bias and Errors: Are Crews Better than Individuals?," *International Journal on Aviation Psychology* 10 (2000): 85–97, 94.

53. 15 U.S.C. § 1681b(3) (2012).

54. Federal Trade Commission, "Employment Background Checks and Credit Reports, FTC Facts for Consumers," May 2010.

55. Federal Trade Commissioner Julie Brill has expressed her grave concerns about the data brokerage industry and other companies whose dossiers can have an impact on employment matters without consumers having any opportunity to know what is in those records and to correct inaccuracies. Remarks of Federal Trade Commissioner Julie Brill at the National Cyber Security Alliance Data Privacy Day, Washington, DC, January 26, 2012, http://www.ftc.gov/speeches/brill/120126datarivacyday.pdf.

56. Michelle Alexander, *The New Jim Crow: Mass Incarceration in the Age of Colorblindness* (New York: New Press, 2012), 15–16.

57. Telephone interview with "Beneeta," January 25, 2014 (notes on file with author).

58. Eric Owens, "Nude 'Revenge Porn' Photos Land Christian School Teach on Paid Leave," Daily Caller, December 7, 2013, http://dailycaller.com/2013/12/07/nude-revenge-porn-photos-land-christian-school-teacher-on-paid-leave/.

59. "Married Christian School Teacher Who Resigned When Her Nude Photos Surfaced on 'Revenge Porn' Sites Is Charged with Lying to Police That Her Phone Was Stolen," *Daily Mail* (U.K.), February 1, 2014, http://www.dailymail.co.uk/news/article-2549947/Married-Christian -school-teacher-resigned-nude-photos-surfaced-revenge-porn-sites -charged-LYING-police-phone-stolen.html.
60. David Wagner, "How to Prosecute a Revenge Porn Profiteer," National Public Radio (KPBS San Francisco), December 17, 2013, http://www .kpbs.org/news/2013/dec/17/how-prosecute-revenge-porn-profiteer/.

8. "Don't Break the Internet" and Other Free Speech Challenges

1. In presenting a story on revenge porn forums, the CNN correspondent Anderson Cooper said, "Online, people say things they would never say under their real names. It's free speech so they have the right to say whatever they want." "Part I of @AC360 Exclusive Interview with Man behind 'Jailbait'—Ex-Reddit Troll Michael Brutsch," CNN Press Room (blog), October 18, 2012 (9:58 P.M.), http://cnnpressroom.blogs .cnn.com/2012/10/18/part-1-of-ac360-exclusive-interview-w-man behind-jailbait-ex-reddit-troll-michael-brutsch/. See also Bryan Bishop, "Violentacrez Apologizes: I Was Playing to an Audience of College Kids," The Verge, October 18, 2012, http://www.theverge. com/2012/10/18/3523434/violentacrez-michael-brutsch-apologizes -cnn.
2. Ronald J. Deibert, *Black Code: Surveillance, Privacy, and the Dark Side of the Internet* (Toronto: Random House, 2013), 106.
3. Cornelius Frolick, "Revenge Porn Websites Ensnare Ohioans," *Norwalk (OH) Reflector*, October 7, 2013, http://www.norwalkreflector. com/article/3626786.
4. Reno v. ACLU, 521 U.S. 844 (1997)
5. Danielle Keats Citron, "Fulfilling Government 2.0's Promise with Robust Privacy Protections," *George Washington Law Review* 78 (2010): 825.
6. Rebecca MacKinnon, *Consent of the Networked: The Worldwide Struggle for Internet Freedom* (New York: Basic Books, 2012), 6.
7. Jeffrey Rosen, *The Unwanted Gaze: The Destruction of Privacy in America* (New York: Random House, 2001).

8. Jack M. Balkin, "Some Realism about Pluralism: Legal Realist Approaches to the First Amendment," *Duke Law Journal* (1990): 375–430, 383–384.

9. Samantha Masunaga, "Scarlet Letter: Sex Columnists Under Fire," *Hyphen Magazine,* Summer 2013, http://www.hyphenmagazine.com /magazine/issue-27-sex-summer-2013/scarlet-letters.

10. Skype interview with Zoe Yang, November 30, 2011 (notes on file with author).

11. Email to author from Zoe Yang, February 26, 2014 (on file with author). Yang explained, "Just last week I got an anonymous email from my stalker (I've come to believe it's one individual) threatening my little brother, whose identity he's apparently uncovered. Over the years, he's exposed, harassed, and defamed multiple people close to me." Ibid.

12. Neil M. Richards, *Intellectual Privacy: Civil Liberties and Information in the Digital Age* (New York: Oxford University Press, 2014).

13. Whitney v. California, 274 U.S. 357, 378 (1927) (Brandeis, J., concurring).

14. Richards's book *Intellectual Privacy* provides a compelling account of the self-governance theory of the First Amendment and Justice Brandeis's important contributions to it.

15. Ibid.

16. Whitney, 274 U.S. at 378 (Brandeis, J., concurring).

17. Jack M. Balkin, "Digital Speech and Democratic Culture: A Theory of Freedom of Expression for the Information Society," *New York University Law Review* 79 (2004): 1–58.

18. Robert D. Putnam, *Bowling Alone: The Collapse and Revival of American Community* (New York: Simon and Schuster, 2000), 338.

19. Helen Norton and I developed a theory of digital citizenship in our article "Intermediaries and Hate Speech," *Boston University Law Review* 91 (2011): 1435–1484.

20. C. Edwin Baker, *Human Liberty and Freedom of Speech* (New York: Oxford University Press, 1989), 54.

21. Procunier v. Martinez, 416 U.S. 396, 427 (1974), *overruled by* Thornburgh v. Abbott, 490 U.S. 401 (1989).

22. Owen M. Fiss, *The Irony of Free Speech* (Cambridge, MA: Harvard University Press, 1996), 15.

23. Steven J. Heyman, *Free Speech and Human Dignity* (New Haven, CT: Yale University Press, 2008), 166.

24. Owen M. Fiss, "Why the State?," *Harvard Law Review* 100 (1987): 781–794, 786 ("Autonomy may be protected, but only when it enriches public debate"); Heyman, *Free Speech and Human Dignity*, 18.

25. Cass Sunstein, *Democracy and the Problem of Free Speech* (New York: Simon and Shuster, 1995), 127.

26. Varian Medical Systems, Inc. v. Delfino, 6 Cal. Rptr. 3d 325, 337 (Ct. App. 2003).

27. Solove powerfully made this point with regard to privacy tort protections in his book *The Future of Reputation*. As he argued, privacy torts have the potential to chill speech, but they also serve to protect people's ability to engage in expressive activities free from fear of social disapproval. Daniel J. Solove, *The Future of Reputation: Gossip, Rumor, and Privacy on the Internet* (New Haven: Yale University Press, 2007), 130.

28. Abrams v. United States, 250 U.S. 616, 629 (1919) (Holmes, J., dissenting).

29. John Durham Peters, *Courting the Abyss: Free Speech and the Liberal Tradition* (Chicago: University of Chicago Press, 2005), 132.

30. Solove, *The Future of Reputation*, 132.

31. New York Times v. Sullivan, 376 U.S. 254 (1964).

32. Texas v. Johnson, 491 U.S. 397, 414 (1989).

33. In *Cohen v. California*, 403 U.S. 15 (1971), the Supreme Court concluded that the defendant engaged in constitutionally protected speech when he wore a jacket into a courtroom with "Fuck the Draft" written on its back. The Court explained that a governmental interest in regulating offensive speech could not outweigh the defendant's First Amendment right to freedom of speech.

34. United States v. Alvarez, 132 S. Ct. 2537, 2550 (2012).

35. Ibid., 2544. The Court has articulated complex constitutional standards for some of these categories, like defamation, erecting a matrix of fault and damage rules based on whether a plaintiff is a public or private figure. Gertz v. Robert Welch, Inc., 418 U.S. 323, 346–349 (1974). As the free speech scholar Rodney Smolla puts it, the well-defined categories of speech falling outside the First Amendment's coverage entail elaborate standards of review, and some constitutional protection is afforded

certain types of libelous and obscene speech. Rodney A. Smolla, "Categories, Tiers of Review, and the Roiling Sea of Free Speech Doctrine and Principle: A Methodological Critique of *United States v. Alvarez,*" *Albany Law Review* 76 (2013): 499–526, 502.

36. Virginia v. Black, 538 U.S. 343, 359 (2003). Most appellate courts apply an objective standard that focuses on whether it was reasonably foreseeable to the speaker (or the listener) that the statement would be interpreted as expressing a serious intent to hurt another. See, e.g., United States v. Syring, 522 F. Supp. 2d 125, 129 (D.D.C. 2007). A small number of courts require proof that the defendant subjectively intended to threaten the victim. United States v. Twine, 853 F.2d 676, 680 (9th Cir. 1988).

37. Watts v. United States, 394 U.S. 705 (1969) (per curiam). The Court's first foray into the true threats doctrine involved a speech made during an anti–Vietnam War protest. At the Washington Monument, eighteen-year-old Robert Watts told a crowd, "I have already received my draft classification. . . . I am not going. If they ever make me carry a rifle the first man I want to get in my sights is L.B.J." The response was laughter. Given the setting, the audience's playful reaction, and the conditional nature of the threat, Watts's speech was deemed political hyperbole, not a true threat.

38. Kurt Opsahl, "Georgia Court Censorship Order Threatens Message Boards Everywhere," EFF Blog, March 26, 2013, https://www.eff.org /deeplinks/2013/03/georgia-court-order-threatens-message-boards -everywhere.

39. United States v. Jeffries, 692 F.3d 473 (6th Cir. 2012).

40. Kenneth L. Karst, "Threats and Meanings: How the Facts Govern First Amendment Doctrine," *Stanford Law Review* 58 (2006): 1337–1412, 1345.

41. Virginia v. Black, 538 U.S. 343, 359 (2003).

42. Planned Parenthood v. Am. Coal. of Life Activists, 23 F. Supp. 1182, 1184–94 (D. Or. 1998).

43. Karst, "Threats and Meanings," 1079–1080.

44. Because the site lacked a literal articulation of a threat and concerned a political message about the justification of violence against abortion providers, dissenting judges contended that the site could be understood as a true threat only if the speakers or their associates carried out the

threatened harm. Planned Parenthood of Columbia/Willamette v. Am. Coal. of Life Activists, 290 F.3d 1058, 1079, 1089 (9th Cir. 2002) (en banc) (Kozinski, J., dissenting).

45. In the revenge porn victim's case, the harassing posts would not qualify as unprotected incitement as the Court understands it because criminal activity would not necessarily be imminent. Stalking and physical attacks could happen at any time: an hour, a week, or a year after the posts first appeared. Time remained for counterspeech, hypothetically speaking, although it is hard to imagine what one could say. The revenge porn victim could deny wanting to have sex with strangers, but readers of the posts likely would not see her response. Of course, nothing the poster said related to the spread of ideas, no matter how distasteful. But no matter, if time for a response and the imminence of violence remain the central questions, then the incitement exception is inapplicable.

46. Eugene Volokh, "One-to-One Speech vs. One-to-Many Speech, Criminal Harassment Laws, and 'Cyberstalking,'" *Northwestern University Law Review* 106 (2013): 731–794, 754.

47. Randall P. Bezanson and Gilbert Cranberg, "Institutional Reckless Disregard for Truth in Public Defamation Actions against the Press," *Iowa Law Review* 90 (2005): 887–929.

48. Rice v. Paladin Enterprises, 128 F.3d 233, 239–244 (4th Cir. 1997).

49. United States v. Sayer, No. 2:11-CR-113-DBH, 2012 WL 1714746, at *2–3 (D. Me. May 15, 2012).

50. United States v. Petrovic, 701 F.3d 849, 852–853 (8th Cir. 2012).

51. The Seventh Circuit upheld a criminal solicitation conviction as constitutional where the defendant posted a juror's personal information on his neo-Nazi organization's website next to the assertion that the juror was in a relationship with a man of a different race. United States v. White, 698 F.3d 1005 (7th Cir. 2012). It found that in context, the speech amounted to unprotected criminal solicitation given his previous call for violence against others, including jurors, such that a reasonable jury could conclude that in broadcasting the information on a neo-Nazi site, it was specifically designed to reach as many white supremacist readers as possible so that someone could kill or harm the juror.

52. *Rice*, 128 F.3d at 248.

53. Eugene Volokh, "Crime-Facilitating Speech," *Stanford Law Review* 57 (2005): 1095–1122, 1129.

54. United States v. Alvarez, 132 S. Ct. 2537, 2544 (2012) (Kennedy, J., plurality opinion).
55. New York Times Co. v. Sullivan, 376 U.S. 254, 301–302 (1964).
56. Curtis Pub. Co. v. Butts, 388 U.S. 130, 155 (1967).
57. Solove, *The Future of Reputation,* 126.
58. Gertz v. Welch, Inc., 418 U.S. 323 (1974).
59. Curtis Publ'g v. Butts, 388 U.S. 130, 155 (1967).
60. Time, Inc. v. Firestone, 424 U.S. 448, 453–454 (1976).
61. Dun & Bradstreet v. Greenmoss Builders, 472 U.S. 749 (1985).
62. Landmark Communications Inc. v. Virginia 435 U.S. 829, 838 (1978). See Michael Coenen, "Of Speech and Sanctions: Toward a Penalty-Sensitive Approach to the First Amendment," *Columbia Law Review* 112 (2012): 994 (explaining that the "severity of the penalty imposed—though of central importance to the speaker who bears it—does not normally affect the merits of his free speech claim. . . . Speech is either protected, in which case it may be punished, or unprotected, in which case it may be punished to a very great degree.").
63. New York Times Co. v. Sullivan, 376 U.S. 254, 301–302 (1964). To further demonstrate the point, the Court rejected Justice Stevens's proposal to bar criminal prosecutions for obscenity. To be sure, the vagueness doctrine may have greater salience in criminal cases than in civil cases. I address concerns about vagueness in discussing the constitutionality of my proposed revenge porn statute.
64. Garrison v. Louisiana, 379 U.S. 64 (1964).
65. Volokh, "One to One Speech vs. One-to-Many Speech," 752.
66. Smith v. Daily Mail Publ'g Co., 443 U.S. 97, 103 (1979); Florida Star v. B.J.F., 491 U.S. 524 (1989).
67. Smith v. Daily Mail Publ'g Co., 443 U.S. 97, 102 (1979).
68. Florida Star, 491 U.S. at 533.
69. Bartnicki v. Vopper, 532 U.S. 514, 518 (2010).
70. Ibid.
71. Neil M. Richards, "The Limits of Tort Privacy," *Journal on Telecommunications and High Technology Law* 9 (2011): 357–384.
72. See, e.g., Quigley v. Rosenthal, 327 F.3d 1044, 1067–1068 (10th Cir. 2003) (upholding civil penalties under federal Wiretap Act for the disclosure of the contents of an intercepted phone call concerning a woman's private discussion with friends and family regarding an ongoing

dispute with a neighbor because the intercepted call involved purely private matters).

73. Michaels v. Internet Entertainment Group, 5 F. Supp. 2d 823 (C.D. Cal. 1998). See Solove, *The Future of Reputation*, 129, 160; Daniel J. Solove, "The Virtues of Knowing Less: Justifying Privacy Protections against Disclosure," *Duke Law Journal* 53 (2003): 967–1066, 988–998 (arguing that the disclosure tort can be reconciled with the First Amendment where the speech addresses private concerns).

74. Michaels v. Internet Entertainment Group, 840, 841.

75. See Neil M. Richards, *Intellectual Privacy: Civil Liberties and Information in the Digital Age* (New York: Oxford University Press, 2014).

76. *Bartnicki* 532 U.S. at 541.

77. See "Weiner Apologizes for Lying, 'Terrible Mistakes,' Refuses to Resign," CNN Politics, June 7, 2011 (6:54 A.M.), http://www.cnn.com/2011 /POLITICS/06/06/new.york.weiner/.

78. In *Intellectual Privacy*, Richards argues that naming celebrities as adulterers may be one thing, but publishing high-resolution videos of their sex acts is another. As he explains, we do not need to see celebrities naked to discuss their infidelity (38).

79. Cohen v. Cowles Media Co., 501 U.S. 663 (1991); Neil M. Richards and Daniel J. Solove, "Privacy's Other Path: Recovering the Law of Confidentiality," *Columbia Law Review* 96 (2007): 123–182.

80. Eugene Volokh, "Florida 'Revenge Porn' Bill," The Volokh Conspiracy (blog), April 10, 2013 (7:51 P.M.), http://www.volokh.com/2013/04/10 /florida-revenge-porn-bill/.

81. United States v. Stevens, 599 U.S. 460 (2010).

82. Ibid.

83. Fla. Star v. B.J.F., 491 U.S. 524, 533 (1989).

84. Hustler Magazine v. Falwell, 485 U.S. 46 (1988).

85. Snyder v. Phelps, 131 S. Ct. 1207, 1220 (2011).

86. Cyberbullying and Other Online Safety Issues for Children, Hearing on H.R. 1966 and H.R. 3630, H. Comm. on the Judiciary, Subcomm. on Crime, Terrorism and Homeland Security, 111th Cong. 44–45 (September 30, 2009) (statement of Professor Robert M. O'Neil). The typical intentional infliction case involved a cruel joke or hoax: someone would send a telegram or letter expressing feigned condolences for the death of the person's close relative, when in fact the relative was in

perfect health. Over the years, victims of vicious pranks have successfully sued for intentional infliction of emotional distress.

87. Hustler Magazine v. Falwell, 485 U.S. 46 (1988).

88. Geoffrey Stone, "Privacy, the First Amendment, and the Internet," in *The Offensive Internet: Speech, Privacy, and Reputation,* ed. Saul Levmore and Martha Nussbaum (Cambridge, MA: Harvard University Press, 2011), 174–194. Relatedly, Volokh argues that cyber harassment statutes fail because they cover one-to-many speech that is "generally constitutionally protected even when some . . . viewers are likely to be offended." Volokh, "One-to-One Speech," 743. In making that argument, he relies on Supreme Court cases involving protests about public matters, such an anti–Vietnam War messages like "Fuck the Draft."

89. State v. Vaughn, 366 S.W.3d 513, 519, 521 (Mo. 2012) (considering a First Amendment challenge to sections of Missouri's harassment statute and ruling one provision unconstitutional because it restricted speech that did not constitute traditionally regulable harassment and finding another provision constitutional because the legislature apparently intended to bar a course of conduct causing emotional distress, which the court considered a term of common understanding); People v. Borrelli, 91 Cal. Rptr. 2d 851, 859, 860 (Ct. App. 2000) (finding California's stalking statute did not infringe on constitutionally protected free speech and explaining that, in order to be penalized, "the defendant must willfully engage in the prohibited conduct with the intention of inflicting substantial emotional distress on the person"); United States v. Shepard, No. CR 10-1032-TUC-CKJ, 2012 WL 113027, at *8 (D. Ariz. Jan. 13, 2012) (finding that Section 2261A is not facially vague, despite the statutorily undefined phrase *substantial emotional distress*, because the statute's specific intent requirement gives fair notice of what is prohibited, as defendant must necessarily know his or her own intention and the phrase can be understood by a person of ordinary intelligence).

90. Naomi Harlin Goodno, a law professor, writes that statutes aimed at cyberstalking will not be unconstitutionally overbroad if they prohibit willfully engaging in a harassing course of conduct because this ensures that perpetrators will have the requisite specific intent to commit a crime. Naomi Harlin Goodno, "Cyberstalking, a New Crime: Evaluating the Effectiveness of Current State and Federal Laws," *Missouri Law Review* 72 (2007): 125–198, 155.

91. See, e.g., United States v. Petrovic, 701 F.3d 849, 856 (8th Cir. 2012); United States v. Sayer, No. 2:11-CR-113-DBH, 2012 WL 1714746 (D. Me. May 15, 2012) (finding application of Section 2261A(2)(A) constitutional because the defendant's speech constituted true threats, solicitation, and defamation); United States v. Shepard, No. CR 10-1032-TUC-CKJ, 2012 WL 1580609, at *5 (D. Ariz. May 4, 2012) (rejecting a First Amendment defense to charges brought under Section 2261A(2)(A) after finding the subject of harassment was not a public figure and thus, as a matter of defamation jurisprudence, the defendant's writings about the subject were unprotected speech); see also United States v. White, 698 F.3d 1005 (7th Cir. 2012) (finding that a neo-Nazi's posting of a juror's phone number, former address, and homosexuality on a white supremacist website was constitutionally unprotected criminal solicitation); State v. Benham, 731 S.E.2d 275 (N.C. Ct. App. 2012) (unpublished table decision) (upholding a conviction for misdemeanor stalking based on online postings with an abortion provider's name, photograph, personal information, and missive that he was "WANTED . . . by Christ to Stop Killing Babies," which amounted to a true threat).
92. United States v. Cassidy, 814 F. Supp. 2d 574, 579–83 (D. Md. 2011).
93. Volokh, "One-to-One Speech vs One-to-Many Speech," 754
94. Wisconsin v. Mitchell, 508 U.S. 476 (1993); R.A.V. v. City of St. Paul, 505 U.S. 377 (1992).
95. *In re* Anonymous Online Speakers, 661 F.3d 1168 (9th Cir. 2011).
96. McIntyre v. Ohio Elections Comm'n, 514 U.S. 334 (1995).
97. Hurley v. Irish-Am. Gay, Lesbian & Bisexual Grp. of Bos., 515 U.S. 557 (1995).
98. See, e.g., NAACP v. Alabama, 357 U.S. 449, 462 (1958). The cyber law scholar Michael Froomkin has done important work on the importance of anonymity and technologies, laws, and legal arguments that riok anonymous communications. Michael Froomkin, "Lessons Learned All Too Well: The War on Anonymity," Center for Democracy & Technology (blog), May 9, 2011, https://www.cdt.org/blogs/lessons-learned-too-well-evolution-internet-regulation.
99. Indeed the Court has gone much further, allowing the state to obtain the Ku Klux Klan's membership list to deter violence. New York *ex rel.* Bryant v. Zimmerman, 278 U.S. 63 (1928).

100. See, e.g., Doe v. Cahill, 884 A.2d 451, 457 (Del. 2005); Nathaniel Gleicher, Note, "John Doe Subpoenas: Toward a Consistent Standard," *Yale Law Journal* 118 (2008): 320–368, 354.

101. My colleague James Grimmelmann has been incredibly helpful in talking with me about the problems associated with unmasking. See also James Grimmelmann, "The Unmasking Option," *Denver Law Review Online* 87 (2010): 24–25.

102. James Bamford, "The NSA Is Building the Country's Biggest Spy Center," *Wired Magazine*, March 15, 2012, http://www.wired.com /threatlevel/2012/03/ff_nsadatacenter/all/1; Michael Isikoff, "The Whistleblower Who Exposed Warrantless Wiretaps," *Newsweek*, December 12, 2008, http://www.newsweek.com/whistleblower-who -exposed-warrantless-wiretaps-82805.

103. Barton Gellman and Laura Poitras, "U.S., British Intelligence Mining Data from Nine U.S. Internet Companies in Broad Secret Program," *Washington Post*, June 6, 2013 (10:51 A.M.), http://www.washington post.com/investigations/us-intelligence-mining-data-from-nine-us -internet-companies-in-broad-secret-program/2013/06/06/3a0c0da8 -cebf-11e2-8845-d970ccb04497_story.html; Glenn Greenwald, "NSA Collecting Phone Records of Millions of Verizon Customers Daily," *Guardian* (U.K.), June 5, 2013, http://www.guardian.co.uk/world/2013 /jun/06/nsa-phone-records-verizon-court-order.

104. See generally Daniel J. Solove, *Nowhere to Hide: The False Tradeoff Between Security and Privacy* (New Haven, CT: Yale University Press 2012).

105. Richards, *Intellectual Privacy.*

106. My colleague David Gray and I have written a number of articles exploring the Fourth Amendment implications of surveillance technologies. Danielle Keats Citron and David Gray, "Addressing the Harm of Total Surveillance: A Reply to Professor Neil Richards," *Harvard Law Review Forum* 126 (2013): 262–274; David Gray and Danielle Keats Citron, "The Right to Quantitative Privacy," *Minnesota Law Review* 98 (2013): 62–144; David Gray and Danielle Keats Citron, "A Shattered Looking Glass: The Pitfalls and Potential of the Mosaic Theory of Fourth Amendment Privacy," *North Carolina Journal of Law and Technology* 14 (2013): 381–429; David Gray, Danielle Keats Citron, and Liz

Clark Rhinehart, "Fighting Cybercrime after United State v. Jones," *Journal of Criminal Law and Criminology* (forthcoming).

107. My previous work argued in favor of traceability anonymity, a requirement that site operators configure their sites to collect and retain visitors' IP addresses. Danielle Keats Citron, "Cyber Civil Rights," *Boston University Law Review* 89 (2009): 61–125, 123. I argued that traceability anonymity would permit posters to comment anonymously to the outside world but allow their identity to be traced in the event they engage in unlawful behavior. Mandatory data retention laws do run the risk of abuse, most significantly by governments engaging in surveillance practices. My related work on quantitative privacy and fusion centers has convinced me that the potential downside of data retention laws, without concomitant privacy guarantees, is not worth the price. Danielle Keats Citron and Frank Pasquale, "Network Accountability for the Domestic Intelligence Apparatus," *Hastings Law Journal* 62 (2011): 1441–1494; Gray and Citron, "The Right to Quantitative Privacy." The cyber law and privacy scholar Paul Ohm helpfully and generously discussed these concerns with me.

9. Silicon Valley, Parents, and Schools

1. This scenario is drawn from the actress Gwyneth Paltrow's experience with a stalker. "10 of the Scariest Celebrity Stalkers," BuzzFeed, January 22, 2013 (4:16 P.M.), http://www.buzzfeed.com/sevenpsychopaths/10-of-the-scariest-celebrity-stalkers-8rf6.

2. Erica Newland, Caroline Nolan, Cynthia Wong, and Jillian York, "Account Deactivation and Content Removal: Guiding Principles and Practices for Companies and Users," Berkman Center for Internet & Society and The Center for Democracy & Technology, September 2011, 5, http://cyber.law.harvard.edu/sites/cyber.law.harvard.edu/files/Final_Report_on_Account_Deactivation_and_Content_Removal.pdf (quoting Shirky).

3. Rebecca MacKinnon, *Consent of the Networked: The Worldwide Struggle for Internet Freedom* (New York: Basic Books 2012), 10.

4. Ellen Nakashima, "Harsh Words Die Hard on the Web," *Washington Post*, March 7, 2007, A1.

5. Telephone interview with Hemanshu Nigam, June 22, 2010 (notes on file with author). Nigam led MySpace's safety, security, and privacy team for more than four years. He came to MySpace after prosecuting Internet crimes for the Department of Justice and holding security positions at Microsoft and the Motion Picture Association of America. Berkman Center for Internet & Society, "Enhancing Child Safety & Online Technologies."

6. Angi Becker Stevens, "Dear Facebook: Rape Is No Joke," *Ms. Magazine* (blog), September 19, 2011, http://msmagazine.com/blog/2011/09/19 /dear-facebook-rape-is-no-joke/.

7. Dave Lee, "Facebook Bows to Campaign Groups over 'Hate Speech,'" BBC News, last modified May 29, 2013 (10:13 A.M.), http://www.bbc .co.uk/news/technology-22701082.

8. Yaakov Lappin, "'Kill a Jew' Page on Facebook Sparks Furor," *Jerusalem Post,* July 5, 2010, 5.

9. Community Connect, Inc., "Statement to the Technical Advisory Board" (2008), last accessed July 15, 2013, http://cyber.law.harvard.edu /sites/cyber.law.harvard.edu/files/Community_Connect%20feedback .pdf (describing efforts to promote Internet safety on behalf of five social network sites, including BlackPlanet.com, the largest online community for African Americans).

10. Telephone interview with Hemanshu Nigam, June 22, 2010 (notes on file with author).

11. I explored some of the ideas in this discussion in an article I coauthored with Helen Norton, "Intermediaries and Hate Speech: Fostering Digital Citizenship for Our Digital Age," *Boston University Law Review* 91 (2011): 1435–1484. Some insights also stem from my work as a member of the Inter-Parliamentary Coalition against Cyber Hate, led by the hate speech expert Chris Wolf and Speaker of the Knesset Yuli Edelstein.

12. Marne Levine, "Controversial, Harmful and Hateful Speech on Facebook," Facebook, May 28, 2013 (4:51 P.M.), https://www.facebook.com /notes/facebook-safety/controversial-harmful-and-hateful-speech-on -facebook/574430655911054. Facebook's guidelines for its safety staff, leaked to the press, go into a bit more detail. Cyber harassment and bullying include attacks based on someone's status as a sexual assault victim and persistent contact with users who have said they want no further

contact. "Abuse Standards 6.2: Operation Manual for Live Content Moderators," accessed December 17, 2013, http://www.scribd.com/doc /81863464/odeskstandards. It is unclear if those policies are still operational, as Facebook fired the company responsible for drafting those guidelines. Jeffrey Rosen, "The Delete Squad," *New Republic*, April 29, 2013, http://www.newrepublic.com/article/113045/free-speech-internet -silicon-valley-making-rules#.

13. "Community Guidelines," Tumblr, last modified March 22, 2012, http://www.tumblr.com/policy/en/community.

14. "Hate Speech and the Beliefnet Community," Beliefnet, accessed December 17, 2013, http://www.beliefnet.com/Skipped/2004/06/hate -speech.aspx.

15. Chuck Cosson, March 17, 2012, comment on Danielle Citron, "Actualizing Digital Citizenship with Transparent TOS Policies: Facebook Style," Concurring Opinions (blog), March 16, 2012 (9:41 A.M.), http:// www.concurringopinions.com/archives/2012/03/actualizing-digital -citizenship-with-transparent-tos-policies-facebooks-leaked-policies .html.

16. Abraham H. Foxman and Christopher Wolf, *Viral Hate: Containing Its Spread on the Internet* (New York: Palgrave Macmillan, 2013), 120.

17. Interview with Dave Willner, May 7, 2012 (notes on file with author).

18. Berkman Center for Internet & Society, "Enhancing Child Safety & Online Technologies."

19. Rosen, "The Delete Squad," 23.

20. Miguel Helft, "Facebook Wrestles with Free Speech and Civility," *New York Times*, December 13, 2010, B1.

21. Technology Advisory Board Report, Submissions of Social Network Sites, Appendix E, Statement of Google's Orkut (2008), http://cyber.law .harvard.edu/sites/cyber.law.harvard.edu/files/ISTTF_Final_Report -APPENDIX_E_SNS.pdf.

22. Rosen, "The Delete Squad," 23.

23. Emily Bazelon, *Sticks and Stones: Defeating the Culture of Bullying and Rediscovering the Power of Character and Empathy* (New York: Random House, 2013), 288.

24. Elaine Edwards, "Facebook and Department of Education Meet over 'Cyber Bullying' Issue," *Irish Times*, June 7, 2013 (10:55 A.M.), http:// www.irishtimes.com/news/technology/facebook-and-department-of

-education-meet-over-cyberbullying-issue-1.1419642 (subscription required).

25. Helft, "Facebook Wrestles with Free Speech and Civility."

26. Bazelon, *Sticks and Stones,* 266.

27. Teresa Nielsen Hayden, "Virtual Panel Participation," Making Light (blog), January 27, 2005 (5:25 P.M.), http://nielsenhayden.com/making light/archives/006036.html.

28. David A. Hoffman and Salil K. Mehra, "Wikitruth through Wikiorder," *Emory Law Journal* 59 (2009): 151–210, 182.

29. Bazelon, *Sticks and Stones,* 267.

30. Newland, "Account Deactivation and Content Removal."

31. "Appealing Video Strikes," YouTube, accessed December 17, 2013, https://support.google.com/youtube/answer/185111?hl=en.

32. Danielle Keats Citron, "Technological Due Process," *Washington University Law Review* 85 (2008): 1249–1313.

33. Center for Democracy and Technology, "Campaign Takedown Troubles: How Meritless Copyright Claims Threaten Online Political Speech," September 2010, http://www.cdt.org/files/pdfs/copy right_takedowns.pdf.

34. Clay Shirky, *Cognitive Surplus: Creativity and Generosity in a Connected Age* (New York: Penguin Press, 2010), 165.

35. Jonathan Zittrain, *The Future of the Internet—And How to Stop It* (New Haven, CT: Yale University Press, 2008), 134–135. Wikipedia also enlists volunteer editors, called "third opinion Wikipedians," who resolve disputes between editors. Wikipedia's guidelines advise them to "read the arguments, avoid reckless opinions, be civil and nonjudgmental, offer neutral opinions, and monitor the page after offering an opinion." Hoffman and Mehra, "Wikitruth through Wikiorder."

36. Dennis Scimeca, "Using Science to Reform Toxic Player Behavior in *League of Legends,*" *Ars Technica,* May 16, 2013 (8:30 A.M.), http://arstech nica.com/gaming/2013/05/using-science-to-reform-toxic-player-behav ior-in-league-of-legends/.

37. E-mail from Julie Martin, associate general counsel, Mozilla, to author, August 11, 2010 (on file with author).

38. Jaron Lanier, "You Are Not a Gadget," *New Media and Society* 13 (2011): 510–513.

39. Berkman Center for Internet & Society, "Enhancing Child Safety & Online Technologies."

40. Christopher Wolf, "Sunday Dialogue: Anonymity and Incivility on the Internet," *New York Times*, November 27, 2011, SR2.

41. Levine, "Controversial, Harmful and Hateful Speech."

42. Danielle Keats Citron, letter to the editor, "Sunday Dialogue: Anonymity and Incivility on the Internet," *New York Times*, November 27, 2011, SR2.

43. Erving Goffman, *Interaction Ritual: Essays on Face-to-Face Behavior* (Garden City, NY: Anchor Books, 1967).

44. Audrey, a sixteen-year-old virtual-world user, explains that an avatar is a "performance of you"; that is, the avatar is your "own little ideal person. . . . You can create who you want to be." Sherry Turkle, *Alone Together: Why We Expect More from Technology and Less from Each Other* (New York: Basic Books, 2011), 191. Lisa Nakamura has done insightful work on the visual culture of avatars and the "passing" of avatars as a different gender, ethnicity, or race. Lisa Nakamura, *Digitizing Race: Visual Cultures of the Internet* (Minneapolis: University of Minnesota Press, 2008); Lisa Nakamura, *Cybertypes: Race, Ethnicity, and Identity on the Internet* (New York: Routledge, 2002).

45. Turkle, *Alone Together*, 191.

46. Beth Coleman, *Hello Avatar: Rise of the Networked Generation* (Boston: MIT Press, 2011), 71, 119.

47. Ibid.

48. Texted comments and one's voice can also signal one's gender or race, which in turn can impact the behavior of bigots. Some contend that the prejudice-reducing effects of contact are negligible in online spaces due to the "absence of face-to-face, personal interaction and the individuation and empathy it engenders." Jack Glaser and Kimberly B. Kahn, "Prejudice, Discrimination, and the Internet," in *The Social Net: Human Behavior in Cyberspace*, ed. Yair Amichai-Hamburger (New York: Oxford University Press, 2005), 247–274. Often called the "contact hypothesis," studies find that direct contact and interaction among groups can reduce stereotyping and prejudice. Thomas F. Pettigrew and Linda R. Tropp, "Does Intergroup Contact Reduce Prejudice? Recent Meta-Analytic Findings," in *Reducing Prejudice and Discrimination*,

ed. Stuart Oskamp (Mahwah, NJ: Lawrence Erlbaum, 2000), 93–114. Specific conditions must exist for contact to reduce intergroup bias, such as equal status, sanction by an authority, common goals, and a noncompetitive relationship. Gordon W. Allport, *The Nature of Prejudice* (Reading, MA: Addison-Wesley, 1954).

49. Erving Goffman, *Gender Advertisements* (New York: Harper and Row, 1979).

50. Jennifer Stromer-Galley and Rosa Mikeal Martey, "Visual Spaces, Norm Governed Places: The Influence of Spatial Context Online," *New Media and Society* 11 (2009): 1041–1060, 1049, 1054.

51. Rosa Mikeal Martey and J. Stromer-Galley, "The Digital Dollhouse: Context and Social Norms in The Sims Online," *Games and Culture* 2 (2007): 314–334.

52. Foxman and Wolf, *Viral Hate;* James Grimmelmann, "The Google Dilemma," *New York Law School Law Review* 53 (2008–2009): 939–950, 942–943.

53. Saeed Ahmed, "Google Apologizes for Results of 'Michelle Obama' Image Search," CNN.com, November 25, 2009 (12:05 P.M.), http://www .cnn.com/2009/TECH/11/25/google.michelle.obama.controversy-2/.

54. Frank Pasquale, "Rankings, Reductionism, and Responsibility," *Cleveland State Law Review* 54 (2006): 115–140.

55. Ernest W. Adams, "A Call to Arms for Decent Men," Jezebel, September 5, 2012 (1:30 P.M.), http://jezebel.com/5938972/a-call-to-arms-for -decent-men.

56. "McAfee Digital Deception Study 2013: Exploring the Online Disconnect between Parents & Pre-teens, Teens and Young Adults," May 28, 2013, http://www.mcafee.com/us/resources/reports/rp-digital-de ception-survey.pdf?culture=en-us&affid=0&cid=122416.

57. Jan Hoffman, "As Bullies Go Digital, Parents Play Catch Up," *New York Times,* December 5, 2010, A1.

58. Berkman Center for Internet & Society, "Enhancing Child Safety & Online Technologies."

59. Telephone interview with Hemanshu Nigam, June 22, 2010 (notes on file with author).

60. "What Went Wrong in Steubenville?," NoBullying.com, accessed December 17, 2013, www.nobullying.com/what-went-wrong-in-steuben ville/.

61. Susan Donaldson James, "'Misty Series' Haunts Girl Long after Rape," ABC News, February 8, 2010, http://abcnews.go.com/Health/internet-porn-misty-series-traumatizes-child-victim-pedophiles/story?id=9773590#.UeWbAI2cfTo. A woman named Amy told the press of learning that a video of her being raped by her uncle at age four was widely circulated online, "Every day of my life, I live in constant fear that someone will see my pictures, recognize me and that I will be humiliated all over again."

62. "Columbia University Study: Facebook Users Either Sharing Too Much, or Too Little," *Baltimore Sun*, April 11, 2011 (2:31 P.M.), http://weblogs.baltimoresun.com/news/technology/2011/04/columbia_university_study_face.html.

63. Eileen Ambrose, "Want a Scholarship? Watch What You Post Online," *Baltimore Sun*, March 19, 2012, http://articles.baltimoresun.com/2012-03-19/business/bs-bz-ambrose-scholarships-20120319_1_central-scholarship-bureau-national-scholarship-providers-association-privacy-settings.

64. "McAfee Digital Deception Study."

65. Turkle, *Alone Together*.

66. danah boyd, Eszter Hargittai, Jason Schultz, and John Palfrey, "Why Parents Help Their Children Lie to Facebook about Age: Unintended Consequences of the 'Children's Online Privacy Protection Act,'" *First Monday*, November 2011, http://journals.uic.edu/ojs/index.php/fm/article/view/3850/3075.

67. Bazelon, *Sticks and Stones*, 43.

68. Hoffman, "As Bullies Go Digital."

69. Ellen Kraft and Jinching Wang, "Effectiveness of Cyberbullying Prevention Strategies: A Study on Students' Perspectives," *International Journal of Cyber Criminology* 3 (2009): 513–535.

70. Bazelon, *Sticks and Stones*.

71. Telephone interview with Julia Angwin, June 17, 2013 (notes on file with author).

72. "Protecting Children in the 21st Century Act Amendment," Federal Communications Commission, August 11, 2011, http://www.fcc.gov/document/protecting-children-21st-century-act-amendment.

73. Bazelon, *Sticks and Stones*, 213.

74. Bethel School Dist. No. 403 v. Fraser, 478 U.S. 675, 681 (1986).

75. John Dewey, "The School as Social Centre," *Elementary School Teacher* 3 (1902): 73–86, 76.

76. *Youth Safety on a Living Internet: Report of the Online Safety and Technology Working Group*, June 4, 2010, 29, http://www.ntia.doc.gov/legacy /reports/2010/OSTWG_Final_Report_060410.pdf.

77. Bazelon, *Sticks and Stones*, 213–214.

78. Dian Schaffhauser, "Teaching Parents Digital Citizenship at Katy ISD," *Journal*, May 11, 2010, http://thejournal.com/articles/2010 /05/11/teaching-parents-digital-citizenship-at-katy-isd.aspx.

79. Mike Donlin, "You Mean We Gotta Teach That Too?," in *Cyberbullying Prevention and Response: Expert Perspectives*, ed. Justin Patchin and Sameer Hindjuga (New York: Routledge, 2012), 111–126.

80. Bazelon, *Sticks and Stones*, 42.

81. A Thin Line, http://www.athinline.org.

Conclusion

1. Telephone interview with Holly Jacobs, July 27, 2013 (notes on file with author).

2. Email from Kathy Sierra to author, July 18, 2013 (on file with author).

3. Anita Sarkeesian, "Harassment via Wikipedia Vandalism," Feminist Frequency (blog), http://femfreq.tumblr.com/post/24919530277/harass ment-via-wikipedia-vandalism.

4. Fred Strebeigh, *Equal: Women Reshape American Law* (New York: Norton, 2009), 384.

Acknowledgments

Many people generously helped me with this project. I am incredibly grateful to those who shared their cyber harassment experiences with me. Their trust and time has meant the world to me.

A wonderful community of colleagues and friends helped shape the ideas in this book. Deserving special mention are Gabriella Coleman, Leslie Meltzer Henry, Helen Norton, Neil Richards, Max Siegel, Daniel Solove, and David Super. They spent hours critiquing drafts and brainstorming ideas with me. I am grateful for the feedback of Anisha Ahooja, Julia Angwin, Jack Balkin, Taunya Banks, Derek Bambauer, Ann Bartow, Emily Bazelon, Steve Bellovin, Richard Boldt, danah boyd, Ryan Calo, Bryan Choi, Julie Cohen, Deven Desai, Dissent Doe, Martha Ertman, Lisa Fairfax, Ed Felten, Mary Anne Franks, Susan Freiwald, Barry Friedman, Michael Froomkin, Don Gifford, Nathaniel Gleicher, Eric Goldman, Leigh Goodmark, David Gray, Rebecca Green, James Grimmelmann, Leslie Harris, Woodrow Hartzog, Mike Heintze, Debbie Hellman, Chris Hoofnagle, Sherrilyn Ifill, Robert Kaczorowski, Lee Kovarsky, Kevin Linskey, Alice Marwick, William McGeveran, Helen Nissenbaum, Paul Ohm, Frank Pasquale, Scott Peppet, Whitney Phillips, Amanda Pustilnik, Joel Reidenberg, Joseph Reagle, David Robinson, Catharine Ross, Lee Rowland,

Jana Singer, Sonja Starr, Katharine Strandburg, Kasia Szymborski, David Thaw, Kaimi Wegner, Robin West, Dave Willner, Chris Wolf, and Greg Young. Participants in the Privacy Law Scholars Conference (2012, 2013), the Columbia University Computer Science Distinguished Speaker Series, and Denver University Law Review's Cyber Civil Rights Symposium provided helpful critiques as well.

The University of Maryland Francis King Carey School of Law has been wonderful to me. My students provided invaluable research assistance. They include Andrew Ahrens, Joshua Chazen, Marissa Clark, Lucia Cooke, Claire Costantino, Adam Farra, Joshua Fraser, Nina Gleiberman, Megan Hindle, Stephanie Malcolm, Zachary Ostro, Eshawn Rawlley, Maram Salaheldin, Susan Schipper, Miriam Sievers, Richard Starr, Ryan Steidl, and Fei Teng. Pamela Bluh found sources for me in seconds. Susan McCarty provided her expert editing and citation help every step of the way. Cameron Connah and Alice Johnson were outstanding research fellows. Charles Pipin helped me figure out copyright permissions. My assistant Frank Lancaster was always there to lend a hand in all aspects of the work. Associate deans Mark Graber and Max Stearns were insightful sounding boards for my ideas. Dean Phoebe Haddon and Dean Karen Rothenberg generously supported my research.

I was fortunate to work with the advocacy groups Without My Consent and Cyber Civil Rights Initiative. Their leaders have been an incredible source of insight and inspiration: Mary Anne Franks, Holly Jacobs, Erica Johnstone, Charlotte Laws, and Colette Vogele. Carrie Goldberg is a phenomenal lawyer working hard to represent cyber harassment victims and providing us with inspiration.

At Harvard University Press, my editor, Elizabeth Knoll, was a constant source of insight and ideas. She believed in the project from the start, and her enthusiasm was key to pushing this project forward. Joy Deng provided wonderful support and assistance throughout the project.

My eternal thanks and love to my husband, daughters, sister and her family, mother, and stepfather. They provided endless encouragement and inspiration. And to my father, whose bravery is always with me—he left us too early, but his guidance has remained.

Index